AFRICAN AMERICAN WORKERS
AND THE APPALACHIAN COAL INDUSTRY

AFRICAN AMERICAN WORKERS AND THE APPALACHIAN COAL INDUSTRY

Joe William Trotter Jr.

West Virginia University Press / Morgantown

ISBN 978-1-959000-12-9 (paperback) / 978-1-952271-18-2
(cloth) / 978-1-952271-19-9 (ebook)

Library of Congress Control Number: 2021947905

Book and cover design by Than Saffel / WVU Press.
Cover image: *Untitled, Appalachia* © 1952–2002 Milton Rogovin.
Courtesy of the Center for Creative Photography, University of
Arizona Foundation.

This book is dedicated with love to my cousin
Willie Frank "Pete" Foster

CONTENTS

———

PREFACE

When I proposed this volume to the West Virginia University Press in the fall of 2019, the devastation of Covid-19 was just months away. Hence, the impact of the pandemic did not figure into my rationale for wanting to publish this book. My motivation for producing this volume stemmed from the impending thirtieth anniversary of my book, *Coal, Class, and Color: Blacks in Southern West Virginia, 1915–32* (University of Illinois Press, 1990). I hoped to use this collection of essays to reflect on my personal and professional journey to the notion of proletarianization (class formation) in scholarship on Black coal miners in the southern Appalachian coalfields; explore the transformation of research on the topic since publication of *Coal, Class, and Color*; and suggest directions that the next wave of research on the topic might take. These objectives remain core elements in the book's raison d'être, but the disproportionate impact of the coronavirus pandemic on people of African descent represents an even more compelling rationale for publishing these essays at this particular time in the history of the region and the nation.

During the early phases of the pandemic, media reports downplayed the potential impact of the virus on poor and working-class Black communities. Evidence of widespread racial disparities in sickness and death from the disease soon dispelled such thinking. Over the past several months, growing numbers of scholars, media, and public policy analysts from a variety of fields have located the roots of these disparities in the concentration of Black people in the most dangerous, unhealthy, and underpaid work, housing, and living conditions in the geography and political economy of the nation. While these debates and discussions accent the need for historical perspectives on these racialized issues, they are unfolding without sufficient attention to African American health care activism designed to creatively combat disease, restore their own health, and insure their survival in the face of substantial trauma. These conversations also elide the precise ways that socioeconomic, labor, and environmental conditions undermined the health and well-being of the African American community in particular places at specific moments in time.[1]

By focusing on a variety of issues in the history of African American workers in the Appalachian coal industry, this book calls attention to the ways that a better sense of history can deepen our understanding of the roots of the coronavirus among other epidemics and pandemics in African American history. A few illustrations from the West Virginia coalfields underscore this point. First and perhaps most important, in southern West Virginia, loading coal over a lifetime took its toll on the health of Black miners and exposed them to a wide variety of diseases, particularly tuberculosis during the industrial age. Some Black miners "literally broke themselves down loading coal." According to one miner, Pink Henderson, "My daddy got so he couldn't load coal. He tried to get company work [light labor, often outside] but the doctor turned him down, because he couldn't do nothing. He broke his self down. . . . My brothers done the same thing. They used to be the heavy loaders."

Coal loaders also endured the persistent inhalation of coal dust and particles of coal, black lung or "miners' asthma," a slow killer of miners as it was called in those days. Inadequate housing also took its toll on the health of Black miners and their families. In 1927–1928, the West Virginia Bureau of Negro Welfare and Statistics (BNWS) reported that tuberculosis was a far greater cause of death among Black people than mine accidents. Described as that "great scourge of the Negro race," tuberculosis accounted for 13 percent of African American health-related deaths compared to less than 8 percent among whites. The BNWS concluded that improvement in Black miners' health required better "living conditions—proper housing, wholesome food and sanitation," the "prerequisites of good health."

In addition to charting the health conditions of Black coal miners, this volume also recalls how Black miners, their families, and their communities mobilized movements designed to fight racial inequality in the health care system and counteract the impact of insufficient wages to fully support their families with healthy diets and living conditions. Across the coalfields, as part of their strategy for combatting disease as well as hunger, miners and their families not only cultivated their own vegetable gardens but also maintained a few hogs, chickens, and sometimes a cow for fresh milk and butter. Most important, however, they also collectively used their vote to demand greater access to public funds to serve their education, social welfare, and health needs. They not only worked through the state's leading Republican legislators but also elected their own numbers to public office. During the early post–World War I years, they sent three Black men, one a miner, to the House of Delegates in Charleston.

They effectively used their political influence within the Republican Party to secure the establishment of two all-Black colleges (West Virginia State College and Bluefield State College); homes for the African American elderly, deaf, and blind residents; and a tuberculosis facility.

In other words, looking back over this collection from the vantage point of current debates and the quest for knowledge to address the challenges of COVID-19, this book illuminates both the conditions that repeatedly exposed African Americans to the most destructive impact of disease as well as some of the most important strategies that they devised to help themselves. In addition, as noted at the outset of this preface, *African American Workers in the Appalachian Coal Industry* also responds to the need for an assessment of the field since the closing decade of the twentieth century, along with ideas for moving scholarship forward into the third decade of the twenty-first century and beyond.

In addition to illustrating key themes, topics, and changes in the history of Black coal miners over time, this book recalls the theoretical underpinnings of my work on Black labor and working-class history thirty years ago. At the outset of my career, I employed the notion of working-class formation or proletarianization as a process by which southern Black migrants made the transition from agricultural labor to wage-earning work in the manufacturing sector of the nation's expanding urban industrial economy.[2] Encouraged by a groundswell of new work employing notions of working-class formation, I embarked upon a case study of Black workers in southern West Virginia, a rural-industrial region of the Upper South. I hoped to deepen our understanding of proletarianization as a process that cut across regional lines, while retaining certain distinctive features from place to place. Various Marxist formulations of class formation shaped my understanding of the proletarianization process, but I was most impressed by profound differences in the experiences of Black and white workers under the impact of global capitalism. An extensive body of scholarship emphasizes how European and Euro-American workers experienced movement into the wage-earning workforce almost exclusively as a process of downward mobility and "immiseration." White workers entered the world of wage-earning labor as a desperate last resort, as they increasingly lost access to landownership as independent farmers on the one hand and control over specialized skills as autonomous craftsmen on the other. As suggested by the history of Black coal miners in West Virginia, people of African descent helped to build the capitalist economy as enslaved workers before the Civil War and, thereafter, as members of the free but disfranchised and unequal sharecropping and rural proletariat.

Unlike their white counterparts, as Black workers rapidly entered the wage-earning industrial workforce during the era of the Great Migration, they experienced movement into the industrial working class as a somewhat pro-gressive process of upward socioeconomic mobility. They moved from life and work in previously rigid systems of human bondage and suppression of human and civil rights (with few passageways to equality and social justice) into a closer relationship with the predominantly white labor movement, higher wages, and access to new forms of labor organizing and protests against injustices previously unavailable to them. African American working-class formation nonetheless entailed deeply entrenched patterns of inequality, injustice, and misery along the color line. It was the persistence of inequality during the urban industrial age that underlay the rise of the Modern Black Freedom Movement nationwide during the middle to late twentieth century.

The process of African American proletarianization converged across re-gional lines under the impact of the Great Migration. Massive rural to urban Black population movements transformed the Black population from a pre-dominantly rural southern population into a new national African American population, spread almost equally across the urban North and West on the one hand and the South on the other.

As a West Virginian by birth and member of a coal-mining family of fourteen children, I was drawn to the history of Black coal miners in the Mountain State. In addition to my scholarly and intellectual interests, I studied coal miners as a means of better understanding the history of my own family and the coal-mining community—which collapsed as the demand for coal declined in the years after World War II. Before I graduated from high school, my family moved from Vallscreek, West Virginia, to Newcomerstown, Ohio, a small industrial town south of the Akron-Canton metropolitan area.[3]

In many ways that I had not imagined growing up in a coal town in the southern Appalachian region, my research on Black miners revealed that indus-trial working-class formation defined African American life in the coalfields as elsewhere in twentieth-century America. But it also differed enormously from Black working-class formation in other parts of the nation, North and South. Unlike their kinsmen in the Deep South and other parts of the Upper South and Border States, African Americans in West Virginia retained the vote, endured fewer recorded incidents of mob lynching, and entered a workforce that placed their wages on a nearly equal par with their white fellow miners. While Blacks reported greater access to the rights of citizens, including the right to vote, in the urban North and West none could claim, as West Virginians did, the election of three Black men (one a coal miner) to the state legislature and the passage of an antilynching law during the 1920s. Moreover, when the popular Black state legislator Ebenezer Howard Harper died in office in 1927, Governor

Howard M. Gore appointed Mrs. Minnie Buckingham Harper to serve out her husband's term. In making the announcement of Harper's appointment, Gore acknowledged her as "the first woman of the Negro Race to become a member of a legislative body in the United States."[4]

While the concept of proletarianization illuminated important similarities and differences in the experiences of Black workers across regional lines, it left important dimensions of working-class life in the shadows. These included most notably the role of women and gender relations and the significance of paid and unpaid labor in the household, domestic, and personal service sectors of the industrial economy. While acknowledging the contributions of proletarianization to our knowledge of Black labor and working-class history, a growing number of studies helped to close these gaps during the final years of the twentieth century and the opening of the new millennium.[5]

Over the past three decades, scholarship on the class, gender, and racial dynamics of working-class formation established the intellectual foundation for a reformulation of the concept of proletarianization itself. In her recent LAWCHA presidential address, Julie Greene builds upon this scholarship to suggest a new transnational model for future research on African American and U.S. labor and working-class history. Based on "social reproduction" and "social formation" theories, Greene outlines a compelling conceptual framework for the next generation of labor and working-class history.[6] In addition to the hard work of theory building, empirical research, and production of new knowledge, however, young scholars of the next generation are already facing fresh new challenges during the age of the coronavirus pandemic.

But that is not all. Young scholars are also both witnessing and participating in massive grassroots street protests against police brutality and stiff white supremacist resistance movements. They are also demanding the abolition of systemic racism in American society, culture, and politics. Amid these sweeping changes in U.S. and global history, it is my hope that the history of Black miners will offer inspiration for moving forward during this difficult moment in the history of the nation and the world.

This miner manually lifts a huge piece of coal into the waiting train car. Ordinarily, he would have used a shovel—one in the background to the left and another in the foreground to the right. Courtesy of the Eastern Regional Coal Archives, Craft Memorial Library, Bluefield, West Virginia.

Introduction

———

THE BLACK MINER IN U.S. LABOR HISTORY

———

Until the final third of the twentieth century, enslavement, reconstruction, and the rise of Jim Crow dominated scholarship on the African American experience. As the Great Migration transformed African Americans from a predominantly rural to a predominantly urban industrial people, research on the massive movement of Southern rural Blacks into the nation's major urban centers gained increasing attention. But migration to urban America was by no means a one-stop process from rural to large urban industrial areas. From the outset of the emancipation years following the Civil War, sharecroppers, farm laborers, and general laborers gradually moved into rural-industrial lumber, railroad, and coal-mining communities. The West Virginia bituminous coal industry became a major magnet of Black migration to rural-industrializing America. Focusing primarily on Black migration, labor, and community formation in southern West Virginia, this volume calls attention to the place of coal mining in the rise of the Black industrial working class and the role of race in the development of the U.S. working class.

Historiography and Debates

Research and writing on Black coal miners had their genesis in early twentieth-century reactions to white supremacist scholarship on the subject. As early as 1909, Yale University geographer George T. Surface conducted a study of Black miners in Kentucky, Tennessee, Virginia, and West Virginia. He concluded that the "great majority" of Black migrants were "irregular" in labor and "unstable" in residence. Surface also sanctioned systematic labor discrimination against Black workers in the coal industry. Accordingly, early twentieth-century Black scholars like W. E. B. Du Bois, Carter G. Woodson, Charles Wesley, Abram Harris, and their white allies defended Black coal miners against such racist stereotypes. They concluded that Southern Black migrants were not genetically "irregular in labor," "unstable in residence," or incapable of meeting the knowledge and skill requirements of industrial production. Early twentieth-century scholars also helped to establish Black migration and labor studies as systematic scholarly fields of historical inquiry.[1]

Even as scholars like Du Bois, Woodson, Harris, and others defended Black miners against racist perspectives on their lives as workers and as Black people in a predominantly white political economy, they initially accented the vitality, skills, and education of a small segment of the Black working class, what Woodson described as the migration of the "talented tenth."[2] In the years following World War II, however, the advent of the Modern Black Freedom Movement and the rise of the "New Labor History" transformed our understanding of the masses of Black coal miners, not just the skilled and highly educated few. Following the lead of Herbert Gutman, one of the principal pioneers in the study of the U.S. working class "from the bottom up," increasing numbers of post–World War II scholars documented the development of Black coal-mining communities as well as patterns of interracial cooperation in the labor movement, particularly the United Mine Workers of America (UMW). Studies by Stephen Brier and Daniel P. Jordan offered groundbreaking studies of interracial unionism in the southern West Virginia coalfields. In his essay, "Interracial Organizing in the West Virginia Coal Industry: The Participation of Black Mine Workers in the Knights of Labor and the United Mine Workers, 1880–1894," historian Stephen Brier concluded that "Perhaps the most striking aspect of this episode in American working class history is the fact that southern West Virginia Black miners, many recently migrated from the cities and farms of Eastern Virginia, came to view interracial union organization as the vehicle through which they could fight for their liberation both as workers and as Black people."[3]

Daniel Jordan documented the outbreak of class warfare during the UMW's effort to organize the unorganized Black and white miners in Mingo, Logan, and other southern West Virginia counties following World War I. He concluded that the "Mingo War" was a unique "interracial affair." It was "neither conducted along racial lines nor marked by racial violence; as such, for the times, it was certainly atypical." David A. Corbin's *Life, Work, and Rebellion in the Coal Fields* (1981) and my own book *Coal, Class, and Color* (1990) documented racial and class dynamics in the development of coal-mining communities in southern West Virginia. Whereas Corbin, Jordan, and Brier underscored how class often "trumped" race in the southern West Virginia coalfields, *Coal, Class, and Color* not only documented substantial interracial cooperation, it emphasized how the rise of the rural industrial Black proletariat and the building of Black communities unfolded within the larger context of a racially segregated social order, reinforced by the ideas and actions of white workers and elites alike.[4]

By the late 1980s and early 1990s, a growing number of scholars challenged emerging class over race perspectives in many of the new coal-mining labor studies in West Virginia and nationwide. Following the lead of labor attorney and civil rights activist Herbert Hill and historian David Roediger, these scholars emphasized the persistence of working-class "white privilege" and the very tenuous nature of interracial cooperation in coal, steel, and other U.S. manufacturing firms during the Industrial Age. As Roediger put it in his influential book, *The Wages of Whiteness*, by the end of the Civil War, working-class whiteness, with deep roots in the antebellum years, was "firmly established and well poised to remain a central value, founded . . . not just on 'economic exploitation' but on 'racial folklore,' " as the nation matured as a predominantly urban-industrial society during the late nineteenth and early twentieth centuries.[5]

In the meantime, over the past three decades, a variety of studies continued to flesh out the themes of interracial cooperation, conflict, family, and community building among Black people in the Mountain State. These studies include, most notably, James Green's *The Devil is Here in These Hills* (2015); Cero M. Fain's *Black Huntington* (2019); and Christopher Wilkinson's *Big Band Jazz in Black West Virginia* (2012).[6] In his comprehensive study of the southern West Virginia labor-capital mine wars of the early twentieth century, the late labor historian Jim Green built upon the contributions of a wide range of published studies, as well as his own extensive primary archival research on the subject. *The Devil is Here in These Hills* is the most detailed account to date of the West Virginia mine wars of the early twentieth century and the fight for democracy among people who ironically were known by their motto—"Mountaineers Are Always Free." In 2016, PBS aired Randall McLowery's documentary film, *The Mine Wars*, based mainly on Green's book and in consultation with the author.[7]

While Green's book and the documentary film reiterated the importance of working-class solidarity in the fight for democracy and social justice in the coalfields, most recent studies deepen our understanding of family, community, and institution-building activities among Black miners in the Mountain State. Historian Cicero Fain breaks new ground in his study of Black life in Huntington. He employs the conceptual, theoretical, and methodological insights of late twentieth- and early twenty-first-century scholars of Black migration and urban community formation. Whereas most research on Black miners focuses on small, primarily company-owned towns, Fain documents the development of a Black urban-industrial community in the Mountain State. He also emphasizes the primacy of race, "not class," in the rise of Black Huntington.

Fain finds little evidence of interracial working-class cooperation before the turn of the twentieth century. Before the onset of World War I, however, Huntington's "colored citizens of the East End" established the city's first African American local of the Socialist Party of America and supported efforts to build bridges between Black and white workers in the city. Until then, in a telling chapter on the development of the Black working class, he succinctly concludes, "Estranged from white workers, blocked by white management, and disdained by a small but growing class of Black leaders, Black workers found no incentive to leave the psychic refuge of race as the prime modality of consciousness."[8]

Like Fain, music historian Christopher Wilkinson deepens our understanding of the heretofore little understood African American music and dance culture in the coalfields and cities of the Mountain State. Focusing on the rise of big band music in West Virginia—including the state's larger urban centers like Huntington, Wheeling, and Parkersburg as well as the Winding Gulf, Pocahontas, Williamson-Logan, and Kanawha New River coalfields of southern West Virginia—Wilkinson carefully documents the spread of big band music in West Virginia before the advent of the big band era during the mid-to-late 1930s and 1940s. He forcefully and convincingly concludes that Black West Virginians had facilitated this cultural innovation in dance music and dancing through a complicated interplay between their own community-based cultural values, dance styles, and music sensibilities and the regular booking of big bands from New York City, Chicago, Pittsburgh, and elsewhere to play in coal towns and cities across the state.

A series of rich and highly textured personal recollections reinforce the insights of recent historical studies of African Americans in the southern Appalachian coalfields. Specifically, the memoirs of Robert Armstead, Memphis Tennessee Garrison, and my brother Otis Trotter deepen our understanding of the class, racial, and gendered dimensions of Mountain State Black life.[9]

In his important memoir, *Black Days, Black Dust* (2002), the first penned by an African American coal miner, Armstead recalls a remarkable forty-year career as a coal miner in the region. Because his life as a miner covered the heyday of the Modern Black Freedom struggle and beyond, his memoir illuminates the bittersweet mix of declining coal-mining employment for Black workers and the gradual upward mobility of a few who remained as the coal-mining industry nearly disappeared. Beginning his mining career as an underground laborer, setting timber for mine roofs, Armstead later became a machine operator, fore-man, and finally safety director.

Born in McDowell County in 1890 to former slaves Wesley Carter and Cassie Thomas Carter, Memphis Tennessee Garrison launched her public schoolteach-ing career in 1908 and continued to serve her community, the state, and nation until her death in 1988. Garrison later recalled how she desired to become a lawyer, but her parents could not afford the cost of law school. Married to a coal miner, she became an active member of the local branch of the National Association for the Advancement of Colored People (NAACP) and influenced the organization's civil rights struggles across the state and nation.

For his part, Otis Trotter opens his story with the challenge of recovering an image of his father in the absence of an existing family photograph of him. He writes, "There is no photograph of my father. My family and I possess no still images of him captured in time, which we can cherish as a tangible connection to the past. . . . He lives in our hearts and minds, and his impact on our family continues to be felt across the generations." [10] *Keeping Heart* goes on to relate numerous episodes in the Trotter family's history in McDowell County during the Great Depression, World War II, and the 1950s. Most important, however, Trotter's *Keeping Heart* underscores how his congenital heart disease and the quest for life-saving medical treatment helped to crystalize the family's decision to move from the coalfields to a small industrial town in eastern central Ohio south of the Akron-Canton metropolitan area.

The proliferation of research on West Virginia's Black miners was closely in-tertwined with the explosion of studies on African American coal miners across the United States. This scholarship includes studies of Kentucky, Alabama, Tennessee, and other locations in the North and West. [11] In her creative study of Black coal miners and their families in eastern Kentucky, historical sociologist Karida L. Brown analyzes two generations of Black residents of the region's coal-mining communities: (1) the first generation of Deep South rural Blacks who migrated into the coalfields during the interwar years; and (2) the children of the first generation who spearheaded movement out of the coal region into the major urban centers across the nation in the years after World War II. Brown convincingly argues that both groups of migrants moved under the same im-perative—the search for "freedom and citizenship." [12]

Focusing on the Birmingham district of Alabama, labor historian Daniel Letwin explored the development of interracial unionism among Black and white miners in a Deep South industrial city and its surrounding coal-mining towns. He shows how interracial organizing in the Alabama coalfields ebbed and flowed with the business cycle of the state's coal industry. During each boom period, new spurts of interracial organizing emerged. In relatively rapid succession during the late nineteenth and early twentieth centuries, coal miners rallied across the color line around the Greenback Labor Party, the Knights of Labor, and finally the United Mine Workers of America.[13]

For her part, historian Ellen Curtin documented the experiences of convict miners, including women, in the Alabama coalfields. Rather than following the usual emphasis on the convict leasing system as a highly exploitative scheme that offered prisoners little room for resistance and self-expression, Curtin accents the preprison culture, attitudes, and behavior that many incarcerated Black men and women took behind prison walls: "Certain characteristics that appear to transfer into prison include racial pride, acting in concert, expectations of justice, and a recognition of the potentially impartial power of the law. All of these qualities aided prisoners in their struggle to survive."[14]

In addition to the experiences of Black miners and their families in Kentucky, Alabama, and elsewhere in the South, studies of Black coal miners in Washington State; Ferber, Texas; and especially Buxton, Iowa, have also illuminated sharp contrasts in the experiences of Black miners from place to place within and across regions.[15] Near the town's founding at the turn of the twentieth century, African Americans soon made up 55 percent of Buxton's five thousand residents, but their proportion declined to 40 percent as the Great Migration got underway and continued to decline into the 1920s. Whereas the Great Migration reinforced the expansion of Black coal-mining communities in most places, Buxton experienced the reverse. Focusing on the little-known, small coal town of Ferber, Texas, Marilyn D. Rhinehart shows how miners developed a "subterranean community" that cut across racial and ethnic lines and helped to forge amicable and less violent social relations in the aboveground community life of the town than elsewhere. But she offers little explanation for the town's ethnically and racially divided housing market.[16]

Conclusion

As new studies emerged on African American coal miners across the country, they established the intellectual and empirical foundation for the publication of new and more diverse syntheses on the subject. Labor historians Paul Nyden, Ronald Lewis, and Priscilla Long advanced broad general narratives and comparative syntheses of Black coal miners in U.S. labor and working-class history.[17] To some extent, more recently, historian Michael Goldfield's study, *The Southern Key*, reinforces these efforts.[18] Together, these studies illuminate the transformation of class, ethnic, race, and to some extent gender relations in the U.S. coal industry over more than a century of time. Building partly upon Nyden's pioneering history of Black coal miners in America, labor historians Ronald L. Lewis and Priscilla Long offer broader and more complete syntheses of race and ethnicity in the development of the U.S. coal industry. Lewis's *Black Coal Miners in America* is a stellar study of Black coal miners across the North and South. Employing a "comparative regional approach," he documents the emergence of distinct patterns of "race, class, and community conflict" in the bituminous coal industry of the United States. These distinct coal-mining experiences included what Lewis calls, respectively, "expropriation" and "exploitation" in the ante- and postbellum South; "exclusion" in the industrial North; a measure of "equality" in the central Appalachian coalfields of southern West Virginia; and the emergence of "elimination" in the recent period of deindustrialization and global restructuring of the U.S. economy.

Training her sight on the development of the U.S. coal industry in the Western states, Priscilla Long reinforces Lewis and Nyden's effort to integrate Black workers into a broader and more comprehensive understanding of the U.S. coal industry, race, and class conflict. Unlike Lewis and Nyden, however, she accents the role of women and gender as well. She opens her provocative narrative of the nation's coal industry with the words of Mary "Mother" Jones: "Pray for the dead and fight like hell for the living." Nonetheless, Long treats the coal industry as part of the international spread of capitalism from England to the United States. She places "the emergence of a new system of classes" and class relations at the center of her analysis. In her study, miners sometimes forged remarkably unified, alternative communal visions for America that clashed with capitalist commitments to private profit and individualism. But these visions repeatedly withered under the pressure of a diverse and deeply fragmented coal-mining working class. As she concludes, gender, race, culture, nationality, religion, and other issues "divided working people a hundred times over."[19]

While acknowledging the many failures of industrial workers to organize and sustain interracial labor movements, Michael Goldfield argues that such failures were by no means inevitable, especially among coal miners. Focusing roughly on the middle third of the twentieth century, he documents the emergence of coal miners as the "vanguard" of the radical interracial labor movement within and beyond the South. Even as they launched their own militant campaigns, most notably in Birmingham, Alabama, and Paint Creek and Cabin

Creek, West Virginia, miners assisted organizing efforts among other workers, particularly in steel, which they saw as key to the "security of their own union." [20]

Over the next decade, hopefully, as studies employing global methodologies and perspectives comes to fruition, they will lay the groundwork for the development of new and more transnational syntheses on African American workers in the Appalachian coalfields. This collection of essays aims to encourage and reinforce that process.

————

Chapter 1

AFRICAN AMERICANS IN WEST VIRGINIA

————

Ninety years ago, editor and publisher A. B. Caldwell published *The History of the American Negro: West Virginia Edition*, volume 7. Appearing on the heels of the Great Migration of African Americans out of the rural South and into the nation's major urban industrial centers, this volume of biographical portraits celebrates the achievements of Black West Virginians and reinforces the very hopeful social, cultural, and political outlook of the emerging "New Negro" of the 1920s. Membership in Black churches and fraternal orders, Republican Party politics, and local chapters of the NAACP figure prominently among the activities of the state's Black "men of distinction." Specifically, Caldwell pursues these biographies with an eye for the accomplishments of "representative" African American "leaders" in a wide range of professions and lines of work, for the "inspiration and encouragement" of the next generation of Black Mountaineers, and for the benefit of "future historians" of the state's Black past. On each of these counts—as a source of inspiration, a call for race advancement, and a document for future historical study—the West Virginia Edition represents a major contribution to knowledge.

Through the lens of biography, the *West Virginia Edition* underscores key themes in the state's African American history. From the onset of statehood in 1863 through the publication of Caldwell's book sixty years later, these themes included the ambiguous legacy of slavery and freedom, new patterns of class and racial inequality, and persistent movements for full citizenship and equal rights across the color line. In 1861, when Virginia seceded from the Union and joined the Confederacy, western Virginians opposed secession, remained in the Union, and created a new state. After becoming a state in 1863, however, West Virginia did not become a symbol of emancipation for enslaved and free Blacks.

While the Mountain State enacted a law for the gradual emancipation of en-slaved Black children after they reached adulthood, West Virginia nonetheless entered the Union as a slaveholding state. Before the constitutional convention approved gradual emancipation, the original provision stated, "No slave shall be brought or free person of color come into this state for permanent residence after this constitution goes into effect." Because of this provision, and under the impact of the Civil War, West Virginia's Black population actually dropped from over 21,000 in 1860 to nearly 17,000, or 3 percent of the total population by the war's end. In February 1865, however, West Virginia abolished chattel slavery nearly a year ahead of the Thirteenth Amendment.

Despite West Virginia's ambiguous legacy of slavery and freedom for Black people, African Americans from declining tobacco-growing areas of Virginia and other Upper South states gradually moved into the Mountain State. Beginning slowly during the Civil War with notable newcomers such as Booker T. Washington and his stepfather Washington Ferguson, Black migration to the Mountain State accelerated during the late nineteenth and early twentieth centuries as the state's bituminous coal industry dramatically expanded. Under the impact of industrialization, the Black population increased from 25,800 in 1880 to over 64,000 in 1910 and to nearly 115,000 in 1930, about 6 percent of the state's total. At a time when most industrial firms in the nation excluded Black workers from employment, both the railroad and coal industries hired large numbers of African Americans to open up the bituminous coalfields of southern Appalachia. African Americans helped lay track for the Chesapeake & Ohio (C&O), the Norfolk & Western, and the Virginian. Work on the C&O also produced the Black folk hero John Henry, who powerfully contested the steam drill during work on the Big Bend tunnel at Talcott, present-day Summers County. Following the completion of each rail line, substantial numbers of Black railroad men remained behind as part of the expanding coal mining labor force. Blacks made up more than 20 percent of all West Virginia coal miners from the 1890s through the early twentieth century.

Whereas the majority of Black migrants moved to West Virginia from the nearby states of Virginia, Kentucky, and Tennessee before World War I, rising numbers of Black migrants from the Deep South states of Alabama, Georgia, and Mississippi supplanted the Upper South sources of Black migrants during and after World War I. African American workers helped to increase coal pro-duction from less than 5 million tons in 1885 to nearly 40 million tons in the southern counties of the state alone by 1910. Although the industry would experience recurring up- and downswings in the demand for coal, southern West Virginia mines produced over 120 million tons in 1925.

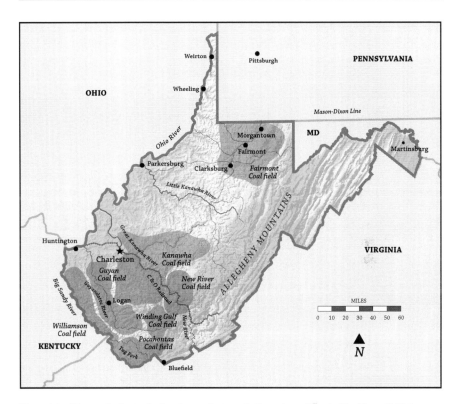

Map of the Mountain State during the early twentieth century. Created by Than Saffel.

Coal companies launched aggressive recruitment drives to bring Southern Black workers into the coal mines. During the war years, one company advertised for workers in the Williamson-Logan coalfields: "Miners Wanted: The Ideal Mining Town of the State. YMCA, Three Schools, Splendid Churches, Shower Baths, Playground, [and] Base-ball Parks." Black migrants to the Mountain State were by no means simply pulled by the forces of industrial labor demands or pushed by the economic decline of tobacco farming in their old homes; they were also agents in their own movement into the state. African American kin and friendship networks played a pivotal role in the Great Migration of Blacks into the Mountain State. In visits back South, coal miners invariably recruited additional relatives for the coalfields. In his investigation of Black migration during World War I, the U.S. attorney for the Southern District of Alabama remarked, "It is the returned [N]egroes who carry others off."

Deep South Blacks not only fueled the production of coal, they also helped to transform the culture and politics of the Mountain State. Their achievements, however, were closely intertwined with the pioneering political struggles of Blacks from Virginia and other Upper South states, beginning during the Civil War and continuing through the late nineteenth and early twentieth centuries. Black West Virginians, such as Martin R. Delany, served in the Union forces of Ohio, Pennsylvania, and other Northern states. Born in Charlestown, Jefferson County, Delany became a medical officer and attained the rank of major in the Union Army. Based partly upon their service in the Union forces, Blacks in the Mountain State claimed a role in bringing about their own emancipation and the collapse of slavery across the South.

Like their counterparts elsewhere in postbellum America, Black West Virginians confronted a long hard road to full citizenship rights. The fight for ratification of the Fifteenth Amendment resulted in fierce opposition from ex-Confederates working through the state's Democratic Party. Democrats refused to support the measure because it enfranchised Blacks and disfranchised former Confederates. Before Black men could secure the suffrage in West Virginia, Democrats succeeded in passing the Flick Amendment, extending the suffrage to ex-Confederates. In 1870, as elsewhere in the South, the Democratic Party presented itself as the "white man's party." At the state's constitutional convention in 1872, the Democrats also led the fight to disfranchise Black citizens, but failed. The new constitution enfranchised Blacks by a vote of 36 to 30.

Unlike their counterparts in other Southern states, Blacks in West Virginia not only won the franchise but also maintained it through the rise of Jim Crow during the late nineteenth and early twentieth centuries. Nonetheless, they achieved only partial victory. The new state constitution denied Blacks the right to serve on juries and mandated racially segregated institutions, particularly in public schools. Specifically, the segregationist clause stated, "White and colored shall not be taught in the same school." Accordingly, West Virginia sanctioned a racially stratified and unequal social order that would spread into a broad range of social service organizations and public accommodations. The state's Jim Crow order would frame the African American Freedom Movement through the mid-twentieth century. Although the incidence of mob violence was less prevalent in West Virginia than elsewhere in the postbellum and segregationist South, African Americans nonetheless confronted white supremacist campaigns and the outbreak of racial violence. In the early aftermath of World War I, in addition to the lynching of two Black miners at Chapmanville, Logan County, local chapters of the revitalized Ku Klux Klan emerged in Logan, Mercer, Kanawha, and other counties of the state. At the same time, Black men, particularly those accused of raping white women, faced summary justice before the law and sometimes died at the hands of the state, despite insufficient evidence of their guilt.

In line with West Virginia's segregationist law that "white and colored shall not be taught in the same school," this is a segregated West Virginia Department of Mines extension class for Black miners in the 1950s. Courtesy of West Virginia and Regional History Collection, West Virginia University, Morgantown, West Virginia.

African Americans in the Mountain State did not take racial and class inequality sitting down. Black Mountaineers waged an ongoing fight against efforts to curtail their citizenship rights. In 1872, for example, over sixty Black residents of Jefferson County presented a petition to the constitutional convention requesting the right to serve on juries in the state's courts of law. Additionally, since the Black percentage of the state's total population remained among the lowest in the Union, Black West Virginians carefully built alliances with selected white Republican leaders and forcefully advanced their claims for equal treatment. Some of their white allies eloquently argued for the rights of Blacks in their public speeches. In a speech supporting the right of Blacks to testify in court, Governor Arthur Boreman stated, "Until this act of justice is done, all other guarantees are fruitless, and these unfortunate people are left to the mercy of anyone who chooses to inflict injury upon them." Other white Republicans supported the enfranchisement of Blacks on the basis of their service in defense of the Union during the Civil War: "In war you send the Negro to the front . . . in peace you impose upon him all the duties of citizenship; why not let him vote? Republicanism makes no distinction before the law on account of race or color."

Under the impact of the Great Migration, African Americans increased their influence in the politics of the state and heightened their demands for equal rights. During the 1890s and 1910s, Blacks increased their proportion of the state's voting-age male population from negligible numbers following the Civil War to about 17 percent. As they made the transition to the new industrial era, African Americans also diversified their institutional and political responses to inequality. Black business and professional men took the top leadership positions, and African American workers and women also influenced the development of the Black community. Church membership, mainly in Baptist and African Methodist Episcopal (AME) bodies, rose from less than 15,000 in the pre–World War I years to nearly 33,000 in 1926. Black fraternal orders and mutual benefit societies also enrolled rising numbers, reaching a peak of about 32,000 members before declining during the late 1920s. Established in 1903 under the leadership of Rev. R. H. McKoy, the Golden Rule Beneficial and Endowment Association not only served Blacks in West Virginia but also developed branches in Kentucky and Virginia.

In addition to a broad range of churches, fraternal orders, and social clubs, Mountain State Blacks built strong ties to influential national Black civil rights and political organizations. West Virginia branches and affiliates of the National Association for the Advancement of Colored People and the Universal Negro Improvement Association (UNIA, i.e., the Garvey Movement) proliferated. By the mid-1920s, southern West Virginia alone counted no less than eight local chapters and divisions of the UNIA, while the NAACP reported a dozen active chapters in the region by the beginning of the Great Depression. Even as Blacks joined larger national campaigns for social justice, they also deepened their efforts to build solidarity among themselves as West Virginians. These efforts gained potent expression in the work of the closely aligned McDowell County Colored Republican Organization (MCCRO) and the Black weekly newspaper, the *McDowell Times*. Under the editorship of Matthew Thomas Whittico, a graduate of Lincoln University in Pennsylvania, the *McDowell Times* offered African Americans an alternative to the biased reporting of the white press. In Whittico's words, "The white press champions the cause of all people except the Negro, and upon the question of his rights . . . it is left to the Negro papers to wage an unceasing warfare upon the enemies of the Negro." Whittico also coined the popular phrase, "The Free State of McDowell." This phrase not only accented the paper's location in the state's largest center of Black population, it also underscored the determination of Mountain State Blacks to fight for and secure full citizenship for Blacks in West Virginia and the nation.

The proliferation of Black institutions facilitated the political mobilization of the state's Black population. Partly because they retained the right to vote at a time that other Southern Blacks faced increasing disfranchisement, African Americans in West Virginia exercised considerable influence in the politics of the state. Through their alliance with the Republican Party, Black voters largely insured the election of certain white Republicans to state and local positions, but they also insisted on nominating and electing their own numbers to public office. In 1918, three African American men served in the West Virginia State Legislature. Black state representatives included the Charleston attorney T. G. Nutter, the Keystone attorney Harry J. Capehart, and the coal miner John V. Coleman of Fayette County. Based upon their growing political influence in the state, by the onset of the Great Depression, African Americans had secured access to a variety of state-supported Black institutions: the Bureau of Negro Welfare and Statistics; two state colleges (Bluefield State and West Virginia State); a large number of public grade, middle, and high schools; and a plethora of social welfare institutions serving the state's Black handicapped, elderly, and tuberculosis patients, to name a few. Moreover, Black legislators had spear-headed passage of a pioneering antilynching law as well as a statute to prevent the showing of racially inflammatory films such as *The Birth of a Nation*.

African American political unity was by no means unproblematic. As elsewhere, the development of West Virginia's Black community entailed substantial tensions and social conflicts along class, cultural, and gender lines. By the late 1920s, for example, as increasing numbers of Blacks from the Deep South entered the coalfields, Blacks born in Virginia and West Virginia looked down upon the newcomers as less educated and modern than their Upper South counterparts. During the late 1920s, according to one study of race relations in the coalfields, West Virginians regarded the Southerners as "crude," "emotional," and "mean" and tended to avoid them.

While Black men took most decision-making positions, African American women provided indispensable leadership in the development of Black churches, fraternal orders, and social clubs. In his entry on Margaret A. W. Thompson, one of the three women listed in volume 7, Caldwell notes Thompson's extraordinary role as president of the state's Black Woman's Baptist Convention. She had served as president for twenty-four years: "The work has taken her into every part of the state and there is not a colored woman in West Virginia who is better known than Mrs. Thompson." Under her leadership, membership in the organization increased from under one hundred to more than fifteen hundred. Similarly, Hattie A. Washington, a second Black woman featured in the Caldwell volume, not only served as president of the state Federation of Women's Clubs in West Virginia but also took an active part in the benevolent Daughters of Rebecca and the fraternal Order of St. Lukes. Like other Black women religious leaders, Washington combined church work with club work, including the Woman's Improvement League.

In addition to their religious, club, and lodge work, Black women also fueled the political and civil rights activities of the Black community, both before and particularly after the enfranchisement of women in 1920. In 1927, Minnie Buckingham Harper became the first Black woman to serve in a state legislature in the United States when she completed the term of her deceased husband, E. Howard Harper of McDowell County. Memphis Tennessee Garrison, a public schoolteacher and civil rights activist, influenced the work of the local and state NAACP; she also shaped the work of the national organization when she spearheaded the NAACP's Annual Christmas Seal fundraising campaign under the powerful motto, "Merry Christmas and Justice for All." Garrison also served as secretary of the local Gary branch of the NAACP from 1921 through the remainder of the decade. At the same time that she worked with the NAACP, Garrison worked hard for the McDowell Colored Republican Organization; she also spearheaded a movement to replace the male secretary of the organization with a female. This movement split the MCCRO along gender lines, with men voting against and women voting for placing a woman in the secretary's post. Between 1926 and 1930, the predominantly male MCCRO defeated efforts of women to gain the position. In other organizations as well, Black women made their tremendous contributions to the life of the state against the barriers of gender and sex, as well as race and class.

Despite significant internal social cleavages and conflicts before the depression years, Black West Virginians experienced perhaps their most hopeful moment in the state's history during World War I and the 1920s. The Great Depression of the 1930s and the technological transformation of the coal industry (particularly the increasing use of mechanical coal-loading machines) set in motion the long-term outmigration of Blacks from the Mountain State to the industrial cities of the Northeast and Midwest. While the state's Black and white populations both dropped in the wake of the coal industry's decline, Blacks suffered disproportionate losses. By 1980, Blacks accounted for only 3 percent of the state's dwindling coal-industry workforce and about the same proportion of the state's total population. According to one Black miner, management "always put them [loading machines] where Blacks were working first." Black men, he said, could not "kick" against the machines.

As growing numbers of Blacks and whites left the state in the years after World War II, West Virginia's Jim Crow order gradually crumbled. Similar to the rise of the modem civil rights movement elsewhere, efforts to integrate the schools and open up public accommodations to Blacks and whites on an equal basis met stiff white resistance in some places. In Greenbrier County, for example, civil rights leaders faced intimidation and threats of violence from local white supremacist groups. For the most part, however, the increasing outmigration of Blacks and whites tempered resistance to the desegregation movement in the Mountain State. Unlike other southern states, by the mid-1970s the predominantly Black Bluefield State College and West Virginia State College had become predominantly white institutions. Moreover, at the grade school and high school levels, African American residents decried the swift dismantling of Black schools in the wake of the increasing consolidation of Black and white schools. According to R. Charles Byers, professor of education at West Virginia State College, the fall of Black high schools was a "heart-breaking" development, "but what was more deplorable was the injustice that took place in West Virginia. The artifacts, trophies, books, yearbooks, and records now referred to as memorabilia were burned or placed away in boxes and forgotten."

During the closing years of the twentieth century, African Americans continued their uphill struggles for social justice in the institutional, political, social, and economic life of the state. After a brief recovery in the coal industry during the national energy crisis of the early 1970s, the industry plunged downward again by the close of the twentieth century. Beginning during Roosevelt's New Deal coalition of the 1930s, the state's Black and white voters had supported the Democratic Party in national elections, but a majority of the state's white population voted Republican in the presidential elections of 2000, 2004, and in 2008, when the nation elected Barack H. Obama the first president of African American descent. In 1998, however, the state had elected a Marshall University professor, Marie Reed, the second Black woman to serve in the West Virginia House of Representatives, and the first Black woman to gain election to that office in her own right.

By the beginning of the twenty-first century, Black Mountaineers not only continued their fight to improve conditions and open up opportunities for the state's small African American population, they also mobilized their resources to recover and preserve the history of Blacks during the height of the segregationist era. In 1988, the First Baptist Church of Charleston hosted the First Annual Conference on West Virginia's Black History. Sponsored by the Alliance for the Collection, Preservation, and Dissemination of West Virginia's Black History, the annual conference underscored the state's loss of a broad range of historic institutions. Black Mountaineers and their white supporters not only decried the loss of recent Black history and culture through the closing of Black schools and the reverse integration of historically Black colleges, they also lamented the dismantling of key state-supported Black institutions such as the West Virginia Bureau of Negro Welfare and Statistics, which closed its doors in 1956 and thus removed a key agency in the fight to improve the socioeconomic status of Blacks across the state.

Reissue of Caldwell's *West Virginia Edition* in 2012 offers a fine opportunity for us to reassess recent changes in the state's Black history against the advances in African American life and race relations during and after World War I. Yet, despite its extraordinary contributions to knowledge, volume 7 exhibits certain limitations and blind spots. At a time when the vast majority of Southern Blacks entered the labor force before graduating from high school, this volume features the careers of men who had obtained high school, college, and even MA and PhD degrees from such diverse institutions as Howard University, Penn State, and Yale. It not only downplays the contributions of poor and working-class Black men, it also largely overlooks the vital role of Black women at all levels of the social structure. Only three Black women appear among the 118 entries. Nonetheless, this volume shows how the lives of Black men and women, both elites and workers, were closely intertwined within the larger context of the expanding Jim Crow order.

The segregationist system presented extraordinary challenges to the state's Black population across class, status, and gender lines, but West Virginia nonetheless seemed a great beacon of hope for large numbers of Black people during the first third of the twentieth century. Black men gained a substantial foothold in the bituminous coal industry; their numbers also helped to elect three Black men to the state legislature during the early post–World War I years. Moreover, while the movement for a federal antilynching law faltered, Black legislators spearheaded the passage of such a law in the Mountain State. As suggested by recent developments in African American history in West Virginia, the ninetieth anniversary publication of A. B. Caldwell's *History of the American Negro, West Virginia Edition* is an exceedingly timely and welcome event. It offers an extraordinary opportunity to reflect on the state's African American experience during the opening decade of another century—the era of Barack Obama.

———

MIGRATION TO SOUTHERN WEST VIRGINIA

———

The Great Migration of Blacks to northern, southern, and western cities is receiving increasing scholarly attention, but large numbers of Blacks moved to the southern Appalachian coalfields of Kentucky, Tennessee, Virginia, and especially West Virginia. The African American population in the central Appalachian plateau increased by nearly 200 percent between 1900 and 1930, from less than 40,000 to more than 108,000.[1] Black migration to southern Appalachia, as elsewhere, was deeply rooted in the social imperatives of Black life in the rural South, as well as the dynamics of industrial capitalism. This chapter examines the origins, sources, and consequences of Black migration to the Mountain State. It also suggests how Southern Blacks helped to organize their own movement and transformation into a new class of industrial workers.

Black migration to West Virginia accelerated as the Mountain State underwent a dramatic industrial transformation. The entire state produced only 5 million tons of coal in 1887, but coal production in southern West Virginia alone increased to nearly 40 million tons in 1910, about 70 percent of the state's total output. As coal companies increased production, the state's Black population increased from an estimated 25,800 in 1880 to more than 64,000 in 1910.[2] Like industrialization in other Southern states, bituminous coal mining helped to transform the region's largely subsistence economy into a dependent industrial economy, with growing links to national and international markets.[3] Between the 1890s and early 1930s, Blacks made up over 20 percent of the state's total coal-mining labor force.[4]

African American migration to the Mountain State built on antebellum and early postbellum roots. Booker T. Washington was among ex-slaves who migrated into the coalfields and worked in the mines. During the Civil War, Washington Furguson escaped from slavery and followed Union soldiers into the Kanawha Valley. After the Civil War, he sent for his wife, Jane, and her children, including the young Booker T., "who made the trip overland in a wagon, there being no railroad connection as yet with old Virginia." Booker T. Washington later described his tenure in the mines as an unpleasant experience. "Work in the coal mines I always dreaded. . . . There was always the danger of being blown to pieces by a premature explosion of powder, or of being crushed by falling slate. Accidents from one or the other of these causes were frequently occurring and this kept me in constant fear." [5]

Although Blacks had entered the region in the antebellum and Reconstruction eras, it was not until the railroad expansion of the 1890s and early 1900s that their numbers dramatically increased, giving rise to a new industrial proletariat. Black workers helped to lay track for every major rail line in the region. In his assessment of Black labor on the Chesapeake and Ohio (which produced the Black folk hero John Henry), sociologist James T. Laing concluded that "this important road was largely built by Negro laborers from Virginia." Upon completion of the Chesapeake and Ohio in 1873, many Blacks remained behind "to work in the newly opened coal mines of the New River district." The ex-slave James Henry Woodson from nearby Virginia eventually took a job on the labor crew of the Chesapeake and Ohio Railway shops and thus paved the way for his young son Carter G. Woodson's brief stint in the mines of the Kanawha- New River field. The younger Woodson later moved out of coal mining, earned a PhD degree from Harvard University, and founded the Association for the Study of Negro Life and History. [6]

In 1892, Blacks played "fully as large a part" in the building of the Norfolk and Western Railroad as they did in constructing the Chesapeake and Ohio. As in the case of the Chesapeake and Ohio, following the completion of the Norfolk and Western, many Black railroad men "remained to work in the coal fields" of the Pocahontas Division. Black labor on the Virginian Railroad and the subsequent opening of mines in the Winding Gulf field followed a similar pattern. "When the Winding Gulf Field . . . opened up through the building of the Virginian Railroad in 1909 the Negro again played the part of pioneer." [7] While a few individuals like Carter G. Woodson and Booker T. Washington eventually moved out of coal mining, gained substantial education, and became part of the national Black elite, most Black migrants finished out their careers as part of the expanding Black industrial proletariat. Under the impact of World War I, working-class Black kin and friendship networks would intensify, bringing a new generation of Southern Black workers into the coal industry. [8]

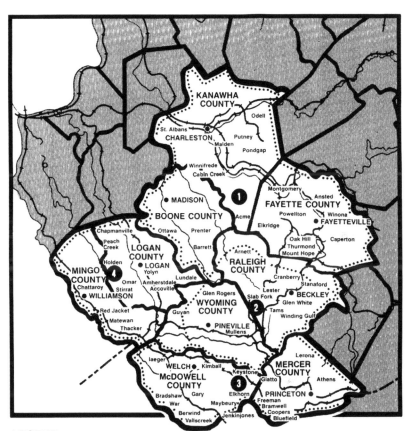

LEGEND

Approximate boundaries are shown by dotted lines.

1 Kanawha–New River Field: Kanawha, Fayette, and Boone Counties and part of Raleigh County

2 Winding Gulf Field: most of Raleigh and Wyoming Counties

3 Pocahontas Field: McDowell and Mercer Counties

4 Williamson-Logan Field: Logan and Mingo Counties and part of Wyoming County

Data Sources: Adapted from Otis K. Rice, *West Virginia: A History* (Lexington University Press of Kentucky, 1985); Cortez Donald Reece, "A Study of Selected Folksongs Collected in Southern West Virginia" (PhD diss., University of Southern California, 1955); and Philip M. Conley, *History of the West Virginia Coal Industry* (Charleston: Education Foundation, 1960).

Southern West Virginia. Reproduced with permission from Joe William Trotter Jr., *Coal, Class and Color: Blacks in Southern West Virginia, 1915–32* (Urbana: University of Illinois Press, 1990), 74.

Spurred by the labor demands of World War I, the Black population in southern West Virginia increased by nearly 50 percent, from just over forty thousand in 1910 to nearly sixty thousand in 1920. The percentage of West Virginia Blacks living in the southern counties increased from 63 to nearly 70 percent. At the same time, the Black coal mining proletariat increased from eleven thousand in 1915 to over fifteen thousand during the war years, rising from 20 to nearly 25 percent of the labor force, as immigrants declined from 31 to 19 percent. Led by Virginia with over 34 percent in 1920, Blacks from the Upper South states accounted for 56 percent of the state's Black total.

Black migration to southern West Virginia during World War I was part of the first wave of the Great Migration of Blacks northward out of the South. As elsewhere, the majority were young men between the primary working ages of twenty and forty-four, though the sex ratio evened out over time (as did the white ratio). Nonetheless, a substantial imbalance continued through the war years, at 125 males to every 100 females in 1920. One contemporary observer argued that the Mountain State not only received the earliest but also the "best" of the migrants. "We got the vanguard . . . those who came voluntarily and were not encouraged to leave on account of strained relations or the strain of living." In reality, however, the majority of Blacks entered West Virginia precisely because of the "strain of living" and often "strained relations" in other parts of the South.[9]

In the Upper South and Border States, Black farmers abandoned the land in growing numbers. During World War I, John Hayes moved his family from rural North Carolina to McDowell County, his daughter tersely recalled, "because he got tired of farming." For similar reasons, in 1917, John Henry Phillips moved his family from a small farm in Floyd County, Virginia, to Pageton, McDowell County. During World War I, Salem Wooten's family owned a farm in Henry County, Virginia, near Martinsville. The family raised wheat, corn, some live-stock, and especially tobacco for the market.[10]

Tobacco farming, Wooten recalled, was "back-breaking labor. Tobacco is a delicate crop and it's a lot of hard work. . . . If you did that all day, it was very tiresome." With thirteen boys and five girls in the family, the Wootens managed to make ends meet during the war and early postwar years. The young men, however, "wanted to get away from the farm." The elder Wooten fought in vain to keep his sons on the land. Shortly after his discharge from the army in 1918, the oldest son migrated to southern West Virginia, setting in motion a process that would eventually bring seven of his younger brothers into the coalfields.[11]

With the labor demands of the bituminous coal industry intersecting with the boll weevil and destructive storms on Southern farms, hundreds of Black sharecroppers and farm laborers from the Deep South also migrated to southern

West Virginia. The Deep South states of Alabama, Georgia, South Carolina, and Mississippi sent increasing numbers of Black migrants to southern West Virginia. Indeed, among contributing states, the Deep South state of Alabama was third, making up over 6 percent of West Virginia Blacks in 1920.

Under the deteriorating agricultural conditions in the Deep South, some white landowners eased their tenacious grip on Black farm laborers and helped to stimulate out-migration. In a revealing letter to the U.S Department of Justice, Alexander D. Pitts, U.S. attorney for the Southern District of Alabama, explained: "There has been no corn (and little cotton) made and this country only raises cotton and corn, you can readily see that the negroes have nothing to eat. The planters are not able to feed them and they are emigrating."[12]

Black miners averaged $3.20 to $5.00, and even more, per eight-hour day, compared to a maximum of $2.50 per nine-hour day for Southern industrial workers. Black Southern farm laborers made even less, as little as $0.75 to $1.00 per day. It is no wonder, as one migrant recalled, that some Blacks moved to southern West Virginia when "they heard that money was growing on trees."[13]

In 1916, Thornton Wright's family moved from a sharecropping experience in Montgomery, Alabama, to the coal-mining community of Accoville, Logan County. At the same time, a Union Springs, Alabama, migrant wrote from Holden, Logan County, "I make $80 to $90 per mo. with ease and wish you all much success. Hello to all the people of my home town. I am saving my money and spending some of it." Writing in a detailed letter to his friend, another Alabama migrant wrote back from Omar, Logan County, "You can make I dollar heaire quicker than you can 20 ct theaire in Alla."[14]

Important social, cultural, and political factors reinforced the attractiveness of West Virginia as a target of Black migrants. Racial lynchings were fewer, education opportunities were greater, and voting was not restricted by race as elsewhere in the South. In his letter back home, one migrant, W. L. McMillan, enclosed a flyer announcing a political rally, bearing the bold captions, "Republican Speaking Mr. Colored Man Come Out And Bring Your Friends to Hear." "Now listen," McMillan concluded, "I will vote for the president on the [11th]of this mont[h;] Collered man tick[e]t stands just as good as white man heare." Although it frequently overstated the case, during the 1920s the Bureau of Negro Welfare and Statistics (BNWS), a state agency, repeatedly emphasized the political and social attractions of West Virginia.[15]

Though most Blacks came to West Virginia from agricultural backgrounds, many had already made a substantial break with the land. As opportunities in Southern agriculture steadily declined, rural Blacks increasingly moved into Southern nonfarm industries, especially lumber, coal, and railroad work, before coming to West Virginia. Before bringing his family to Pageton, McDowell County, John Henry Phillips had alternated between work in a local sawmill and farm labor. Salem Wooton recalled that one of his brothers worked in a furniture factory in Martinsville, Virginia, before migrating to southern West Virginia. Before migrating to Coalwood, McDowell County, Pink Henderson and his father were coal miners in the Birmingham district of Alabama. Alabama coal operators were infamous for the highly unjust contract labor and convict lease systems of employment. Taken together, these systems placed miners—mainly Blacks—at a severe disadvantage, protected management, and helped to drive numerous Alabama miners to West Virginia. Commenting on the low wages in Alabama mines, Henderson stated, "That's why we came to West Virginia. They wasn't paying nothing [in Alabama]. They was paying more here in West Virginia mines than they was down there."[16] Since they entered the mines from industrial or semi-industrial backgrounds, Black men like the Hendersons, Phillips, and Wooten experienced a less radical change than farm laborers did.

In addition to the economic conditions from which they came, the recruitment and advertising campaigns of coal companies provided important stimuli to the Black migration. In the spring of 1916, the United States Coal and Coke Company, a subsidiary of the U.S. Steel Corporation, advertised for workers at Gary, McDowell County: "Wanted at once / 1000 Miners and Coke Drawers / 11 mines and 2000 coke ovens working Six Days Per Week / Five Percent Increase in Wages / Effective May 8, 1916." At the height of World War I, such advertising intensified. In the summer of 1917, the King and Tidewater Coal and Coke Company at Vivian, McDowell County, frantically announced, "10 Automobiles Free / Men Wanted: miners and Day Men Money without limit to be made with Ten Automobiles given away free."[17]

Professional labor recruiters for the coal companies also encouraged Southern Blacks to move to the coalfields. During World War I, E. T. McCarty, located in the Jefferson County Bank Building, Birmingham, Alabama, recruited Black coal miners for major southern West Virginia coal producers. His clients included the New River Coal Company and the New River and Pocahontas Coal Corporation. In Bessemer, Alabama, the renowned Jones and Maddox Employment Agency also served a variety of coal companies in the region. These agents carefully calculated their messages, skillfully aiming to uproot Blacks from their tenuous foothold in the Southern economy: "Do you want to go North where the laboring man shares the profits with the boss? Are you satisfied with your condition? Are you satisfied with your pay envelope? Are you

This is an early twentieth-century view of the Gary, West Virginia, coal mines of the U.S. Coal and Coke Company, a subsidiary of the U.S. Steel Corporation. For over thirty years, U.S. Steel secured its coal and coke supplies from its southern West Virginia mines. Courtesy of the Ancella Bickley Collection, West Virginia State Archives, Division of Culture and History, Charleston, West Virginia.

making enough wages [to] take care of you in the times of distress? If you are not satisfied we want you to come to see us." [18]

Coal companies also enlisted the support of middle-class Black leaders. Especially important was the local Black weekly, the *McDowell Times*, which circulated in West Virginia and nearby Virginia. During World War I, the *McDowell Times* editorially proclaimed, "Let millions of Negroes leave the South, it will make conditions better for those who remain." In lengthy articles, the *Times* celebrated the movement of Blacks into the various coal camps like those of Glen White, Raleigh County. "The old saying that 'All roads lead to Rome' surely has its modern analogy. . . . 'All railroads seem to lead to Glen White' for every train drops its quota of colored folks who are anxious to make their homes in the most beautiful spot in the mining district of West Virginia." *Times* columnist Ralph W. White stated simply, "To one and all of them we say WELCOME." [19]

Despite the optimistic portrayals of the *McDowell Times*, a substantial degree of private and public coercion underlay the recruitment of Black labor. Operators often advanced the migrants transportation fees, housing, and credit at the company store. Using privately employed Baldwin-Felts detectives, some coal operators were notorious for their violent control of Black workers. One Black miner recalled, "I can show you scars on my head which were put in there by the Baldwin-Felts men in 1917. There was four of them jumped me until they thought me dead, but I didn't die. They kicked two or three ribs loose—two or three of them—on Cabin Creek."[20]

The operators' autonomy over company-owned land was strengthened in 1917 when the West Virginia Legislature enacted a law to "prevent idleness and vagrancy . . . during the war and for six months thereafter. All able bodied men between 18 and 60 years of age, regardless of color, class or income must toil thirty-five hours each week to support themselves and their dependents."[21] Failure to work as prescribed could result in arrests and sentences to work for the county or city for six months. Neutral in its class and racial provisions, however, the law received the enthusiastic endorsement of middle-class Black leaders like T. Edward Hill, who approvingly exclaimed, "So the boys who 'toil not' in McDowell County have 30 days to make up their minds [to work in the mines or on public road crews]. . . . Don't crowd boys."[22]

Moreover, West Virginia had passed a prohibition law in 1914, and some of the prohibition arrests, convictions, and sentences to hard labor on county road projects were scarcely veiled efforts to discipline and exploit the Black labor force. Even the local Black weekly soon decried the arrest of what it condescendingly called "a lot of ignorant men and depriving their families of support for months and in some cases years." According to the state commissioner of prohibition, southern West Virginia had the highest incidence of arrests, convictions, and sentences to hard labor on county road projects.[23]

Although some Black miners felt the impact of public and private coercion, most migrants chose southern West Virginia voluntarily, using their network of kin and friends to get there. After arriving, they often urged their Southern kin and friends to join them. Acute contemporary observers understood the process. In his investigation of the great migration, the U.S. attorney for the Southern District of Alabama reported that at least 10 percent of those who had left had returned, but half of the returnees had come back for relatives and friends. "It is the returned negroes who carry others off."[24]

Coal companies soon recognized the recruitment potential of Black kin and friendship networks and hired Black miners to recruit among relatives and friends. During World War I, the Rum Creek Collieries Company hired Scotty Todd as a labor recruiter. On one trip back to Alabama, the company gave Todd enough money to bring fifty men to West Virginia. Several relatives and friends returned to the state with Todd, including his younger brother Roy. At Hollow Creek, McDowell County, the company added a second and then a third shift.

When one newcomer asked why, the superintendent's reply, although highly paternalistic, revealed the familial pattern of Black migration: "If you stop bringing all your uncles and . . . aunts and cousins up here we wouldn't have to do that. We got to make somewhere for them to work. . . . They can't all work on day shift. They can't all work on evening shift."[25]

As suggested above, coal mining was an overwhelmingly male occupation, with few opportunities for Black women outside the home. Yet, Black women played a crucial role in the migration process. Before migrating to southern West Virginia during the war years, Catherine Phillips married John Henry, who worked in a nearby sawmill in rural western Virginia. Catherine raised crops for home consumption, performed regular household chores, and gave birth to at least three of the couple's eight children. In 1917, she took care of the family by herself for several months, while John Henry traveled to southern West Virginia, worked in the coal mines, and finally returned for her and the children.[26]

Nannie Bolling, more than a decade before she moved with her family to southern West Virginia, married Sam Beasley in rural North Carolina. Sam eventually traveled to Gary, McDowell County, and worked in the mines for several pay periods, leaving Nannie to take care of the couple's four children until he returned for them. In a family group, including her husband, four children, and one grandparent, Vallier Henderson traveled from Jefferson County, Alabama, to McDowell County during World War I. The Hendersons traveled with a party of three other Alabama families, along with their household furnishings, and the trip took nearly seven days by rail. Upon reaching McDowell County, the families made a time-consuming and arduous horse-and-wagon trip into the mountains of Coalwood.[27] Back women—desiring to hold their families together, escape rural poverty, and gain greater control over their destinies—played a key role in the migration to southern West Virginia.[28]

Involving a web of legal entanglements and debts, some Blacks found it more difficult than others to escape Southern sharecropping arrangements. In such cases, their kin and friends served them well. Notwithstanding deteriorating conditions in the Southern economy, Southern landowners and businessmen often resisted the Black migration. They feared a permanent loss of their low-wage labor pool. Thus, for many Black migrants, white resistance necessitated a great deal of forethought, planning, and even secrecy. In his effort to ascertain the character and extent of Black migration from Mississippi, Jasper Boykins, a U.S. deputy marshal, reported, "It is very difficult to get the names and addresses of any of the negroes going away. It seems that this movement is being conducted very quietly."[29] Another investigator likewise observed, "I, myself, went to see the families of several negroes who have left and they are loath to tell where these people have gone. Of course, I did not tell them what I want to know. . . . They are secretive by nature."[30] Black migrants were by no means "secretive by nature," but many of them were secretive by design, and for solid reasons. The coercive elements of Southern sharecropping would die hard.

Yet not all Black migrants to southern West Virginia received the blessings of their kin. In deciding to leave their Southern homes, some young men moved despite the opposition of their fathers, who sought to keep them on the land. Scotty Todd and his brother moved to West Virginia when their father rejected their effort to bargain: they had requested a car in exchange for staying on the farm.[31] Salem Wooten's father also fought a losing battle to keep his sons on the land. The oldest son "slipped away," and his brother later vividly recalled the occasion:

> My father sent him over in the field to do some work. . . . And he packed his clothes, what few he had, and slipped them over there at the edge of the field and worked a little bit, well something like a half an hour in the field. Then he went to the cherry tree, ate all the cherries he could eat. Then he came down the tree and got his little suitcase, and he had to cross Smith River to get what we called the Norfolk and Western Railroad Train . . . into Roanoke [VA] from there into West Virginia. . . . He had money enough. . . . He came to McDowell County."[32]

Such family tensions undoubtedly punctuated the lives of numerous Blacks as they made their way into coalfields during the war and early postwar years.

Whereas the vigorous recruitment of Black workers characterized the war years, in the economic downturn of the early 1920s Black miners suffered rising unemployment. The Bureau of Negro Welfare and Statistics reported that the two years from July 1, 1921, to June 30, 1923, "were the most unsettled and dullest in the coal industry of this state for many years." Numerous Black miners like John Henry Phillips moved to farms in Virginia and North Carolina, until work in West Virginia was "more plentiful and wages higher." At the same time, other Black miners left the state for Pennsylvania and other Northern industrial centers.[33]

More important, as the United Mine Workers of America accelerated its organizing activities in the aftermath of World War I, coal companies intensified their efforts to retain a solid cadre of Black labor. As early as June 1920, the Williamson Coal Operators Association addressed a full-page advertisement to Black workers. The statement emphasized "the discrimination practiced against their race in the unionized fields," where the United Mine Workers held contracts with the operators of the northern Appalachian mines. Logan County coal operators developed a pamphlet for Black workers that exaggerated the virtues of coal mining in the area. "You are now living in the best coal field in the country, working six days a week in perfect harmony and on the seventh day resting, where there are churches and schools furnished by the coal company, while in the so-called Union fields, churches and schools are not furnished. . . . You are getting better pay than any other field and better coal." [34]

During the early postwar years, the Bureau of Negro Welfare and Statistics (BNWS) reinforced the operators' lively campaigns to keep Black workers. Under its Black director, T. Edward Hill, an attorney and business manager of the *McDowell Times*, the bureau often served the labor needs of the bituminous coal industry. In 1921, for example, the bureau proudly proclaimed credit for deterring over one hundred Black men from joining the violent "Armed March" of miners on Logan and Mingo Counties. Equally important, the bureau recognized the cyclical swings of the coal industry. When work was "irregular and wages reached a certain minimum," the bureau observed that hundreds of Black miners moved to nearby Southern farms until work resumed at higher wages. In an effort to help stabilize the Black labor force, the BNWS advocated the permanent resettlement of Southern Blacks on available West Virginia farmland. [35]

As the coal industry recovered between roughly 1923 and 1928, Black migration to the region also resumed. The Black population in southern West Virginia increased from close to sixty thousand in 1920 to nearly eighty thousand in 1930. By 1925, the Black coal-mining labor force had increased to an estimated 20,300, about 27 percent of the labor force, as immigrants continued to decline to less than 14 percent. When Black workers left the area during the economic downturn and coal strikes of the early postwar years, other Blacks, some serving as strikebreakers, had slowly filled their places. It was during this period that the Deep South states of Alabama, Georgia, and South Carolina dramatically increased their numbers. Alabama moved up from third to second place in the number of West Virginia Blacks born elsewhere. Blacks born in Alabama now made up nearly 10 percent of the number born in other states. Unlike the Black migration to the industrial North, however, the Upper South and Border States of Virginia, North Carolina, Tennessee, and Kentucky continued to dominate the migration stream to West Virginia. [36]

Established Black kin and friendship networks played a key role in stimulating the new cycle of Black migration into the coalfields. Born in Leesville, Virginia, Sidney Lee visited relatives in the region for several months off and on, before moving to Omar, Logan County, in 1926. Beginning at age fifteen, Lee had alternated between work on the Virginian Railroad and farm labor, before taking his first permanent job loading coal in southern West Virginia. Lester Phillips (son of John Henry and Catherine Phillips) returned to southern West Virginia to work in the mines shortly after his sister married a Pageton, McDowell County, man during the late 1920s. Salem Wooten's oldest brother, after migrating to southern West Virginia from Virginia in the early postwar years, assisted seven of his younger brothers to enter the coalfields, most arriving during the mid-to-late 1920s. The youngest, Salem Wooten, was the last to arrive. He migrated during the early 1930s. According to Elizabeth Broadnax, she and her mother moved from North Carolina to Capels, McDowell County, during the 1920s because her brother lived and worked there.[37]

The growing importance of Black kin and friendship networks was also reflected in the rising number of West Virginia–born Black miners. In increasing numbers, Southern-born fathers taught their West Virginia–born sons how to mine coal. This process gained momentum during the 1920s. In 1923, Virginia-born miner James B. Harris took his fifteen-year-old son into the mines at Giatto, Mercer County. The young Charles T. Harris entered coal mining from a coal-mining family, he later recalled, "as a career. I never even thought about it. Just coal mining was all I knew. My father was a coal miner." Three years later, with his father and cousin, Preston Turner loaded his first ton of coal at the Winding Gulf Colliery Company. Under the shadow of the impending depression, Lawrence Boling entered the mines of Madison, Boone County, in 1930. While Gus Boling had hoped to educate his son, he now relented and carried the young man into the mines. Lawrence Boling later recalled, "My dad and I talked it over. . . . Things were tough in the mines. . . . I seen I didn't have a chance to go to college even if I finished high school. So I decided at that point that I wanted to work in the mines and would be helping him too. I went in with him. . . . He was responsible for me for a certain length of time."[38]

During the 1920s, like most of their white counterparts, Afro-Americans entered the mines primarily as unskilled coal loaders. They worked mainly in underground positions, called "inside labor," as opposed to outside or surface works. In 1922 and again in 1927, the BNWS reported that more than 90 percent of Black miners worked as manual coal loaders or as common day laborers. The percentage of Black laborers declined during the Great Depression. Yet, according to Laing's survey of twenty coal-mining operations, over 75 percent of Black miners continued to work in such positions in 1932.[39]

Under the impact of the Great Depression of the 1930s, Blacks shouldered a disproportionate share of the unemployment and hard times. Their percentage in the state's coal-mining labor force dropped from over 22 percent in 1930 to about 17 percent in 1940. The depression and World War II also unleashed new technological and social forces that transformed the coal industry and stimulated massive out-migration in the postwar years. Although coal companies had installed undercutting machines in their mines during the 1890s, the hand loading of coal remained intact until the advent of the mechanical loader during the late 1930s. Loading machines rapidly displaced miners during the 1940s and 1950s. As one Black miner recalled, "The day they put the loading machine on our section, the coal leaders went in to work but the boss was already there and he said that the men not on his list could pick up their tools and leave." A Black miner recalled that the mine management "always put them [loading machines] where Blacks were working first." Black men, he said, could not "kick" against the machines.[40]

Mechanization decimated the Black coal-mining labor force. The percentage of Black miners dropped steadily to about 12 percent in 1950, 6.6 percent in 1960, and to 5.2 percent in 1970. By 1980, African Americans made up less than 3 percent of the state's coal miners. To be sure, the white labor force had also declined, dropping by nearly 36 percent, but the Black proportion had declined by over 90 percent. Under the leadership of John L. Lewis, the United Mine Workers of America adopted a policy on technological change that reinforced the unequal impact of mechanization on Black workers. As Lewis put it, "Shut down 4,000 coal mines, force 200,000 miners into other industries, and the coal problem will settle itself."

As the state's Black coal-mining labor force declined, racial discrimination persisted in all facets of life in the Mountain State. In 1961, according to the West Virginia Human Rights Commission, most of the state's public accommodations—restaurants, motels, hotels, swimming pools, and medical facilities—discriminated against Blacks. Moreover, applications for institutions of higher learning contained questions on race and religion, designed to exclude so-called undesirable groups. Finally, and most importantly, as Blacks lost coal-mining jobs, they found few alternative employment opportunities. The state's Human Rights Commission reported, "Numerous factories, department stores, and smaller private firms had obvious, if unwritten, policies whereby Blacks were not hired or promoted to jobs of importance or positions in which they would have day-to-day contact with white clientele."

Building upon the traditions bequeathed by preceding generations, many African Americans again responded to declining economic and social conditions by adapting migration strategies. Many moved to the large metropolitan areas of the Northeast and Midwest. Smaller networks of West Virginia Blacks emerged in cities such as Cleveland, Chicago, Detroit, and New York. Others moved to the nearby Upper South and border cities of Washington, D.C., and

Alexandria, Virginia. Still others moved as far west as California. Indicative of the rapid out-migration of West Virginia Blacks, the state's total African American population dropped from a peak of 117,700 in 1940 to 65,000 in 1980, a decline from 6 to 3 percent of the total.

Still, other West Virginia Blacks remained behind and struggled to make a living in the emerging new order. The dwindling number of African Americans did not sit quietly waiting for things to change under them. Charles Brooks, a Black miner from Kanawha County, served as the first president of the Black Lung Association, which in 1969 marched on the state capital in Charleston to demand compensation for miners suffering from the disease. In 1972, the Black Lung Association also played a key role in the coalition of forces that made up Miners for Democracy, a rank-and-file movement that resisted the growing autarchy of the United Mine Workers of America's top leaders like Tony Boyle. As early as the mid-1930s, along with Blacks elsewhere in America, West Virginia Blacks had reevaluated their historic links to the Republican Party and found it lacking. They joined the Democratic Party and helped to buttress the volatile New Deal coalition of Northern urban ethnic groups, organized labor, and devotees of what was known as the "solid South." As suggested by their disproportionately declining numbers in the coal industry, however, the Black alliance with the Democratic Party produced few lasting benefits in the Mountain State.

Although characterized by enduring patterns of class and racial inequality, the history of African Americans in West Virginia is not one but many stories. The first generation faced the challenge of transforming themselves from slaves into citizens in the larger body politic. While this goal was only partially realized and would persist over the next century, the next generation confronted its own unique challenge. During the late nineteenth and early twentieth centuries, African Americans in the Mountain State faced the difficult transition from life in Southern agriculture to life in coal-mining towns. Despite important class and gender differences between Black men and women and between Black workers and Black elites, African Americans built upon the traditions of their predecessors, bridged social cleavages, and protected their collective interests. Like preceding generations, the current generation is reckoning with the impact of mechanization, the decline of the coal industry, and the massive out-migration of Blacks to cities throughout the nation. How well they succeed in building upon the lessons of the past is yet to be seen.

Black migration to West Virginia was inextricably interwoven with the larger processes of industrialization and class formation in modern industrial America. Their experiences were shaped by the dynamics of class, race, and region. Yet, until the decline of the coal industry, southern West Virginia between World War I and the Great Depression offered a unique setting for the development of Black life. Blacks in the Mountain State faced fewer incidents of mob violence, less labor exploitation, and, since they retained the franchise, fewer constraints on their civil rights than their southernmost kinsmen. In 1918, for example, three Black men, one a coal miner, served in the state legislature from southern West Virginia. Nonetheless, their socioeconomic footing remained volatile, as reflected in the significant economic contributions of Black women, work in the deadly Hawk's Nest Tunnel, and substantial geographic mobility throughout the period. Still, through their southern kin and friendship networks, Black coal miners played a crucial role in organizing their own migration to the region. They facilitated their own entrance into the industrial labor force and to a substantial degree shaped their own experience under the onset of industrial capitalism.

Chapter 3

———

INEQUALITY IN THE WORKPLACE

———

Our knowledge of urban Black workers has increased considerably over the past several decades, but the rise of a Black industrial proletariat was not limited to cities.[1] Large numbers of Southern Blacks migrated to the coalfields of Kentucky, Tennessee, Virginia, and West Virginia. Although they entered rural settings, they performed industrial work and mirrored the larger transformation of the African American working class. Thus, a focus on the experiences of Black coal miners in southern West Virginia between World War I and the early years of the Great Depression has broader significance. It not only reveals the dynamics of class and racial inequality in the bituminous labor force and the Black miners' response, but, perhaps most important, it illustrates the comparative dimensions of proletarianization in different regions of the nation.

During the 1920s, like most of their white counterparts, African Americans entered the West Virginia mines primarily as unskilled coal loaders. As before the war, they worked mainly in underground positions, called "inside labor," as opposed to doing outside or surface work. In 1921, and again in 1927, the West Virginia Bureau of Negro Welfare and Statistics reported that more than 90 percent of Black miners worked as manual coal loaders or as common day laborers. The percentage of Black laborers declined during the Great Depression. Yet, according to James T. Laing's survey of twenty coal-mining operations—covering McDowell, Mercer, Fayette, Raleigh, Kanawha, and Logan Counties—75 percent of Black miners still worked in these positions in 1932 (Tables 3.1, 3.2, and 3.3).[2]

Coal loading was the most common, difficult, and hazardous inside job and thus was more readily available. Yet Blacks often preferred it because it paid more than other manual labor jobs and "provided the least supervision with the greatest amount of personal freedom in work hours." As one Black miner recalled, because coal loaders were paid by the ton, they could increase their wages simply by increasing their output.[3] On the other hand, while the average wage rates for coal loading were higher than most outside jobs, like other inside work, it was subject to greater seasonal fluctuations and presented greater health hazards.

Table 3.1. Black Coal Miners in West Virginia by Job Classification, 1921

	Number	Percent
Loaders	2,876	44.4
Inside and outside men (mainly common laborers)	3,376	52.1
Motormen	182	2.8
Skilled mechanics (mainly undercutting machine)	36	0.5
Foremen and other bosses	7	0.1
Officers and welfare workers	6	0.1
Total	6,483	100.0

Source: West Virginia Bureau of Negro Welfare and Statistics, Biennial Report, 1921–1922 (Charleston), 57–58.

Table 3.2. Black Coal Miners in West Virginia by Job Classification, 1927

	Number	Percent
Day laborer[s]	2,233	29.4
Coal loaders	4,674	61.4
Drivers	125	1.6
Brakemen	34	0.4
Trappers	10	0.1
Motormen	321	4.2
Machine-operators	215	2.8
Carpenters	8	0.1
Fireboss	1	—
Total	7,621	100.0

Source: West Virginia Bureau of Negro Welfare and Statistics, Biennial Report, 1927–1928 (Charleston), 17–19.
Note: Table sample was 7,621.

Table 3.3. Mining Occupations by Race and Ethnicity in Twenty Coal Operations of Five Southern West Virginia Counties, 1932

Occupation	American-Born Blacks		Immigrants		Whites	
	Number	Percent	Number	Percent	Number	Percent
Coal loaders	1,410	76.8	626	87.6	1,329	52.7
Machinemen	36	1.9	18	2.5	172	6.5
Motormen	85	4.6	16	2.2	199	7.6
Brakemen	128	6.9	7	0.9	169	6.4
Trackmen	109	5.9	36	5.0	177	6.7
Tipplemen	24	1.3	6	0.8	293	11.2
Other	43	2.3	5	0.7	224	8.5
Totals	1,835	100.0	714	100.0	2,613	100.0

Source: James T. Laing, "The Negro Miner in West Virginia" (PhD diss., Ohio State University, 1933), 195.

Note: The table included the following counties: McDowell, Mercer, Raleigh, Fayette, Kanawha, and possibly Logan.

Although coal loading was classified as unskilled work, it did require care and skill. For the novice especially, the apparently simple act of loading coal into a waiting train car could not be taken for granted. Watt Teal's father taught him important techniques for preserving his health as well as his life, such as carefully pacing his work. As Watt himself concluded, "There is a little art to it." [4]

Coal loading involved much more than merely pacing the work, though. It took over an hour of preparation before the miner could lift his first shovel of coal. The miner deployed an impressive range of knowledge and skills: the techniques of dynamiting coal, including knowledge of various gases and the principles of ventilation; the establishment of roof supports to prevent dangerous cave-ins; and the persistent canvassing of mines for potential hazards. Referring to the training he received from his brother, Salem Wooten recalled, "The first thing he taught me was . . . my safety, how to set props and posts. Wood posts were set up to keep the slate and rocks from caving in on you . . . safety first." [5]

Coal loading was not the only job that Blacks entered. Small numbers of them worked in skilled positions as machine operators, brakemen, and motor-men. In its 1921–1922 report, the BNWS proudly announced its success, al-though modest, in placing "three machine men, two motormen . . . [as well as] 57 coal loaders and company men." Labor advertisements sometimes specified the broad range of jobs available to African Americans: "Coal Miners, Coke Oven Men, Day Laborers, Contract Men and Helpers, Motormen, Track Layers. Machine Runners, Mule Drivers, Power Plant Men, and other good jobs to offer around the mines." According to statewide data, the number of Black motor-men and machinemen (or mechanics) increased nearly 50 percent, from 218 in 1921 to 536 in 1927 (see tables 3.1 and 3.2). Although their numbers declined thereafter, some Blacks retained their foothold in skilled positions through the 1920s, with machine running being the most lucrative. Between 1926 and 1929, for example, Roy Todd and his brothers worked as machine operators at the Island Creek Coal Company, at Holden, Logan County. On this job, Roy Todd recalled, he made enough money to buy a new car, bank $100 monthly, pay his regular expenses, and still have "money left over."[6]

However skillful Black coal loaders may have become, coal loading took its toll on their health. Some men literally broke themselves down loading coal. Pink Henderson painfully recalled, "My daddy got so he couldn't load coal. He tried to get company work [light labor, often on the outside], but the doctor turned him down, because he couldn't do nothing. He done broke his self down. . . . My brothers done the same thing. They used to be the heavy loaders." Moreover, all coal loaders, Black and white, careful and careless, were subject to the inherent dangers of coal mining such as black lung disease, then commonly called "miners' asthma," a slow killer of miners caused by constant inhalation of coal dust. Explosions were the most publicized and dramatic cause of miners' deaths, but roof and coal falls were the largest and most consistent killer (Tables 3.4 and 3.5). All coal miners and their families had to learn how to live with the fear of death, although few fully succeeded. As one Black miner and his wife recalled, reminiscent of Booker T. Washington's experience in the early prewar years, "That fear is always there. That fear was there all the time, because . . . you may see [each other] in the morning and never [see each other] any more in the flesh."[7]

As African Americans abandoned Southern life and labor for work in the coalfields, as the foregoing evidence suggests, their rural and semirural work culture gradually gave way to the imperatives of industrial capitalism. New skills, work habits, and occupational hazards moved increasingly to the fore, gradually supplanting their older rural work patterns and rhythms of "alternat-ing periods of light and intensive labor." With the dramatic expansion of their

Table 3.4. Two Selected Fatal Accident Types by Race and Ethnicity, West Virginia, 1917–1927

	Roof and Coal Falls		Mine Cars	
	Number	Percent	Number	Percent
1917				
Blacks	41	18.9	14	27.5
Foreign-born whites	73	33.4	14	27.5
American-born whites	104	47.7	23	45.0
Total	218	100.0	51	100.0
1921				
Blacks	45	23.0	12	22.7
Foreign-born whites	52	26.5	11	20.7
American-born whites	99	50.5	30	56.6
Total	196	100.0	53	100.0
1925				
Blacks	67	18.8	24	23.6
Foreign-born whites	90	25.1	13	12.7
American-born whites	201	56.1	65	63.7
Total	358	100.0	102	100.0
1927				
Blacks	59	22.1	19	23.8
Foreign-born whites	60	22.3	8	10.0
American-born whites	149	55.6	53	66.2
Total	268	100.0	80	100.0

Source: West Virginia Department of Mines, *Annual Reports, 1917,* 228; *1921,* 346; *1925,* 238; and *1927,* 207.

Table 3.5. Fatal and Nonfatal Mine Accidents by Race and Ethnicity, West Virginia, 1917–1927

	Fatal		Nonfatal	
	Number	Percent	Number	Percent
Blacks	74	18.8	176	17.8
Foreign-born whites	115	29.2	237	23.8
American-born whites	205	52.0	580	58.4
Total	394	100.0	993	100.0
1919				
Blacks	72	20.9	137	16.3
Foreign-born whites	86	28.8*	203	24.3
American-born whites	188	54.3	500	59.0
Total	346	100.0	842	100.0
1925				
Blacks	128	18.7	645	19.1
Foreign-born whites	138	20.1	617	18.1
American-born whites	420	61.2	2,132	62.8
Total	686	100.0	3,394	100.0
1927				
Blacks	168	28.5	644	18.8
Foreign-born whites	96	16.3	554	16.0
American-born whites	326	55.2	2,245	65.2
Total	590	100.0	3,443	100.0

Source: West Virginia Department of Mines, Annual Reports, 1917–1927 (Charleston).

*Includes three unknowns.

numbers during World War I and the 1920s, Black miners increasingly accepted southern West Virginia as a permanent place to live and labor.[8]

The working lives of Black women also underwent change in southern West Virginia, but it was less dramatic. Along with their regular domestic tasks, working-class Black women nearly universally tended gardens. Although the men and boys cleared and broke the ground, women and children planted, cultivated, harvested, and canned the produce: corn, beans, cabbage, and collard and turnip greens. The family's diet was supplemented by a few hogs, chickens, and sometimes a cow.[9] Gardening not only nourished the family but also symbolized links with their rural past and soon became deeply entrenched in the region's economic and cultural traditions. Not yet eleven years old, while confined to a local hospital bed, a young Black female penned her first verse, illuminating the role of the Black women in the life of the coalfields:

> When I get [to be] an old lady,
> I tell you what I'll do,
> I'll patch my apron, make my dress
> And hoe the garden too.[10]

Although Black women maintained gardens and worked mainly in the home, when compared to their white counterparts they had a higher rate of wage-earning domestic service employment. Based on state-level data, in 1920, when 19.8 percent of Black women were gainfully employed, only 10.8 percent of American-born white women, 15.5 percent of American-born white women of foreign or mixed parentage, and merely 8.2 percent of immigrant women were so employed. Recalling her mother's experience during the 1920s, Margaret Moorman opined, "No matter how poor white people are, they can always find a little change to hire a Black woman in their home, and [my mother] did that, she would work occasionally for some of the bosses."[11] When Mary Davis's husband lost a leg in a mining accident during the 1920s, she opened a boardinghouse restaurant, serving Black miners in the area. She rented an eight-room facility, where her family of nine boys and seven girls resided. To supplement Mary's restaurant activities, the family purchased a mule and cultivated a relatively large hillside plot behind the restaurant. In addition to a variety of vegetable crops, the family raised several hogs, chickens, and cows.[12]

Part and parcel of the material services that Black coal miners' wives provided their families were indispensable emotional encouragement and support. Even if exaggerated, the obituaries of Black women suggest their successful interweaving of material and spiritual roles. The 1916 obituary of Maggie E.

Matney, wife of a Black miner and a teacher by training, testified, "Her aim in life was the comfort and happiness of her home. She worked day and night to have these conditions exist there. It was indeed a place where each absent member longed to be. . . . [She planned] minutely the cost and use of every item that entered the family's budget."[13]

Matney's teacher's training must have enabled her to systematize her parental role. Yet working-class Black women placed a high value on children and family; some sought to adopt children when they could not have their own. In 1928, for example, a Black woman in the coal town of Hiawatha, McDowell County, wrote to W. E. B. Du Bois seeking his aid in adopting a child: "I would love for you all to look out for a girl are [sic] a boy [w]ho have not got a good home. . . . We have not got children and we would be so glad to. . . . They would really have a good home." When one Black woman married a coal miner who had recently lost his wife and had two sons, she dreaded the task of stepmothering, until one day she overheard one of her stepsons say to the other, "There is a dusty seat in Heaven waiting for a good stepmother and I believe Mrs. Lulu will get it; for she is a good stepmother."[14]

Family and gender relations in the Black coal-mining community were by no means unproblematic, though. The son of one miner who remarried following the death of his first wife recalled that his stepmother "was very antagonistic toward her three stepsons." As tension built between the children and the stepmother, one of the sons left home at an early age, he said, "in order to avoid the conflict between us." When it came to defining gender roles, working-class Black men endorsed the home as woman's proper and special sphere. In an ad for a wife, one Black miner sought a woman who could "cook, iron, feed his children and hogs, milk his cows, patch his pants, darn his socks, sew buttons on his shirt and in a general way attend to the domestic duties of his palatial home." Working-class Black men were acutely aware of their own tremendous labor value in the coalfields, as well as the small ratio of Black female wage earners. Unfortunately, this awareness, in part, often led Black miners to undervalue the Black woman's contributions to the household economy. "My mother never hit a lick at a snake," exclaimed one second-generation miner when asked if his mother worked outside the home.[15] Nonetheless, in the hostile racial environment of southern West Virginia, Black men and women pooled their resources in the interest of group survival and development.

Although African American coal-mining families gained a significant foothold in the coal industry, not all Blacks who entered the coalfields were equally committed to coal-mining life. Some of the men were actually gamblers, pimps, and bootleggers, reminiscent of John Hardy of prewar fame. Middle-class Black leaders attacked these men as "Jonahs" and "kid-glove dudes," who moved into the coalfields, exploited the miners, and then often moved on.[16] Other Black men, like European immigrants, used coal mining as a means of making money to buy land and farms in other parts of the South. The 1921–1922 report of the BNWS noted that some Black miners continued to work, sacrifice, and save in order "to buy a farm 'down home,' pay the indebtedness upon one already purchased or, after getting a 'little money ahead,' return to the old home." The 1923–1924 report observed that several hundred Blacks in the mines of McDowell, Mercer, and Mingo Counties either owned farms in Virginia and North Carolina or else had relatives who did. In order to curtail the temporary and often seasonal pattern of Black migration and work in the mines, the BNWS accelerated its campaign for the permanent resettlement of Blacks on available West Virginia farmland.[17]

If some Black workers entered the region on a temporary or seasonal basis, shifting back and forth between Southern farmwork and mine labor, it was the upswings and downswings of the business cycle that kept most Black miners on the move. Although there was an early postwar economic depression in the coal economy, it was the onslaught of the Great Depression that revealed in sharp relief the precarious footing of the Black coal-mining proletariat. In December 1930, the Black columnist S. R. Anderson of Bluefield reported that "more hunger and need" existed among Bluefield's Black population "than is generally known. It is going to be intensified during the hard months of January and February."[18] In the economic downturn that followed, the region's Black miners dropped from 19,648 in 1929 to 18,503 in 1931, though the percentage of Blacks in the labor force fluctuated only slightly, hovering between 26 and 27 percent. Black miners desperately struggled to maintain their foothold in the coal-mining region. Their desperation is vividly recorded in the "Hawk's Nest Tragedy" of Fayette County.

In 1930 the Union Carbide Corporation commissioned the construction firm of Rinehart and Dennis of Charlottesville, Virginia, to dig the Hawk's Nest Tunnel, in order to channel water from the New River to Union Carbide's hydroelectric plant near the Gauley Bridge. As local historian Mark Rowh noted, "Construction of the tunnel would mean hundreds of jobs, and many saw it as a godsend. Unfortunately, it would prove the opposite."[19]

Requiring extensive drilling through nearly four miles of deadly silica rock, in some areas approaching 100 percent, the project claimed the lives of an estimated five hundred men by its completion in 1935. African Americans were disproportionately hired for the project, and they were the chief victims. They made up 65 percent of the project's labor force and 75 percent of the inside tunnel crew. According to R. H. Faulconer, president of Rinehart and Dennis, "In the 30 months from the start of driving to the end of 1932, a total of 65 deaths of all workmen, both outside and inside the tunnel occurred, six whites and fifty-nine colored." [20] The depression was not only a period of extensive unemployment, but, as the Hawk's Nest calamity demonstrates, also a time of extraordinary labor exploitation.

If unemployment pressed some men into the lethal Hawk's Nest project, it also required substantial sacrifice from Black women. Pink Henderson recalled that while he worked on a variety of temporary jobs during the early depression years, his wife "canned a lot of stuff," kept two or three hogs, raised chickens, and made clothing for the family. In 1930 the U.S. Census Bureau reported that 57.6 percent of Black families in West Virginia were composed of three persons or less, compared to 37.5 percent for immigrant families and 40.8 percent for American-born white ones; but the difference in household size was offset by the larger number of boarders taken in by Black families. During the late 1920s and early 1930s, for example, Mary Davis not only enabled her own family to survive hard times but also aided the families of unemployed coal miners with her boardinghouse restaurant. "We were pretty fortunate," her son later recalled, "and helped a lot of people." [21]

Black coal miners and their families, the foregoing evidence suggests, were inextricably involved in the larger proletarianization process. As in the prewar years, through their Southern kin and friendship networks, Black coal miners played a crucial role in organizing their own migration to the region, facilitating their own entrance into the industrial labor force and, to a substantial degree, shaping their own experiences under the onslaught of industrial capitalism.

As the bituminous coal industry entered the post–World War I era, however, racial and ethnic competition increased. African Americans found it increasingly difficult to retain their positions in the industry, especially in the few supervisory and skilled positions they had earlier managed to acquire. As manual loaders, they also faced growing discrimination in the assignment of workplaces, a factor that made it hard to keep pace with the production and wage levels of their white counterparts. For the most disagreeable tasks, employers sought Blacks in preference to immigrants and American-born whites. The discriminatory policies of employers, however, were repeatedly reinforced by the racial attitudes and behavior of white workers and the state. Operating on the narrow middle ground between these hostile forces, Black coal miners eventually developed strategies for combating them.

After the war, Black representation among supervisory personnel dropped sharply. Black foremen, for example, increasingly lost ground during the postwar era. In the 1916–1920 period, nearly 10 percent of the supervisory personnel killed or seriously injured were Black men. Over the next five years, no Black fatalities or injuries were reported in this category, indicating a drastic drop-off in the numbers of Blacks holding supervisory positions. As early as 1916, attorney W. H. Harris, a *McDowell Times* columnist, complained, "It has been the practice not to employ Colored men as bosses in the mines. This has been . . . a sort of unwritten law as it were—no matter how capable or efficient they were." [22]

In its 1921–1922 survey of Black miners, the West Virginia BNWS recorded only seven Black foremen and other bosses in the entire state. A similar survey in 1927 produced "only one fire boss." "In late years, many or all of these places were filled by native whites and foreigners," wrote the teacher and political activist Memphis T. Garrison in 1926. [23] Under the impact of the depression, sociologist James T. Laing found, only eleven Blacks were in positions that, even by the most liberal stretch of the term, could be called positions of authority. Two of the eleven were assistant mine foremen; five worked as stable bosses in mines that still used mules; and the remainder held a miscellaneous set of jobs, including foreman over a slate dump, boss mule driver, and head of a "negro rock gang." In practice, employers modified their traditional position that "a Negro is a very good boss among his own color." One contemporary observer noted an emerging pattern when he remarked that "even foreigners are given these positions in preference to native Colored men." [24]

The discriminatory attitudes and practices of state officials reinforced Black exclusion from supervisory jobs. To meet the new standards that had been set on the eve of World War I, West Virginia University expanded its mining extension classes for the training of white foremen. During the war years, enrollments reached over 4,500, accelerated during the 1920s, and by 1930 had climbed to over 20,000. These classes not only trained whites for managerial and supervisory positions but also heightened the racial stratification of the mine labor force. Only in the late 1930s did Blacks receive similar classes, and then on a segregated and inadequate basis. [25] In the war and postwar years, as in the prewar era, caste restrictions continued to limit the occupational mobility of Black workers.

If Blacks found it nearly impossible to gain supervisory jobs, they found it somewhat less difficult to secure positions as machine operators and motormen. The employment of Blacks in unskilled and semiskilled jobs was highly sensitive to the specific labor demands of the bituminous coal industry. During the coal strikes of the early 1920s, for example, company officials hired growing numbers of Black machine operators and frequently praised them for their efficient labor. In 1921–1922, according to the BNWS, employers of skilled Black workers stated that "they are as efficient, more loyal, as regular and take a greater personal interest in their work and in the success of the business than workers of other races." Likewise during the economic upswing of the mid-1920s, the bureau enthusiastically reported, "Not only has the Negro made for himself a permanent place as miner and laborer about the mines, but he is being sought . . . by mine owners to fill positions requiring skill and training."[26]

Although some Blacks gained skilled positions, their path was nonetheless difficult. During the war years, for example, a Logan County engineer informed operators that "where ever one finds a Colored motorman having a white brakeman or machineman a white helper, he may be sure that there is more or less friction between the two. . . . A white man doesn't care to have a Colored for his buddy." Black workers found it especially difficult to secure jobs as mainline motormen, workers who transported loaded coal cars from underground working areas to the surface. In the mines of Hemphill and Coalwood, McDowell County, Pink Henderson bitterly recalled, during the 1920s "the mine foremen wouldn't let the Black[s] . . . run the motor. . . . A white man ran the motor." When the foreman assigned Blacks to motormen jobs, he was careful to specify that they were "running the motor extra," as a temporary expedient, thus preserving for whites a proprietary right to the job.[27] Another Black motorman agreed: "When a white man came there and wanted the job then . . . you had to get down. . . . A Black man had to get down and let the white run."[28]

Highlighting the exclusion of Blacks from jobs on the mainline motor was their employment as brakemen and mule drivers. Among skilled and semiskilled jobs, Blacks gained their strongest foothold in the dangerous brakeman job, which paralleled the hazardous coupling job on the old railroad cars. They worked behind white motormen but continually complained that white men "would not brake behind a Black motorman." Although the use of draft animals steadily declined with the rise of mechanization, some southern West Virginia mines continued to use mules in the underground transportation of coal. During the 1920s, Oscar Davis and later his son Leonard drove mules at the New River and Pocahontas Consolidated Coal Company in McDowell County.[29] Disproportionately Black, the mule drivers worked between the individual working places and the mainline rails, where the "mainline motor," usually operated by white men, pulled the cars to the tipple, the outside preparation and shipment facilities. According to the accident reports of the State Bureau of Mines, between 1916 and 1925 African Americans accounted for over 35 percent of the state's 124 fatal and serious nonfatal accidents involving mule drivers.[30] Gradually, however, the "gathering motors" replaced the mules.

The introduction of the gathering motor, which was ancillary to the "mainline motor," provided increasing opportunities for Blacks after World War I.

As the coal industry entered the depression years of the late 1920s, white resistance to employment of Blacks as skilled workers grew more vocal. Employers increasingly asserted that "the negro is not much good with machinery." At times, according to Laing, "the tone of the employer seemed to imply. . . . a coal cutting machine is a machine—hence, of course, he is no good." At the same time, white workers increased their resistance to the employment of Blacks as machinist helpers, men who had privileged entrée into machinist jobs. When asked if his Black helper was a good worker, one machinist replied, "Yes, he will do his work and half of mine if I want him to." He added that he never "gets familiar" and "keeps his place." The same machinist nonetheless expressed his preference for a white helper, and, as Blacks lost such jobs, those who remained worked under reluctant and blatantly exploitative white bosses.[31] While racism indeed shaped the white workers' responses toward Blacks, white machinists desired white helpers not because Blacks were "lazy," inefficient, or uncooperative, but because they were apparently the opposite and were thus perceived as a threat during a period of increasing mechanization and subsequent economic decline.[32]

In the aftermath of World War I, as racial discrimination excluded Blacks from important skilled, semiskilled, and supervisory positions, it blocked their progress in unskilled jobs as well. As coal loaders paid by the ton, Blacks faced increasing discrimination in the assignment of workplaces. To be sure, Black coal loaders shared a variety of debilitating working conditions with their white counterparts. Low wages, hazardous conditions, and hard work characterized the experiences of all miners regardless of ethnicity or race. Yet, according to the testimonies of Black miners, racism intensified the impact of such conditions on them. "A lot of those mines had unwritten policies. The Blacks would work a certain section of the mines. The [American] whites would work a certain section. The Italians and the foreigners would work a certain section," recalled Leonard Davis. Describing his father's experience during the 1920s and later his own, Davis also said, "At times . . . in certain conditions Blacks would have a good place to load coal. But mostly they were given places where there was a lot of rock, water, and some days you worked until you moved the rock. You didn't make a penny because they weren't paying for moving rock then. You didn't make anything."[33]

During the mid-1920s, Black miners repeatedly complained of poor working conditions. The seams they worked were characterized by excessive rock, water, low coal content, and bad air. They sometimes loaded three to four cars of rock before reaching the "good" coal. From the mid-1920s through the early

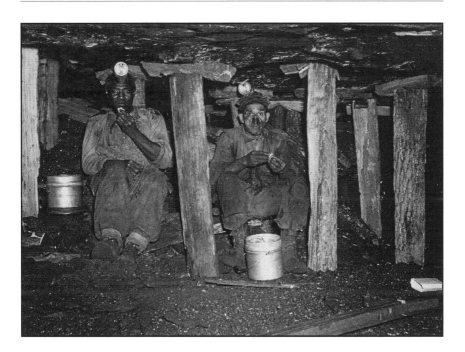

A Black and white miner take an underground lunch break together, despite stiff racial competition and discrimination in the assignment of underground workplaces. Courtesy of the Eastern Regional Coal Archives, Craft Memorial Library, Bluefield, West Virginia.

1930s, Roy Todd recalled, Black miners lost a lot of time and money through "dead work." If there was a rockfall in your area, he said, "you had to clean it up for nothing." The cleanup sometimes took two or three days.[34] Although many observers emphasized the water-free nature of West Virginia mines, in fact work in excessive water was a common problem. Some men loaded coal in hip boots. Even where water was no problem, Black men were disproportionately assigned low seams. They frequently worked in seams as low as two or three feet, loading coal on their knees. "I like it high. . . . I don't like it low," one Black miner exclaimed. "You got to crawl in there."[35] Although they used pads when loading low coal, some men developed calluses on their knees that "looked like they had two kneecaps." According to Lawrence Boling, poor ventilation also hampered the Black coal loader's progress: "Sometimes the circulation of air or no air would be so bad you'd have to wait sometimes up to two hours before you could get back in there to load any coal. I have been sick and dizzy off of that smoke many times. . . . That deadly poison is there. . . . It would knock you out too, make you weak as water."[36]

Compounding the problems of bad air, low coal seams, and water were the difficulties of unmechanized mines. While few mines used pick mining exclusively, traditional methods persisted in portions of mines where use of machines was difficult and unprofitable. During the late 1920s, in one of the few mines relying upon pick methods, Black miners outnumbered the combined total of immigrants and American-born white workers. In such cases the coal was undercut and loaded by hand, thus employing the traditional skill of pick and shovel mining. Recalling his father's employment as an occasional pick and shovel miner, one Black miner said, "My dad would tell me many times that I was [a]sleep when he went to work and [a]sleep when he came back." Another Black miner, Willis Martin of Gary, McDowell County, recalled, "We used to go to work so early in the morning and come home so late that on Sunday morning you'd see a little baby start to crying when he saw the strange man in the house."[37]

While these conditions indeed characterized the experiences of all miners to some extent, racism undoubtedly intensified their impact on Blacks. Surveys of employer attitudes and practices during the late 1920s confirm the role of racism in shaping the coal loader's experience. "The best points of the colored coal loader are that he will work in wet places and in entries where the air is bad with less complaint than the white man," claimed an employer in the Kanawha–New River field. Another employer declared that "in this low coal I would rather have a negro than any other loader."[38]

Reflecting the immigrants' ability to outbid Blacks for the better working areas, one employer exclaimed that "if they [immigrants] do not get the best places in the mine they will not work. . . . That is one thing about the colored man—he will work anywhere." Like American-born whites, immigrants in competition with Black workers increasingly adopted anti-Black attitudes and practices. According to Blacks, some of them exceeded "native whites in this respect." When one immigrant foreman lost his job, Black miners rejoiced, one of them stating, "I just can't stand being Jim-crowed by one of those fellows."[39]

Few workers of either race worked in the less hazardous outside positions, relatively safe from the dangers of explosions, coal dust, poisonous gases, and slate falls. Yet, even more than inside labor, the racial stratification of outside labor increased during World War I and its aftermath. Blacks dominated jobs in the coke yards, the hot, difficult, and most disagreeable of the outside positions, while whites dominated the less demanding phases of outside work, such as the preparation and shipment of coal. In 1910, Blacks had made up 47 percent of the state's coke workers, but in southern West Virginia during World War I and the 1920s, Blacks constituted 65–80 percent of all coke workers, with immigrants and American-born whites making up only 20–35 percent.[40]

Racial discrimination gained concrete expression in the lower average earnings of Black miners. During the economic downturn of the late 1920s, the racial wage gap widened. In 1929, the payrolls of three coal companies revealed an average semimonthly wage of $118.30, with the earnings of whites, both immigrant and American, exceeding those of Blacks by nearly $20.[41] No doubt racial discrimination exacted a similar toll on the earnings of Black miners throughout the postwar period. Despite the debilitating effects of class and racial inequality, Black miners took a hand in shaping their own experience. They developed strategies designed to vitiate the effects of various discriminatory practices that white employers, workers, and the state devised to subordinate them. These strategies included high levels of productivity in the face of white worker competition, solidarity with white workers in the face of capitalist exploitation of all workers, and a growing alliance with Black elites in the face of persistent patterns of racial inequality. Thus, at times their actions appear contradictory and at cross-purposes with each other. Yet, within the highly volatile class and racial environment of southern West Virginia, the Black coal miners' responses in fact had an underlying coherence and logic. As time passed and evidence of white hostility persisted, Black miners placed increasing emphasis on racial solidarity with Black elites as their primary strategy.[42]

In their competitive encounter with white workers, Black miners targeted job performance as one of their most telling mechanisms of survival. Seeking to secure their jobs, Black miners resolved to provide cooperative, efficient, and productive labor. During his career, one Black miner set a record for hand loading. He loaded ninety thousand tons of coal, an amount equal to a seventeen-mile-long train of 1,750 cars, each containing fifty tons.[43] More ordinary Black coal miners also related with pride the number of tons they loaded in a day or week and ultimately over a lifetime. Lawrence Boling later offered crucial insight into the Black miner's contributions to the coal industry, the use of productivity as a strategy of survival, and the Black miner's mentality, when he stated, "As far as I am concerned back in those days, the Black miner was the backbone of the mines. . . . I am proud of my life. . . . I may have worked hard. It was honest."[44]

Up through the job hierarchy, Black miners exhibited a similar resolve to perform well. At the Weyanoke Coal Company, Charles T. Harris transformed the dangerous brakeman job into a status symbol, as well as a mechanism of survival. "I liked the brakeman best . . . because the guys . . . would get together in the pool rooms . . . to see who was the best brakeman and [to] show off.

. . . In fact I done it mostly for a name. . . . They said that I was one of the best brakemen . . . and they called me 'Speed Harris.' " Harris even developed a joke around his job, which captured the inter- and even intraracial competition in the coal-mining labor force: "I said, 'Very few colored people can do what I do but no white at all.' " [45]

In the face of white competition, Black machine cutters and motormen also worked to improve their productivity. In the early 1920s, William Beasley alternated between jobs as a motorman and machine cutter. Later in the decade, using an old standard Goodman machine, he set a record on the undercutting machine, cutting twenty-eight places in eight hours. At times, coal operators used the performance of Black men to raise standards for white workers. The general manager of a large company in McDowell County said, "We try to standardize our work as much as possible. One day one of the groups of [white] coal cutters at a certain mine decided that five places were all that any one man could cut in a day. I went to one of my Negro cutters and told him to go down to that place and we would give [him] all the places he wanted and a $100 [bill] besides. That night this Negro cut 25 places. We standardized at seven." [46]

Black miners not only worked to increase tonnage; they aimed to do so with minimal damage to their health. Even as they pushed to increase output, they sought to avoid lost-time accidents. Like whites, Black miners participated in company-sponsored safety contests. Through such contests, but most of all through day-to-day attention to their own safety, Black miners honed their survival and safety skills. Roy Todd later recalled that he worked in the mines "forty-seven years without a lost time accident." Another Black miner recalled that his father worked in the mines "fifty-one years and he never had a lost time accident." [47] After more than fifty years of coal mining, Charles Harris recalled that his father "never was what you might say sick and he didn't have no bad back, and he didn't have no beat up hands. . . . That's right. I am telling you the truth now." No doubt Harris exaggerated this claim, but it nonetheless suggests insight into the Black miners' attention to their own health and safety. Other Black men simply refused to work in the most dangerous places, reflecting the constant tension in the Black miners' effort to provide productive labor while simultaneously protecting their lives and health. Columbus Avery said, "I'd go in to a place in the morning and inspect it. If it was bad, I wouldn't have anything to do with it. I never was hurt. I just wouldn't go into a dangerous place. They could fire me if they wanted to, but I wouldn't risk my life on a bad tap." [48]

Refusal to work in dangerous places was an aspect of the chronic transience of southern West Virginia's Black coal miners. "They fired me at Pidgeon Creek once because I refused to go into a place I thought was dangerous," Avery said.

Like their white counterparts, in efforts to improve working conditions, increase wages, and gain greater recognition of their humanity, Black miners frequently moved between one mine and another within the region. They regularly traveled through southern West Virginia and farms in other parts of the South. Gradually, they made their way to the mines and steel mills of northern West Virginia, Pennsylvania, and Ohio. "I moved once ten times in ten years. I was high tempered. I would not take nothing off of anyone. I had a lot of pride," Northern Dickerson recalled. Another Black miner said, "I would always be looking for the best job and the most money." [49]

Much of the Black miners' geographic mobility was involuntary, generated by cyclical swings in the coal economy. Moreover, even during good times, coal operators and their supervisory personnel were often arbitrary and callous in their hiring and firing decisions. As Walter Moorman recalled, when miners complained about pay, one foreman retorted, "Don't grumble and stay, grumble and be on your way." In good and bad times, many Black miners took this advice. When one mine foreman told a Black brakeman that he had other brakemen tied up outside "with a paper string, if it rain[s] they'll come in," the brakeman reached up on the motor board, got his lunch bag, said "You get 'em," and quit. [50]

Roy Todd's travels typified the geographical mobility of Black miners. In 1919, he took his first job at the No. 1 mine of the McGregor Coal Company at Slagle, Logan County. He worked there for one year before moving to Island Creek Coal Company at nearby Holden. Beginning at the firm's No. 1 mine, Todd soon moved to No. 8, before going to Trace Hollow for six months, working as a brace carrier on a company-constructed high school building. During the mid-1920s, he worked at several mines in McDowell County, including those of the Carswell Coal Company and the Houston Collier Company at Kimball. During the late 1920s and early 1930s, Todd spent short periods mining in Washington, Pennsylvania, the Fairmont District of northern West Virginia, and Lance and Wheelwright, Kentucky. [51] Thus, Todd, in common with other Black miners, traveled widely, not only from company to company but from mine to mine within the same company, always seeking better seams and safer conditions throughout the multistate eastern bituminous region.

In response to the intrinsic hazards of coal mining, Black coal miners sometimes developed close bonds with white miners, especially during crises surrounding such catastrophes as explosions. Echoing the sentiments of many, one Black miner exclaimed that "when that mine [explosion or accident] come, everybody seem like they were brothers. . . . If one man got killed it throwed a gloom over the whole mine." Even under ordinary circumstances, Black and white miners slowly developed bonds across racial and ethnic lines. Such ties were apparently most prominent among Blacks and immigrants of Italian origins, whom Blacks called "Tallies." Pink Henderson recalled that a "certain bunch of whites would not work with a Black man," but immigrants and Blacks got along "pretty well." Lawrence Boling recalled, "They seemed like they'd rather be with the Blacks than with the whites." While Black coal miners made few comparable remarks about their relationship with American-born white miners, some suggested that Blacks got along better with the West Virginia "mountain whites" than with white workers who migrated into the coalfields from Mississippi and other Deep South states.[52]

However uneven the relationship between Black and white coal miners, union struggles brought about a substantial degree of interracial solidarity among the southern West Virginia coal miners. During World War I, Districts 17 and 29 of the United Mine Workers of America (UMWA) expanded dramatically, covering the Kanawha–New River and Williamson-Logan coalfields, including Kanawha, Fayette, Logan, and Mingo Counties. District 17, the larger of the two, increased its membership from seven thousand in early 1917 to over seventeen thousand within a few months. By the war's end, it claimed over fifty thousand members. Union membership in District 29—covering the southernmost Pocahontas and Winding Gulf fields, including McDowell, Mercer, and Raleigh Counties—increased during the period from fewer than one thousand to six thousand. Black coal miners were prominent among the rank and file, frequently held office in local unions, served on the executive boards of Districts 17 and 29, worked as district organizers, and served as delegates to the biennial meetings of the national body.[53]

Because of language barriers, immigrants sometimes deferred to Black leadership. At the 1921 meeting of the national body, for example, Black delegate Frank Ingham of Mingo County eloquently addressed the gathering on conditions in his area: "I will first say that I am happy to be permitted to speak, not for myself but for Mingo county. . . . The real truth has never been told of Mingo county. It cannot be told. The language has not been coined to express the agonies the miners of Mingo county are enduring today. The world is under the impression that martial law exists there. That is not true. What exists in Mingo is partial law, because it is only brought to bear upon the miners that have joined the union." Even T. Edward Hill, the staunch antiunion director of the Bureau of Negro Welfare and Statistics, confirmed the positive character of interracial unionism in the area: "Negro members of the Executive Board . . . were elected in conventions in which white miner delegates outnumbered negroes more than five to one. The Negro union miners . . . are as staunch and faithful supporters of their organization as any other class of workers."[54]

George Edmunds of Iowa, a Black international organizer, played a key role in helping to unionize Black miners in southern West Virginia. In 1916 Edmunds wrote to West Virginia comrades, expressing intimate knowledge of conditions in the region: "I know so many of you, brothers. We have had some good times and hard times together. On Paint Creek and Cabin Creeks; from Gauley to the Ohio River, I have passed and repassed among you and . . . I always did my best for you and your cause." On one occasion, Edmunds addressed "a large and enthusiastic gathering" at Bancroft, West Virginia, where miners from several other mining towns in the Kanawha–New River district had gathered. On another occasion, he helped to organize a "rousing meeting" at Winnifrede, also located in the Kanawha–New River area. In the early postwar years, Edmunds continued to appear among the slate of speakers at the UMWA membership drives in the region.[55]

The immediate postwar years produced the most dramatic expression of working-class solidarity, culminating in the coal strike of 1921 and the "Armed March" of miners on Logan and Mingo Counties. When coal companies denied workers the right of collective bargaining, armed conflict erupted in Logan and Mingo Counties between more than five thousand union miners on one hand and over twelve hundred local law enforcement officers, strikebreakers, and company-employed detectives on the other. The conflict killed more than one hundred men and led to the declaration of martial law on three different occasions, once in 1920 and twice in 1921. Only the intervention of federal troops ended the brutal warfare. Before the conflict ended, however, many Black coal miners had demonstrated solidarity with their white brothers. The march on Logan and Mingo Counties included an estimated two thousand Black miners, mainly union men from the Kanawha–New River field. The movement eventually attracted Black adherents in the violently antiunion strongholds of Mingo, Logan, and McDowell Counties as well.[56]

In their violent confrontation with capital, Black and white miners developed reciprocal loyalties. Their commitment to each other was sometimes demonstrated in dramatic ways. When law officers and Baldwin-Felts guards dispersed a meeting of union men at Roderfield, McDowell County (leaving four dead and four wounded), Black miner R. B. Page organized a contingent of seventy-five men and marched to help his union brothers. Although the police thwarted his plans, his actions were a testament to the interracial character of the mine workers' struggle. At the height of class warfare, according to the *Charleston Gazette,* "One of the [white] deputies who was killed was John Gore. He was scouting through the woods near Blair [Mountain] and encountered a Negro scout. The negro [sic] opened fire on Gore and the latter fired in return.

The negro was killed." When a white miner "came upon Gore who was bending over the body of the negro searching for identification marks," he shot the officer "through the heart." In an enthusiastic letter to the *United Mine Workers Journal,* a white miner summed up the interracial character of the miners' struggle in southern West Virginia: "I call it a darn solid mass of different colors and tribes, blended together, woven, bound, interlocked, tongued and grooved and glued together in one body." [57]

Given before a U.S. Senate investigation committee, headed by Senator William S. Kenyon of Iowa, the most potent evidence of Black participation in the "Mingo War" was the testimony of Black coal miners themselves. Black miners stood firmly with white workers, and their testimonies reflect the complicated blending of class and racial consciousness. Black men also suffered a large, perhaps disproportionate, share of the violent reprisals from law enforcement officers and private Baldwin-Felts guards. For his union activities, Frank Ingham lost his job and house on several occasions. A veteran miner of fourteen years, in the early postwar years Ingham resisted efforts to divide workers along racial lines. The superintendent at his Mingo County mine fired Ingham when the Black miner urged his fellow workers to ignore the company's promise to reward them for abandoning their white coworkers. "He told me to get out when I told the colored people not to take the white people's places," Ingham told the senators. [58]

Nor was dismissal and eviction Ingham's only punishment. Arrested several times by both federal and local authorities, he was brutally beaten and denied visiting privileges. On one occasion, he testified, a local officer suggested that "what we ought to do with [Ingham] is not take him to jail; but to riddle his body with bullets." At midnight, law officers removed him from jail, stole his money and belongings, took him to an isolated spot, and beat him nearly to death. Federal and state authorities were no less brutal. Ingham said that Major Thomas Davis of the West Virginia National Guard denied him visitors and informed his wife, relatives, and friends that "the next nigger that came over and asked him anything about me that he would put them in [jail] as well." Through it all, however, Ingham emphasized his working-class activities as the fundamental cause of attacks upon him. Even following his brutal beating, he testified, saying "They asked me what I had been in the hands of the mob for and I told them because I belonged to the Union." [59]

Still, basic to Ingham's support of the union was his commitment to his race. When he joined the union and resisted the use of Black strikebreakers, he revealed consciousness of both class and race. Of his decision to oppose efforts to divide Black and white mine workers, he declared, "I did not think that would be a very safe thing to do, from the fact that it would terminate in a race riot, and I would not like to see my people in anything like that, because they were outnumbered so far as Mingo County" was concerned. Ingham said further, "My motive in advising the people was, I am a pioneer colored man in that creek. Before that they had been denied the privilege of working in these mines, and since they have got well established in there, many of them had found employment there. I did not want them to make enemies of the white race by taking their places." [60]

Other Black miners confirmed Ingham's commitment to working-class solidarity within the framework of Black unity. George Echols, a union miner, local UMWA officer, and striker said, "The United [Mine] Workers of America have privileges which are guaranteed by the United States, we have rights to protect us, both Black and white, but they [operators and law officers] do not regard those rights at all. They take those privileges away from us. Now we are asking you to give them back to us. Let us be free men. Let us stand equal." [61] Born in slavery, Echols articulated a distinctive African American perspective. "I was raised a slave," Echols related. "My master and my mistress called me and I answered, and I know the time when I was a slave, and I feel just like we feel now." The remarks of another Black miner, J. H. Reed, likewise expressed the blending of class and racial consciousness. Reed linked his arrest, incarceration, and mistreatment to his activities both as a union man and a Black: "The thing here is that a man here is the same as being in slavery." [62]

Still, in West Virginia as elsewhere, working-class solidarity was a highly precarious affair. To be sure, white miners drew inspiration from Black bondage, using the symbolism of slavery to help buttress the mine workers' case against the operators. Later, one white miner even put the issue in verse. "The boss said stand up boys—And drive away your fears / You are sentenced to slavery—for many long years." [63] Yet the white miners' own heritage of racism placed critical limits on their ability to identify with Black workers.

White workers and employers coalesced to a substantial, even fundamental degree around notions of Black inferiority.[64] In its contract with employees, under a provision on workmanship and methods, the Carbon Fuel Company stipulated that "The miner shall load his coal in every case free from shale, bone, *niggerhead* [i.e., worthless coal] and *other impurities*" (my italics).[65] When the *United Mine Workers Journal* reprinted a racist joke from the operators' *Coal Age*, the racial consensus between operators and coal miners was made even more explicit: "Sambo, a negro [mule] driver . . . was able to gather his trips without speaking to his mule. . . . Mose, another driver [presumably Black] . . . went to Sambo for help and asked Sambo what was needed to teach such tricks.

Sambo said all that was necessary was to know more than the mule." [66] Further highlighting the white racial consensus were distasteful and often vicious stereotypes of Black women. [67]

Cross-class white unity helped to engender a growing bond between workers and Black elites. The activities of the Bureau of Negro Welfare and Statistics, the Black press (especially the *McDowell Times*), and the McDowell County Colored Republican Organization (MCCRO) all evidenced aspects of the growing Black worker–Black elite alliance. Through the strikebreaking activities of T. Edward Hill of the BNWS, for example, some Blacks gained jobs during the massive coal strikes of the early 1920s. The bureau proudly claimed credit for deterring more than one hundred Black miners from joining the "Armed March." Under Hill's leadership, the BNWS nonetheless pursued its strikebreaking function with care, seeking to avoid racial violence. As an added measure of protection for Black workers, Hill, with some success, advocated the use of small, interracial contingents of strikebreakers. "The coal companies that are bringing in workers are having them sent in bunches of not more than 25 and in all crowds brought in to-date there have been whites as well as negroes," he reported in 1922. [68]

Hill not only tried to avoid racial violence in the short run; he also sought long-run job security for the Black miner. Keenly aware of the traditional dismissal of Blacks after strikes, Hill attempted to pry protective agreements from owners. In a letter to the local secretaries of the Coal Operators' Association and the president of the West Virginia Coal Association, Hill wrote that it would be "manifestly unfair to use negro miners in this crisis and then displace them when workers of other races are available." [69] In the coal strikes of 1921–1922, Hill secured an agreement from owners and managers "that, however the strike is settled, the negro miners now being employed" would be retained; or, if they voluntarily left their jobs or were "discharged for cause," their places would be filled by other Blacks. In case operators could not secure other Blacks to take the vacant places, the State Bureau of Negro Welfare and Statistics would "be requested to supply qualified Negroes." M. S. Bradley, president of the West Virginia Coal Association, Hill reported, promised to "lend his personal assistance in seeing that justice is done." The secretaries of the Kanawha and New River Coal Operators' Association endorsed the agreement. Hill believed the operators would keep their word and, until the Great Depression, most of them did. [70]

Such economic concessions, however, were purchased at a substantial price. They were achieved not only at the expense of interracial working-class unity but at the expense of greater racial pride and self-assertion. Although based upon the interplay of concrete class and racial interests, the relationship between Blacks and coal operators was mediated through the increasing rhetoric of welfare capitalism, conditioned by the operators' paternalistic and racist notions of Black dependency. In a 1920 advertisement titled "Discrimination Against the Negro," the Logan County coal operators hoped to convince Blacks that they, not the United Mine Workers of America, were best suited to protect the interest of Black workers. "Colored miners in the Williamson field who have been induced to become members of the United Mine Workers," the operators lamented, "were doubtless not informed about the discrimination practiced against their race in the unionized fields."[71]

The following year, the same operators sponsored a pamphlet aimed directly toward the Black workers. Again the owners informed Blacks that only the company had their best interest at heart. "First," the *UMWJ* warned Black miners, "when they open up a new mine they think of the things that will lead you and your children to the better land. . . . So we can plainly see how kind and true the operators are to the colored people in the Logan fields." As late as 1928, before the U.S. Senate's Coal Investigation Committee, a local coal operator testified that "The negro is not responsible for his position in America. It is the duty of the white man to treat him with justice, mercy, and compassion. . . . I do believe in providing the negroes with every economic and industrial [as opposed to social] opportunity possible."[72]

The Black press supported the operators' portrait of themselves as just and paternalistic employers. In doing so, they also adopted aspects of a larger progressive tradition, which urged corporate America to take a more humane interest in the welfare of its workers. In a detailed description of the Carter Coal Company, the popular *McDowell Times* columnist W. H. Harris presented a telling contrast between what he called the old and new captains of industry: "The old time captain of industry was ob[sessed] with just one idea to get as much labor as possible for the smallest amount of money. . . . In late years the industrial captains have found that . . . the best investment is an intelligent, satisfied class of employees."[73] During the 1920s, the popular Bluefield columnist S. R. Anderson reiterated the same theme in his recurring column "News of Colored People," printed in the white *Bluefield Daily Telegraph*. On one occasion, Anderson reinforced the idea of welfare capitalism "as an expression of the human element in corporate interest upon which we may rely as a 'savor of life unto life' against the wreck of radicalism in labor and corporate insanity."[74] In exchange for employment, housing, credit at the company store, and a gradually expanding variety of recreational and social welfare programs, employers expected deference from all workers, but especially from Blacks.

Under the energetic editorship of M. T. Whittico, the paternalistic theme was a recurring feature of the *McDowell Times*. Describing the miners as "children" and the operators as "parents," the *Times* sometimes took the paternalistic theme to extremes. A *Times* columnist describing R. D. Patterson, general manager of the Weyanoke Coal Company, declared, "He is a father to every man, woman and child on his work—a kind but not overly indulgent one. He gets results because his men believe in him." Moreover, the columnist concluded, Patterson's personality, ideas, and way of doing things permeated the entire fabric of coal camp life. "If you will stop to watch him a little, you will see Patterson reflected in everything on that works. . . . Chamelion-like, he has caused everything about him to become Pattersonized." "On the Winding Gulf," another columnist explained, "the men say that Mr. Tams," a company official, "is the working man's 'daddy.' "[75] Such language helped to perpetuate notions of racial subordination and superordination, suggesting critical limits to the benefits to coal miners of their alliance with Black elites. Yet Black editors, columnists, and other community leaders no doubt exaggerated managerial benevolence as a means of eliciting, as well as describing, the desired corporate behavior.

At times, elite leadership was a good deal more assertive. Under the leadership of the McDowell County Colored Republican Organization during World War I and its aftermath, African Americans escalated their demands for representation in the state bureaucracy. Dominated by the region's small Black elite, the civil rights struggle gave rise to a more urgent articulation of Black demands, with greater attention to the needs of the Black proletariat at work and at home—that is, in the larger community life of coal-mining towns.

In their efforts to move up in the bituminous coal industry, Black miners perceived a great deal of value in the growing political alliance between Black workers and Black elites. It not only promised jobs for highly trained Black miners in the state bureaucracy but also offered hope for the future training of Black workers in the changing bituminous coal industry. Thus, in 1927, for example, the State Department of Mines appointed a Black miner to the position of safety director. A former fire boss in the mines of McDowell County and a graduate of West Virginia State College, the new Black appointee, Osborne Black, was responsible for instructing Black miners in mine safety procedures. Mining experts soon came to regard Black as an effective official.[76]

Upon Black's death nearly two years later, the MCCRO passed a resolution "Paying a tribute of respect" to the miner, who was also an active member of the strongest Black political organization in the region. The MCCRO also urged the State Department of Mines to replace the deceased safety director with another African American miner, which it did. Upon John Patterson's appointment to the post, a contemporary student of Black miners noted that "so far as is known, he is the only Negro safety director in the world." Patterson had prepared for the position by taking correspondence courses from Pennsylvania State University. Moreover, before passing his state mine safety examination and receiving appointment to the state job, Patterson had also worked for several years as "a practical miner" and a mine foreman in Raleigh County.[77]

As suggested by the career of John Patterson, some Black miners benefited from their alliance with Black business and professional people. Yet, Black miners were by no means silent partners. They were highly conscious of the working-class basis of the bourgeois class's livelihood and even regarded it with a measure of suspicion, resentment, and distrust. One Black miner recalled, for example, that a prominent Black attorney gave "more favors to whites" than to Blacks. During the early depression years, in one coal town Black miners complained that the local branch of the NAACP did little to combat racial discrimination in the distribution of relief benefits. They also severely criticized the Black attorney who headed the organization: "Why he's a rich man—he don't worry none about us people up here. . . . He don't care about us po' folks."[78]

Between World War I and the Great Depression, as noted earlier, Black coal miners in southern West Virginia developed a variety of responses to racial inequality in the workplace: high productivity in the face of white worker competition; solidarity with white workers in the face of capitalist exploitation; and, most important, a growing alliance with Black elites in the face of persistent patterns of racial discrimination. Yet, although racial discrimination undercut the Black miners' position in southern West Virginia compared to Black miners farther north and south, Black miners in the Mountain State secured a firm position in the bituminous coal industry. Black coal miners in the North remained few in number and highly dispersed, as employers recruited south, central, and eastern European immigrants. Between 1900 and 1930, Black miners in the northern coalfields of Illinois, Indiana, Iowa, Ohio, and Pennsylvania never exceeded 3 percent of the total. Small numbers also made it impossible for African Americans to wage the socioeconomic and political struggles that Blacks waged in southern West Virginia.

White workers also developed strong labor unions in the Northern fields, a development that reinforced the exclusion of Blacks from mines in the region. In order to defeat the demands of white workers for higher pay and better working conditions, Northern coal operators gradually employed Black workers (some as strikebreakers). From the outset, white workers resisted the use of Black labor. As historian Ronald Lewis notes, not only were African Americans considered "scabs, they were *Black* scabs, and the white miners displayed at least as much hostility to their color as to their status as strikebreakers."[79] On April 10, 1899, in Pana and Virden, Illinois, seven persons lost their lives and fourteen were wounded in a confrontation between Black strikebreakers and white unionists. With little support from state and local authorities, the coal company accepted defeat and deported Black strikebreakers from the area. Still, the number of Black miners in the Northern fields slowly increased from just over five thousand in 1900 to nearly eleven thousand during the 1920s. Paradoxically, given their precarious position within a union stronghold, Black miners in the Northern region soon joined white workers and spearheaded a vigorous tradition of interracial unionism. Indeed, Black labor leaders from these Northern fields later aided the UMWA's campaign to organize Black and white miners in southern West Virginia and elsewhere. As discussed earlier, George Edmunds of Iowa was one of these, but the most renowned of these international Black organizers was Richard L. Davis of Ohio.

If Blacks were largely excluded from Northern mines, they dominated the labor force in the Birmingham district of Alabama. Yet a variety of forces weakened their position in the Deep South and made them more vulnerable to the exploitative dimensions of industrial capitalism than their counterparts in southern West Virginia. They faced the abusive contract and convict labor systems, a program of political disfranchisement (reinforced by a vicious pattern of racial violence, including lynchings and race riots), and a racial wage scale, which placed Black earnings distinctly below those of whites for the same work.

Despite the exceedingly hostile environment for interracial solidarity in the Alabama coalfields, Black and white miners developed a degree of class unity. Beginning with the United Mine Workers of Alabama in the late 1880s and early 1890s and continuing with the Southern campaign of the UMWA during the late 1890s and early 1900s, Black and white miners joined together and fought the exploitative practices of Alabama coal companies, particularly the Tennessee Coal, Iron, and Railroad Company, which became a subsidiary of U.S. Steel in 1907. The UMW of Alabama and the UMWA developed policies that aimed to organize Black and white workers across racial lines. Although local autonomy dictated the growth of separate Black and white unions, Alabama District 20 nonetheless reserved the district vice presidency and three of the seven executive board slots for African Americans. Under the leadership of the UMWA, Black and white miners launched vigorous strikes in 1904, 1908, and 1920–1921. In each case, however, partly because rank-and-file white miners had difficulty surmounting their own racism, coal companies appealed to white fears of racial equality and successfully mobilized private and public power against the union and defeated the strikes.

Conditions in the Deep South coalfields helped to drive many Alabama miners to southern West Virginia. Although they occupied the lowest position in the bituminous labor force, in the Mountain State Black miners gained comparatively greater opportunities than their counterparts further north and south. They gained a solid footing in the coal-mining labor force, received equal pay for equal work, were allowed to vote, confronted fewer lynchings and incidents of mob violence, and waged a vigorous and largely successful political struggle for recognition of their human and civil rights.

Coal miner ministers played a major role in the development of African American coal-mining communities. This is a photo of Rev. Wilford Dickerson and his wife, the former Harriet Boone, of Raleigh County, West Virginia. Courtesy of Mr. and Mrs. North Dickerson, Beckley, West Virginia.

Chapter 4

COMMUNITY FORMATION

The rise and expansion of the bituminous coal industry stimulated the emergence of a Black proletariat in southern West Virginia. Blacks were largely excluded from the Northern industrial labor force between 1880 and World War I. But the coal companies of central Appalachia actively recruited Blacks, along with "native whites" and European immigrants, to make up the labor force for their rapidly emerging industry.[1] The rise of the Black coal-mining proletariat was nonetheless a complex process; it was rooted in the social imperatives of Black life in the rural South as well as in the dynamics of industrial capitalism. In their efforts to recruit and control Black labor, coal operators employed a blend of legal and extralegal measures reinforced by the racist attitudes and practices of white workers and the state. However, Black workers, using their network of family and friends, organized their own migration to the region. In this way, they facilitated their own transition to the industrial labor force and paved the way for the rise of a new Black middle class that helped to gradually transform the contours of African American community life in coal-mining towns.

Under the impact of the coal industry's rapid expansion, southern West Virginia underwent a dramatic transformation during the late nineteenth and early twentieth centuries. While the entire state produced only 5 million tons of coal in 1887, coal production in its southern region alone increased to nearly 40 million tons in 1910, which made up 70 percent of the state's total output that year. The region's population increased just as dramatically, growing from about eighty thousand in 1880 to nearly three hundred thousand in 1910.[2] Immigrants from southern, central, and eastern Europe grew from only fourteen hundred in 1880 to eighteen thousand (6 percent of the total) in 1910. The Black population's growth was even greater, moving from forty-eight hundred in 1880 to over forty thousand in 1910. With 6 percent of the total in 1880, by 1910 African Americans made up 14 percent of the populace thirty years later, over twice the proportion of immigrants in the southern part of the state.[3] West Virginia's concentration of African Americans shifted southward as well. Only about 21 percent of the state's Blacks lived in the southern counties in 1880; by 1910, that figure had climbed to 63 percent. In order to cut costs and keep wages down, some coal operators preferred a mixed labor force of immigrants, Blacks, and American-born whites.[4]

Coal mining transformed African American life and labor. As rural Black men entered the coal mines in growing numbers, their seasonal rhythms of planting, cultivating, and harvesting gradually gave way to the new demands of industrial labor. The techniques of dynamiting coal, a variety of mine safety procedures, and the mental and physical requirements of hand loading tons of coal all increasingly supplanted Black workers' agricultural skills and work habits. Because coal mining evolved in semirural settings, the transformation was not as radical as it might have been; Black coal miners regularly shifted back and forth between farming and work in the coal mines.[5]

At the same time that these transitions were taking place, Black miners and their families also contributed to the formation of Black community in southern West Virginia. Black religious, fraternal, and political organizations dramatically expanded. African American institution-building activities reflected growing participation in the coal economy, rapid population growth, and the effects of racial discrimination; they also reflected and stimulated the rise of a vigorous Black leadership. As elsewhere, however, although the Black community developed a high level of racial solidarity in the process, it failed to fully surmount internal conflict along class lines. Black congregations, fraternal orders, and state and local politics offer the most sensitive barometers of change in these areas within the Black coal-mining community.

The independent African American churches in southern West Virginia had their roots in the early emancipation era. Until the Civil War, Blacks had worshipped in the same congregations as whites, but on a segregated basis. Following the Civil War, as elsewhere in the South, African Americans increasingly separated from white religious institutions. Under the leadership of Reverend Lewis Rice, for example, the African Zion Baptist Church at Tinkerville (Malden) in Kanawha County spearheaded the independent Black Baptist movement in the region. A member of the Providence Association of Ohio, formed in 1868, the African Zion Baptist Church stimulated the rise of new "arms of the African Zion Church" in West Virginia. By 1873, as a result of the church's vigorous organizing activities, West Virginia's Black Baptists seceded from the Ohio conference and formed the Mt. Olivet Baptist Association.

Until he left the region in 1880, Booker T. Washington was a member, a Sunday school teacher, and a clerk of the "mother church" at Malden.[6]

As the processes of Black migration, proletarianization, and institutional racism converged during the late nineteenth and early twentieth centuries, Black religious institutions dramatically expanded. Black membership in West Virginia churches more than doubled, from over seven thousand in 1890 to nearly fifteen thousand in 1906. Although Blacks developed a thriving Presbyterian church in McDowell County, and although the number of African Methodist Episcopal churches increased to more than thirty-five at the turn of the century, Baptists dominated the region's Black religious life. In 1906 the U.S. Census of Religious Bodies reported 148 Black Baptist churches in the Mountain State. New congregations were initiated and new associations rapidly emerged in McDowell, Mercer, Raleigh, Fayette, Mingo, and Logan Counties. The Mt. Olivet Baptist Association was soon followed by the New River Baptist Association in 1884, the Flat Top Baptist Association in 1896, and the Guyan Valley Association in 1913. The Flat Top Baptist Association, located in the Pocahontas Field, became the largest and richest in West Virginia.[7]

Black religious life mirrored and stimulated the growth of an energetic Black ministry. The number of Black ministers increased from 93 in 1900 to 150 a decade later. Black ministers played a major role in harnessing working-class financial resources to pay church debts, although some preached for months without pay. Sometimes their fund-raising efforts were quite successful. In May 1913, for example, under the pastorate of Reverend R. H. McKoy, the Bluestone Baptist Church at Bramwell, Mercer County, "closed one of the most successful [financial] rallies in its history," raising $330 over a two-week period. Under the pastorate of Reverend R. V. Barksdale, in July 1913 the First Baptist Church of Anawalt, McDowell County, raised $400 in a special rally.[8] When a fire destroyed the St. James Baptist Church in Welch, Reverend W. R. Pittard and his congregation launched a spirited rebuilding campaign. Within six months, they had raised nearly $500.[9] Coal companies often gave financial support to Black and white churches, but their assistance was not enough to sustain Black churches. Only the persistence of Black coal miners, their families, and their ministers in contributing to the churches fully explains the churches' success in the coalfields.

If the resources of Black coal miners underlay the material well-being of the church, their spiritual and cultural needs shaped patterns of church worship and participation. Rooted deeply in the religious experience of Southern Blacks, the Black church in southern West Virginia helped to sustain and reinforce the

Black workers' spiritual and communal beliefs and practices through sermons, revival meetings, baptismal ceremonies, and funeral rites. At a May 1914 revival meeting, Reverend C. H. Rollins of the Slab Fork Baptist Church "preached two able sermons to an appreciative audience." Taking his texts from Matthew 7:7 and Zechariah 13:1, he "preached so powerful that we were made to say within ourselves as one of the apostles of old, 'Did not our hearts burn within us as he talked by the way.' " [10] At the Wingfield Baptist Church in Eckman, McDowell County, a huge crowd gathered at the river's edge to witness "the 'plunging under' or the 'Burial in Baptism' " of the new converts. "People from all over the county hearing of the occasion . . . came on every train, both east and west. A densely packed crowd of men and women, boys and girls . . . were there." [11] In mid-1913 a funeral for a Black miner who died in a slate fall was conducted at the Mt. Ebenezer Baptist Church near Gilliam, McDowell County, where he was a member in good standing. Reverend L. A. Watkins preached the funeral sermon to a host of "friends and relatives," selecting his text from John 19:30: "When Jesus therefore had received the vinegar, he said, It is finished: and he bowed his head, and gave up the ghost." The choir sang the deceased miner's favorite hymn, "Will the Waters Be Chilly?" [12] Moreover, besides attending funerals and other local church functions, through frequent visits to their old Southern homes, Black workers renewed their ties with the established religious customs of their past. [13]

As Blacks entered the southern West Virginia coalfields in greater numbers, although they retained important cultural links with their rural past, their religious beliefs and practices underwent gradual transformation. Although the evidence is quite sparse, an educated Black ministry gradually emerged in the prewar years. Under its leadership, emotional services increasingly gave way to ones featuring rational and logical sermons often concerned with improving temporal, social, economic, and political conditions and, above all, with the proper attitude and behavior for racial progress in the new industrial age. [14] These emphases undoubtedly had antecedents in the Southern Black religious experience, but they emerged clearly within the socioeconomic, political, and cultural environment of southern West Virginia.

The growing pool of educated Black preachers included schoolteachers who doubled as ministers, such as Reverend J. W. Robinson, principal of the Tidewater Grade School. In November 1913, Reverend Robinson was installed as pastor of the First Baptist Church of Kimball. "He is one of the best known and ablest men in the state, an advocator of note and a preacher of great ability," the McDowell Times reported. But perhaps the best example of the rising educated Black ministry was Reverend Mordecai W. Johnson, who took the pastorate of the First Baptist Church of Charleston, West Virginia, in 1913. Born in 1890 in Paris, Henry County, Tennessee, Johnson received a bachelor of arts degree from Morehouse College in Atlanta in 1911, where he taught economics and history for a while, and another from the University of Chicago in 1913. In the postwar years he left the First Baptist Church for a position at Howard University, where, in 1926, he became its first Black president. Before leaving, though, Johnson played an important role not only in the religious life of the community but also in the civil rights struggle.[15]

Some influential ministers in southern West Virginia were self-taught. The pastor of several Black churches in Kanawha County, Reverend Nelson Barnett of Huntington, Cabell County, was perhaps the most gifted. Born a slave in Buckingham County, Virginia, in 1842, Barnett migrated to West Virginia in 1873 and eventually became the pastor of churches in St. Albans, Longacre, and Raymond City. Upon his death in 1909, the *Huntington Dispatch* wrote, "He lacked the learning of the schools because he was born a slave. But he was of a studious turn of mind, gifted in speech, could expound the scriptures with an insight truly remarkable, and his preaching was wonderfully effective in bringing men to Christ."[16] The funeral sermon for Barnett, preached by the educated Black minister Reverend I. V. Bryant of Huntington, was even more eloquent: "If by education we mean the drawing out of the latent powers and spreading them in glowing characters upon the canvas of the mind, if by education we mean the proper cultivation of all the faculties, the symmetrical development of the head, the heart, and the hand, together with those combined elements that make the entire man, I positively deny that he was uneducated. . . . He was taught by the Great God."[17]

Formally and informally educated Black ministers helped to transform Black workers' religious beliefs and practices. By appealing to the intellect rather than merely to the emotions of their congregants, they helped to rationalize Black religious services. Reverend Barnett, his eulogizer stated, "preached industry as well as religion, and had accumulated considerable property, owning two or three houses and lots in the city. He was active in all interests for the betterment of his race, and took particular interest in the education of young people who regard him as a father."[18] In his sermon before the Seventeenth Annual Meeting of the Flat Top Baptist Association, Reverend G. W. Woody stressed "the fact that men must work for this world's goods." "In conclusion, Rev. Woody grew more forceful and urged upon the brethren to be patient in the small details of their life's work." Before World War I, Reverend J. H. Hammond of Jenkinjones, West Virginia, became an agent of the *McDowell Times* and received praise for helping with the "educational uplift of his race." And in late 1914, the Baptist minister Reverend J. W. Crockett was elected to the Northfork District School Board of McDowell County.[19]

As Black ministers broadened their interest in the here and now, their sermons before their coal-mining congregations underwent a gradual change. In two sermons at Giatto, a Black Baptist minister was "forceful and practical." At the First Baptist Church of Kimball, Reverend R. D. W. Meadows "preached one of the most profound and scholarly sermons." Another sermon "showed much thought in preparation" and delivery. Still another Baptist minister "preached a strong and scholarly sermon." At a meeting of the Winding Gulf Ministerial and Deacons Union, Reverend T. J. Brandon "gave a high class lecture to preachers and congregation on how they should act in church." On the same occasion, another minister delivered an "able" and "instructive" sermon on the subject "Behave." When the "spirit" threatened to overcome him, another Baptist minister took "pains as to control his voice." Yet however rational and controlled their sermons may have become, Black ministers worked to retain contact with the traditional Black culture and consciousness of Black workers. At the Baptist church in Keystone, Reverend Brown of Kimball preached "quite a deep sermon," but he nonetheless emphasized, "It matters not how much learning one may have, unless they have the Spirit of God they cannot have power to do the best work of life."[20]

The Methodist Episcopal and the African Methodist Episcopal churches were more hierarchical in their administrative structures than were the Baptist churches. Their hierarchies exercised greater control over ministers and congregations in particular, controlling the mandatory movement of ministers from one church to another, and they vigorously promoted an educated Black ministry. These two churches were nonetheless deeply enmeshed within the spiritual traditions of Southern Blacks. Utilizing Baptist ministers, for example, the Methodists often conducted revivals and engaged in spirited meetings similar to those of the Baptists. In April 1914 the Northfork Methodist Episcopal Church conducted a revival that resulted in fifty-one accessions, twenty-six new converts, and twenty-five more converts by letter. Under the pastorate of Reverend W. R. Burger, the *McDowell Times* suggested, the Methodists, like the Baptists, understood how "to shout, sing, preach and pray."[21] Yet over time, Black Methodists and Presbyterians in southern West Virginia, as elsewhere, shed the spiritual and emotional aspects of their religious traditions more rapidly than did the Baptists. Within three years of Reverend James Gipson's transfer from the AME Kentucky Conference to Williamson, West Virginia, Gipson developed a reputation as "a hard worker, constructive in mind and progressive in spirit." Under his leadership, the congregation grew from eight to forty members and moved from an inadequate public hall near the railroad tracks to a new brick building in a previously all-white area. The church's assets grew from a mere forty-four cents to over $800, the minister's salary not included; and, starting with no church auxiliaries, a "flourishing" array of them was begun.[22]

Under the pastorate of Reverend R. P. Johnson, the small Presbyterian church of Kimball developed a more energetic social orientation. In December 1913, the church held a sacred concert. The program featured a variety of guest speakers who addressed a broad range of religious, political, and social issues. In his speech, attorney H. J. Capehart, the *Times* reported, emphasized the need to make "services so varied and instructive that they will appeal to all classes. He spoke of the gymnasium, the swimming pool, reading room, sewing circle and settlement work as examples of the work being done by adher[e]nts of the new school of thought in religious worship."[23] In an address titled "My Dream of the Future Church," attorney T. E. Hill looked forward to a church that practiced the principles of social justice and equality. "In this institution there will be no color line, the brotherhood of man will be a fact instead of a catch phrase and it will seek to save the bodies as well as the souls of mankind." In another example of the Black church's growing social bent, the pastor Reverend R. P. Johnson developed a vigorous ministry among Black convicts on the road crews of McDowell County and also a Sunday school relief department, which was designed to aid the working-class "poor of our town, especially children whose parents are not able to keep them in school and Sunday school."[24]

In addition to joining churches, Black coal miners participated in an expanding network of fraternal organizations and mutual benefit societies. By World War I, Black fraternal orders included the Elks, the Knights of Pythias, the Odd Fellows, the Independent Order of St. Luke, and the Golden Rule Beneficial and Endowment Association.[25] The Golden Rule Association emerged as one of the most energetic of the prewar Black fraternal orders. Formed in 1903 under the leadership of Reverend R. H. McKoy, the order established headquarters at Bramwell, Mercer County, and served Blacks in southern West Virginia and parts of Kentucky and Virginia. Within one decade the organization proudly celebrated its success: fifty-four subordinate lodges, twenty-six nurseries serving young people aged three to sixteen, more than 5,280 members, and more than $13,000 paid out in death and sick claims. In numerous churches in the coalfields, Reverend McKoy and officers of the Golden Rule Association publicly paid benefits in ceremonies replete with speeches—indeed, sermons—on the value of the order. In July 1913, for example, the organization paid the endowment of one member "before an overflowing congregation."[26] With God's help,

McKoy said, "The continued progress of the Golden Rule Association means the actual progress of the race in a tangible form." [27]

Within the framework of Black religious culture, the fraternal orders offered Black coal miners an opportunity to protect their material interests. The obituary for John Panell, who lost his life in a slate fall at Gilliam, McDowell County, noted Panell's membership in the Grand United Order of Odd Fellows. Samuel Blackwell, who died of injuries sustained in a slate fall, belonged to the Shining Light Association of the Golden Rule Beneficial and Endowment Association. The 1913 obituary of A. H. Hudle described him as "a consistent Christian, a member of the A.M.E. Church . . . [and] a member of the Grand United Order of Odd Fellows and also a Knight of Pythias." [28] All these Black fraternal orders offered mutual aid and insurance plans to their members that promised to cushion them and their families against hard times.

At the same time as fraternal orders addressed the material welfare of Black workers, they repeatedly reinforced the communal and spiritual aspects of their culture. In company and noncompany towns, the fraternal parade, replete with marching band in full regalia, and the annual thanksgiving sermon emerged as prominent features of African American life in the coalfields. In May 1913, for example, at Keystone and Eckman, McDowell County, the Grand United Order of Odd Fellows held their Thirteenth Annual Thanksgiving Parade and Services. Led by Lord's Cornet Band, the order assembled at Lord's Opera House, in Keystone, marched up Main Street, and wound its way to Eckman, where the Odd Fellows then assembled at the Wingfield Baptist Church. There Reverend L. E. Johnson called the service to order, Reverend William Manns read the scripture, and Reverend Dabney "preached one of the most forceful sermons ever heard here." Taking his text from the 133rd Psalm, Reverend Dabney exclaimed, "Behold how good and how pleasant it is for brethren to dwell together in unity." More than one thousand people witnessed the parade and services. [29]

If the fraternal orders helped to reinforce the religious culture of Black workers, they also helped to link Black miners to the larger African American political and civil rights campaign. The fraternal orders invited major political figures to speak at the annual thanksgiving services and parades. [30] In 1913 the Keystone and Eckman Odd Fellows secured Republican governor H. D. Hatfield as their guest speaker. Similarly, at the Twenty-First Annual Meeting of the West Virginia Knights of Pythias, held at Charleston's First Baptist Church, Mayor J. F. Bedell addressed the gathering. [31] In this manner, Blacks used the fraternal orders to subtly and not so subtly advance their political aims.

More important, unlike most of their counterparts in other Southern states, African Americans in West Virginia received the franchise in 1870 and retained it throughout the period between Reconstruction and World War I. During the 1890s and early 1900s, at a time when other Southern Blacks were being disfranchised, Black coal miners in southern West Virginia exercised a growing impact on state and local politics. West Virginia Blacks developed a highly militant brand of racial solidarity, marked by persistent demands for full equality, albeit on a segregated basis.[32] African American unity across class lines was most evident in protests against racial violence. When whites lynched a Black man at Hemphill, McDowell County, in 1896, an aroused Black community, workers and elite members alike, confronted local authorities with demands for justice and protection. Under the leadership of prominent middle-class Blacks, an estimated five to eight hundred Blacks held a mass meeting in the company town of Elkhorn, McDowell County. The group petitioned county and company officials and demanded an investigation. Although the guilty parties were never brought to justice, the Blacks involved did secure public announcements from government and company officials promising an investigation to determine the guilty parties.[33]

Black coal miners and their elite allies supplemented their protest activities with electoral politics. As early as 1873, Charleston appointed its first Black public official, Ernest Porterfield, who served as a regular policeman. In 1877 the former coal miner Booker T. Washington began his public speaking career as a Kanawha County Republican. According to biographer Louis R. Harlan, Washington played a major role in mobilizing the Black vote in the successful campaign to relocate the state capital from Wheeling to Charleston. Washington not only supported the relocation of the capital, a change backed by powerful white Republicans in the state, but he also joined other Blacks in tying the capital campaign to the issue of equity for Blacks within the party and the state. "Washington began his speeches for the capital on June 27, at a rally in Charleston of 'the colored citizens of Kanawha.' . . . A resolution of the meeting claimed 'the right to a fair portion of the public institutions' in their part of the state." Although Washington later abandoned this vigorous political tradition, most Blacks in southern West Virginia did not. Even so, the state's powerful Democratic Party, which called itself the "white man's party," reinforced by the Ku Klux Klan in the early post–Civil War years, kept Black Republican influence at bay." [34]

For the next two decades, Democrats controlled West Virginia's political machinery. The party's constituency included voters in counties that were predominantly agricultural, workers in the industrial centers of northern West Virginia, and, increasingly, the state's powerful industrialists. By the early 1890s the Democrats not only regularly returned their candidate to the governor's mansion but also returned majorities to the state legislature.[35]

The increasing migration of Blacks into the region, however, set the stage for the resurgence of the Republican Party during the late 1890s. By 1910 Blacks made up more than 17 percent of the state's voting-age (male) population. Immigrants made up 13 percent, but their voting potential was actually much lower, for only 11.5 percent of voting-age immigrants were naturalized and eligible to vote. Thus, the rise of the Black coal-mining proletariat gave African Americans the decisive balance of power in Mountain State politics. As early as the gubernatorial election of 1888, for example, the Republican candidate defeated his Democratic opponent by a narrow margin of 110 votes. Democrats contested the vote, arguing that several hundred Black migrants in Mercer and McDowell Counties "had voted without the required period of residence and that many of them were, in fact, migratory or transitory workers with no fixed abode." More than a year later, a special session of the legislature awarded the office to the Democratic candidate by a margin of 237 votes. In the gubernatorial election of 1896, however, the Republican candidate, George W. Atkinson, courted Black voters and won the governorship by more than twelve thousand votes. Although the Democratic Party continued to control the legislature, Republicans made increasing inroads there as well.[36]

Despite the increasing role of Black voters in Republican victories, Blacks fought an uphill battle for recognition within the party. As one state historian has noted, in addition to courting the Black vote, Republicans appealed to mountain whites for vital support by rejecting "unpopular national issues, especially federal intervention in racial matters." Thus they were able to "overcome identification with the Black population and hated Reconstruction policies," which included the enfranchisement of Blacks. For example, even as G. W. Atkinson campaigned for Black votes, he loudly proclaimed his belief in white supremacy. In a letter to the *New York World*, Governor Atkinson affirmed his Southern roots and racial beliefs: "I am a Virginian, and am therefore 'to the manor born.' . . . Southern people will not submit to negro rule. 'They will die first.' This is an old Southern expression, and they mean it when they say it." Within this racist framework, however, Atkinson and similar Republicans made room for an alliance with West Virginia Blacks around the issue of education. Atkinson delivered a scathing attack on Mississippi senator James K. Vardaman, who sought to deprive Blacks of the right to an education: "When he says it is folly to attempt to advance the negro race by education, and in any way qualify them for responsibility and power . . . because by so doing we spoil corn-field hands and make 'shyster' professional men, he simply loses sight of good judgment and fair dealing, and seeks to vent his narrowness, prejudice and spleen against his 'brother in Black.' "[37]

In order to push for greater influence in the Republican Party, forty-nine Black delegates met in Charleston in 1888. They attacked the Republicans for "absolutely" refusing to give Blacks "the recognition" to which they were "entitled, notwithstanding the fact that there are eleven thousand colored voters in the state, nearly all of whom are Republicans." These Black voters were not merely Republicans; more fundamentally, they were coal miners. They added substance to the African American protests against racial injustice within the party of their allies. It was the Black coal miners' vote that enabled middle-class Black politicians to gain increasing access to public office in southern West Virginia.

Over the next decade the expanding proletarian electorate fueled the African American campaign for elective and appointive office. In 1896 Republicans elected Christopher Payne, the first African American, to the state legislature. Born in Monroe County, West Virginia, Payne was, in turn, a teacher, preacher, and attorney. Allied with Nehemiah Daniels, a powerful white Republican and county sheriff, Payne entered the statehouse from Fayette County, signaling the gradual rise of Black power in southern West Virginia. Payne's election also inaugurated a long tradition of Black Republican legislators in West Virginia. Attorney James M. Ellis of Oak Hill, Fayette County, succeeded Payne in the legislative sessions of 1903, 1907, and 1909, while the educator H. H. Railey of Fayette County served in the 1905 session.[38] In 1904 Blacks in the Pocahontas District formed the McDowell County Colored Republican Organization (MCCRO). Over the next decade, the MCCRO claimed credit for a growing number of Black elected and appointed officials. In November 1913 the organization celebrated its achievements: six deputy sheriffs, three guards on the county road, constables and justices of the peace in four districts, members of school boards in three districts, and the state librarian, a post first held by the influential schoolteacher and grand chancellor of the West Virginia Knights of Pythias L. O. Wilson. MCCRO was open to "All Negro Republicans"; in 1913 its officers included the deputy sheriff Joe E. Parsons, president; the attorney S. B. Moon, recording secretary; the educator E. M. Craghead, corresponding secretary; and the attorney A. G. Froe, treasurer.[39] Black coal miners were a powerful springboard for the political ascent of educated Blacks in southern West Virginia.

Nowhere did the political alliance of Black workers and Black elites in the region produce greater results than in the educational system. African Americans ranked education as their first priority. In their expanding electoral activities, they increasingly demanded equal access to the state's educational resources. In rapid succession, during the 1880s and 1890s, the state funded Black public schools in Fayette, McDowell, Mercer, and Kanawha Counties. In

1891 the state legislature established the West Virginia Colored [Collegiate] Institute, a Morrill land grant college for the training of Blacks in "agricultural and mechanical arts." Four years later, the legislature created the Bluefield Colored [Collegiate] Institute by "an act to establish a High Grade School at Bluefield, Mercer County, for the colored youth of the State."[40]

Storer College was the earliest institution to offer West Virginia Blacks an education "above the common school grades." Founded in 1867 at Harpers Ferry, Jefferson County, Storer would remain the only such school for the next twenty-five years.[41] Following the establishment of the Bluefield Colored Institute and the West Virginia Colored Institute, though, Storer declined as a major provider of educational services to Blacks in southern West Virginia.[42] This decline was yet another indication of the shifting center of Black life from northern to southern West Virginia as the Black coal-mining proletariat expanded.

Although the educational strides of Blacks in southern West Virginia proceeded on a segregated and unequal basis, they still symbolized a victorious Black community. As suggested by Howard Rabinowitz in his study of race relations in the urban South, whites increasingly accommodated themselves to Black access to, rather than exclusion from, fundamental resources and human services. Racial separation was not a static phenomenon; it was not entirely imposed by white racism, and it was not uniformly negative in its results. Within the segregationist framework, the rise of the Black coal-mining proletariat spurred the African American struggle for racial equity, facilitated the winning of new concessions, and made racial discrimination in the institutional life of the region less demeaning than it might have been.[43]

Through membership in national Black religious, fraternal, and political organizations, southern West Virginia's Black coal miners and small Black elites also participated in a larger national Black community. The National Baptist Convention, the Colored Bureau of the Republican Party, and the nationwide bodies of the Elks, Masons, Knights of Pythias, and Odd Fellows all helped to create bonds between the region's Blacks and their Southern and Northern counterparts. Through Black ministers like the self-educated Reverend Mr. Barnett of Huntington, Blacks in southern West Virginia were intimately linked to Blacks in northern West Virginia, Ohio, and parts of Kentucky. In addition to pastoring churches in West Virginia, such as the First Baptist Church in Huntington, Barnett also pastored a variety of Black Baptist churches in southern Ohio, including the Tried Stone Baptist Church in Ironton, as well as others in Gallipolis, Glouster, Providence, and other cities. Upon Barnett's death, the New Hope Baptist Church of Ashland, Kentucky, adopted a resolution expressing its "admiration of the many fine qualities of our departed leader." "For a hundred miles around," the *Huntington Dispatch* proclaimed, "Rev. Barnett's name is a household word in negro homes." [44]

Based upon their firm support within the Black coal-mining community, Black elites from southern West Virginia sometimes took prominent leadership positions in national organizations. At its 1913 annual meeting in Atlantic City, New Jersey, and for several years thereafter, for example, the Improved Benevolent Protective Order of the Elks of the World elected Charleston attorney T. G. Nutter as its grand exalted ruler. In 1913 Nutter defeated the incumbent, Armand Scott, of Washington, D.C. It was the mass migration of working-class Blacks to southern West Virginia, along with their rich pattern of visiting states farther south and north, that fundamentally underlay Nutter's victory and the growing participation of southern West Virginia Blacks in the creation of a national Black community. These national linkages were to intensify during World War I and its aftermath.[45]

Although extensive evidence attests to the strength of African American unity across class lines, this unity had its limits. The *McDowell Times* worked for African American solidarity, for example, and yet it also supported the class interests of coal operators and the small Black elites. The editor encouraged Black miners to provide regular and efficient labor and repeatedly warned them against joining unions. In a mid-1913 letter to the editor, one reader dropped his subscription, emphasizing the editor's antiunion position as the reason. The *Times* not only worked to mold workers' behavior to meet their employers' demands but also worked to shape working-class behavior to fit middle-class cultural norms. In an editorial tided "Clean Up and Swat the Flies," the editor admonished Black coal miners to keep their surroundings sanitary, downplaying the failure of operators to pay higher wages or to provide necessary repairs and sanitation facilities.[46]

As Black coal miners faced the limitations of their alliance with the Black elites, they developed distinct strategies of their own. While they did seek to endear themselves to employers by providing regular and efficient labor, they frequently shunned other elite injunctions. Seeking to improve the terms of their labor, Black coal miners often moved from one mine to another, either within southern West Virginia or farther north and south, and often switched between coal mining and farming in nearby Southern agricultural areas, especially Virginia. In the early 1890s, and again in the Paint Creek–Cabin Creek strike of 1913–1914, against the advice of middle-class leaders, numerous Black miners joined white miners in organized confrontations with management. The Paint Creek–Cabin Creek confrontation produced the heroic exploits of "Few

Clothes" Dan Chain, a Black union man. Portrayed by James Earl Jones in the 1987 film *Matewan*, "Few Clothes" was a big man of over 250 pounds, according to available evidence. Labor historian Ronald Lewis claimed that "Dan Chain's size, nerve, and fighting ability made him a favorite among strikers." In 1887, however, when whites lynched a Black man in Fayette County, Black miners initiated their own mass march of some one thousand men, by some estimates three thousand, vowing to retaliate in kind. Although they disbanded without confrontation, James T. Laing noted, "Whites at the mines in the New River Valley were terrified, for the report was sent to them that the Negroes expected to 'clean out' every white person along the river." [47]

While cleavage along class lines was the most prominent division within the Black community, gender inequality was also a significant problem. Emphasizing the home as women's proper sphere, *McDowell Times* editor M. T. Whittico sought to regulate the behavior of Black women, endorsed the removal of married women from teaching positions, and opposed woman's suffrage. In an editorial titled "Split Skirts," the editor urged Black women to shun the "split skirt" and maintain codes of "modesty." The injunction, however, was directed mainly at Black women in coal-mining families: "Only a few of the vulgar variety have been seen in Keystone and none are worn at present by the better class of Colored [women]." [48] On another occasion, the editor threatened to publish a gossip list if Black women failed to attend to their own "home work, social affairs and individual business and stop going from house to house, store to store carrying messages and . . . stirring up strife and generally making trouble." [49] On gender issues, the views of elite Black men expressed by the editor converged with those of the Black proletariat.

Yet, as with class conflicts within the Black community, gender conflict tended to give way to the imperatives of racial solidarity. Black women perceived their class and gender interests in essentially racial terms. [50] Black Baptist, Methodist, and Presbyterian women, through their regional, state, and local auxiliaries, figured prominently in Black religious activities, especially fund-raising campaigns, sacred concerts, musicals, and literary programs. [51] Moreover, under the energetic leadership of Mrs. Malinda Cobbs, by World War I Black women dominated the Independent Order of St. Luke, which diligently worked "to benefit the race." [52]

Although racial hostility, along with an expanding Black consciousness, helped to forge African American unity across class and gender lines, substantial interracial cooperation went on as well. At elite and working-class levels, as discussed earlier, Blacks and whites in southern West Virginia developed interracial alliances. As early as the 1880s, Black miners in the Kanawha–New River

Field joined the Knights of Labor. They served on integrated committees and, during strikes, helped to persuade Black strikebreakers to leave the area.[53] As the United Mine Workers of America supplanted the Knights in the early 1890s, it attracted Blacks from the Pocahontas Field as well as the Kanawha–New River area. Blacks soon gained recognition in the union, not only as members but as officers, too. In 1893 when the white president of District 17 died in office, the Black miner J. J. Wren of Fayette County filled the position. At Freeman, Mercer County, a white official exclaimed, "The Colored miners have been in the lead in this district until they have shamed their white brethren."[54]

Despite the dramatic display of interracial working-class unity during the 1880s and early 1890s, interracial unionism declined during the mid-1890s and resurged only briefly during the 1914 coal strikes.[55] Even during periods of intense interracial organizing, Black members and officers of local unions frequently complained that they were not accorded equal treatment with white unionists. During the 1880s, for example, the Knights of Labor established segregated units, while white members of the UMWA, formed later, sometimes blatantly resisted Black leadership. Such resistance led one Black labor leader to complain, "If your vice president is a Negro . . . he must be treated the same as a white man and unless you do there is going to be a mighty earthquake somewhere." Although interracial working-class unity remained highly volatile, it was nonetheless important in the lives of Black workers.[56]

Black elites developed a corresponding relationship with white elites, mainly coal operators, within the political framework of the Republican Party. As noted earlier, through alliances with Black coal miners on the one hand and white Republicans on the other, Black professional and business people gained election to the West Virginia legislature, appointments to prestigious positions like state librarian, and membership on the board of regents of all-Black colleges.[57] Likewise, in McDowell County, coal operators supported M. T. Whittico's Black weekly, the *McDowell Times,* which became a preeminent promoter of the McDowell County Colored Republican Organization. No less than the alliance between Black and white miners, however, the alliance between Black elites and the coal operators was inequitable, as indicated by the companies' demand that Black leaders like Whittico help to discipline the Black coal-mining labor force. In the hostile class and racial climate of southern West Virginia, neither Black elites nor Black workers could fully articulate their interests in class terms.

Linked to each other through color and culture, Black workers and Black elites forged their strongest bonds, across class lines, with each other. They developed a distinct African American community in the coalfields. In the ongoing struggle between white capital and labor, however, African Americans developed their most consistent alliances with coal operators and their corporate and political representatives rather than with organized labor. For example, Republican governor H. D. Hatfield, speaking in a local Black church in 1913 before a gathering of Black Odd Fellows, declared his "uncompromising purpose to see that every man gets a square deal."[58] Unfortunately, no corresponding white labor leader developed such a close bond with the Black community.

As the Black coal-mining proletariat expanded following the Civil War through the early twentieth century, it established the socioeconomic and demographic foundation for the emergence and growth of the Black middle class, the rise of Black communities in coal-mining towns, and, most important, the emergence of viable political and civil rights struggles. These processes, rooted in the prewar rise of the Black industrial working class, involved the complex dynamics of class, race, and region. Along with new developments, they would reach their peak during World War I and the 1920s.

Chapter 5

ENVIRONMENTAL CONDITIONS

A long with racial stratification in the labor force after World War I, Black miners in southern West Virginia confronted growing inequality in the community life of coal-mining towns. In addition to informal manifestations of public and private racial hostility, legal forms of racial segregation expanded, especially in the state's educational and social welfare institutions. Nevertheless, compared to the status quo in the contemporary South and in prewar West Virginia, race relations and social conditions in the postwar years in southern West Virginia improved. In the Mountain State, unlike other parts of the South, the Black vote not only persisted but increased in significance, lynchings declined, and Black institutions expanded, filling needs left unmet under the earlier pattern of exclusion.

The racial subordination of Afro-Americans in coal-mining towns, perhaps even more than their unequal treatment in the mines, sharply differentiated the lives of Black coal miners from those of their white counterparts. As in the prewar era, racism played a major role in shaping the housing, health, educational, and legal status of Blacks in southern West Virginia. Its most extreme public and private manifestations included the persistence of lynching sentiment, the resurgence of the Ku Klux Klan, and the intensification of racial discrimination in a broad range of public accommodations.

As elsewhere in industrial America, the Great Migration of Blacks to southern West Virginia and their growing participation in the coal economy precipitated white violence against Blacks. On December 15, 1919, a white mob lynched two Black coal miners at Chapmanville, Logan County. Employed at the Island Creek Colliery Company, Ed Whitfield and Earl Whitney were lynched for allegedly murdering a white construction foreman. The mob seized the two men from local deputies, backed them up against a railroad boxcar, riddled their bodies with bullets, and tossed them into a river. Although the governor wired the local prosecutor, Don Chafin, to ensure a full investigation, and although national and local officers of the National Association for the Advancement of Colored People vigorously pushed for one, the county prosecutor and county judges refused to cooperate. Moreover, the white press downplayed the lynching, printing headlines asserting "No evidence warranting indictments." The lynching of Whitney and Whitfield, the Charleston NAACP concluded, "places West Virginia in the class with other communities who believe in mob rule, the Charleston branch feeling keenly the disgrace."[1]

Although lynchings virtually disappeared from the coalfields during the 1920s, throughout the period lynching sentiment seethed just below the surface. Nowhere was this more evident than in the cases of Black men accused of crimes against white women. Reflecting West Virginia's strong cultural prohibition of interracial sexual relations, the state retained its statute forbidding interracial marriage, and its white citizens jealously guarded the vaunted integrity of white women. In 1921 when Leroy Williams faced rape charges in Charleston, Kanawha County, a lynching atmosphere developed, reinforced by inflammatory reporting by the local press, making it necessary for authorities to transport the accused from Charleston to Huntington, Cabell County. The threat of mob violence dictated a speedy trial and the death sentence. Despite the change of venue, Williams was quickly tried, convicted, and sentenced to be hanged. Evidence of Williams's innocence, including the highly inconsistent testimony of the woman involved, was ignored.

Williams's hanging took place in early 1922. Republican Governor Ephraim F. Morgan denied the NAACP's plea for clemency and a reduced sentence of life imprisonment, despite Blacks' strong support of the Republican Party. On September 7 of the same year, Harry Lattimar of Williamson was arrested "on the charge of rape, indicted, tried, convicted and sentenced to hang, by one o'clock of the next day and the same day placed on a train leaving for the state penitentiary." "The actual trial," the Charleston NAACP reported, "only lasted about thirty minutes." At the initial hearing Lattimar pleaded "not guilty" without the advice of legal counsel. When he later received a court-appointed attorney, the public defender assigned "seemed as anxious to have Lattimar convicted as did the prosecuting attorney, and no effort whatever was made in defense of Lattimar," according to the NAACP. Fortunately, under the vigorous protests of Blacks and the legal defense activities of the Charleston NAACP, Governor Morgan commuted Lattimar's sentence to twenty years' imprisonment.[2]

Similar cases continued to occur until the latter part of the decade. When Henry Grogan was accused of raping a white woman in 1928, an intense lynching atmosphere developed and largely dictated the outcome of his case. To elude various lynching mobs, law officers transported Grogan from Beckley, Raleigh County, to Charleston, Kanawha County, and finally to Huntington, Cabell County. While a lynching was avoided, the transfers interfered with Grogan's defense, culminating in his summary conviction and sentence to hang. To no avail, Brown W. Payne, Grogan's Black defense attorney, bitterly petitioned the Raleigh County Court for a writ of error, primarily basing his plea on the failure of officials to inform him of his client's whereabouts when lynching sentiment had required his speedy transfer from county to county. Without contact between the defendant and his lawyer, a proper defense could not be prepared, and racial injustice prevailed.[3]

As suggested above, with its racially biased, inflammatory reporting, the white press worsened the volatile racial climate Blacks faced in coal-mining towns. In the Williamson, Mingo County, rape case, "the local daily paper ran for several days screaming headlines in which the race of the accused was over-emphasized," complained T. Edward Hill, director of the Bureau of Negro Welfare and Statistics. In a similar case, involving a sixteen-year-old Black male and a thirteen-year-old white female, the local press played up the alleged crime as "the most heinous that could be committed." The white press painted a criminal portrait of Blacks in general, and of the Black coal miner in particular, under a plethora of racially explicit headlines: "Negro Murders White Man," "Negro Attacks Girl," "Miner Shot to Death and Murderer Escapes: Both Victim and Slayer are Colored," and "Three Negro[e]s are Dead . . . Whiskey, Pistols and Politics Hold High Carnival," to list only a few.[4]

Racism also intensified during the postwar years with the revival of the Ku Klux Klan. As the Klan expanded nationally in the wake of World War I, important branches emerged in Logan, Mercer, and Kanawha counties. In 1923, when the evangelist Billy Sunday completed a series of revival meetings in Logan County, the local Klan presented him with $1,000 in cash, along with a prepared statement emphasizing its stature as a white supremacist "organization consisting of several hundred of the leading citizens of this country." Until the mid-1920s, the Logan Klan held extensive public meetings, demonstrations, and celebrations—all testimony to its growing strength.[5] In 1924 the Bluefield KKK opened its office and held its first mass meeting at the city's Colonial Theater. "The theatre was packed from pit to dome and many were standing in the aisles," the *Bluefield Daily Telegraph* reported. When the curtains opened, there sat in full regalia a host of local Klan, joined by W. H. Thomas, city mayor. After receiving the mayor's cordial welcome, H. L. Burham, a grand officer of the West Virginia Klan, outlined the organization's white supremacist ideology and its goal of segregation and disfranchisement. "The Klan believes in white supremacy, and will not compromise on this issue," the principal speaker proclaimed. After the Klan led parades through Black sections of some towns, and after several threatening notes to Black homeowners, churches, fraternal orders, and civil rights organizations, the Bureau of Negro Welfare and Statistics targeted the Klan as the "greatest apparent danger to the peace and goodwill between the races in West Virginia."[6]

In the war and postwar years, racial segregation of public accommodations persisted and even intensified. Black coal miners vividly recalled, for example, how theaters in company and noncompany towns alike continued to segregate Black and white patrons. Andrew Campbell remembered "separate sides" for Blacks and whites at the Hippodrome Theater in Keystone, McDowell County. The Weyanoke Theater in Mercer County, Charles T. Harris recalled, had a single floor with a partition dividing the races. In Bluefield, another Black miner recollected, the Granada Theater reserved the balcony for Black patrons and forced them to use a back-alley entrance. Disgusted, they made fun of the balcony, calling it the "buzzard's roost." In addition, claimed another Black miner, whites in the company town of Gary, McDowell County, had better public accommodations and recreational facilities than Blacks. And when segregated public places like theaters became overcrowded, "whites could use the Black section, but Blacks could not cross into white territory."[7]

Hotels excluded Blacks, and restaurants either barred them or served them on a carry-out basis only. In Bluefield in 1917, Black visitors to the Twenty-eighth Annual Meeting of the Bluestone Baptist Sunday School Union lodged with Black families. In the same year, when the Primitive Baptist Association held its second annual meeting in Keystone, out-of-town guests did the same. In fact, every major Black gathering faced the same problem. As for restaurants, those that were white owned and operated excluded Blacks, or, as Pink Henderson recalled, they "served you, but you couldn't come in." These patterns of racial segregation persisted into the mid-1920s.[8]

Such clear-cut manifestations of racism increased in southern West Virginia in all areas of public life, including housing, education, and legal and medical services. Like white miners, as a condition of their employment, Black miners lived in company-owned housing mainly consisting of inadequately constructed wooden homes. Unlike their white counterparts, however, Black miners were increasingly relegated to the worst structures. Black coal miners invariably recall a pattern of segregated and unequal housing, a decided reversal of the earlier pattern of Blacks and whites at least sometimes receiving similar-quality housing. As noted in chapter 1, in the company town of Capels, McDowell County, Blacks and immigrants at first lived in the same newly constructed rows of houses. Then, in the early 1920s, the company constructed a new group of houses. At the same time, one Italian miner recollected, "The company began moving white families from the older section of the town into the newer town, and all new Black miners hired were assigned houses in the older section of town. In a few years, the town's housing was completely segregated."[9] In 1921, North Dickerson recalled, when he moved to Stanaford, Raleigh County, "White foreigners and Blacks lived up here until another superintendent came along, and he forced segregation of the camp." In this case, segregation expanded to "protect" immigrant whites as well as American-born whites. Black miners recalled always living in segregated company housing throughout the 1920s despite their frequent movement from one company town to another.[10]

Black miners often complained that housing was not only segregated but unequal as well. The housing needs of whites, they believed, received the operator's closer attention. In some places, Preston Turner recalled, white miners received "better materials" and "better-built" houses. Substantial evidence suggests that management placed Blacks at the bottom of its list of housing repairs and other amenities. In the early 1920s, Black men at the Winding Gulf Colliery Company "took offence" when the company painted and repaired the houses of whites but overlooked those of Blacks. When Black miners threatened to leave, company officials promised them new housing the next year, when materials would be cheaper.[11]

Obie McCollum of the New York Urban League recalled working with his father, a carpenter, in the company town of Jenkinjones, McDowell County. "In practically all cases, housing for Negroes [was] segregated and inferior. . . . When a Negro asked for flooring instead of rough boards for his porch, he was told that everything must be as it was originally."[12] In his close examination of Black housing of the late 1920s and early 1930s, sociologist James T. Laing concluded that "where segregation is the policy of the company the Negroes are likely to be found in the less favorable locations and in the less desirable houses." Located close to coal tipples and railroad tracks, the worst houses inhabited by Black coal miners and their families were "loosely-built, unpainted, board and batten type with leaking roof affording scant protection from winter drafts." In her survey of company housing in the southern Appalachian region, Margaret Wolfe also concluded that "the inherently unequal concept of 'separate but equal' prevailed during World War I and its aftermath."[13]

Inadequate living conditions plagued both Black and white coal-mining

Some coal towns were racially mixed, but most were segregated along racial and very often ethnic lines as well. This is a photo of a Black community in a congested and unsanitary area along the railroad tracks in Vivian, West Virginia. Courtesy of the Eastern Regional Coal Archives, Craft Memorial Library, Bluefield, West Virginia.

families in the region. According to the U.S. Department of Labor, in 1923 only 11.2 percent of company-owned homes in West Virginia had running water; only 2.5 percent had bathtubs or showers; and only 3.9 percent had inside flush toilets. Of the 402 company-controlled towns in West Virginia, only 28 had a single water outlet for every family; an almost equal number had only a single outlet for every seven families.[14] None of the towns had a complete sewer system, and over 60 percent had outside privies. Large numbers of them were without cesspool equipment, too.[15] Although these conditions confronted working-class Black and white families alike, the dynamics of racial discrimination intensified their impact on Blacks.[16]

While coal-town housing for Blacks was inferior to that for whites, it would be misleading to leave the comparison at that level. Compared to Blacks' prewar experience, and especially compared to conditions farther south, housing gradually improved for Blacks in southern West Virginia during World War I and the 1920s. The *McDowell Times* noted a shift from shanties for single men to family dwellings at the Sycamore Coal Company at Cinderella, Mingo County. "There are 83 houses all well built and of the two-story kind. There is not a shanty upon the operation because the company wants men with families to do their work, therefore they prepared the best accommodations for them."[17] One columnist contrasted the war housing of Blacks at Giatto, Mercer County, to prewar housing. "Houses at that time . . . were mainly rude constructed shelters thrown up here and there on the mountainside. . . . Thirteen years hence visit the same place again and what a wonderful transformation."[18] The employment manager at the Winding Gulf Colliery Company, George Wolfe, informed the owner that only six houses were available at the Superior Mines for new workers and added, "To be frank with you the six empty houses that we have are not fit for any one to live in, they are houses only by the courtesy of the name." Wolfe recommended a vigorous building program to upgrade the company's housing stock.[19]

In the years following World War I, the U.S. Coal Commission found that nearly 80 percent of miners' homes in West Virginia were supplied with electricity, the highest percentage of any mining region in the country. Partly as a device to control labor and also in a response to growing worker power, coal companies intensified their sanitary housing and garden campaigns among Black and white miners. The U.S. Coal and Coke Company emerged at the forefront of these efforts, but with ulterior motives, as revealed in this statement by a company official: "When employees of a company are made to take a great interest in their homes and to have pride in the appearance of them, there is but one result—they become happy and contented, and are not so susceptible to 'hard times' and anarchistic propaganda."[20]

Eventually, some Black coal miners were able to escape dependence on company-owned housing and purchase their own homes outside the company towns. Although West Virginia had one of the lowest rates of Black homeownership in the nation, an estimated 18 to 19 percent of Blacks owned their homes in 1920 and 1930. While some Blacks purchased homes within established municipal areas, most bought them in new unincorporated segregated developments on the edges of towns and cities. During World War I and the 1920s, an increasing number of Afro-Americans bought homes in and around various coal-mining towns, including Keystone, Welch, and Bluefield in the Pocahontas Field; Beckley in the Winding Gulf Field; Charleston in the Kanawha–New River Field; and Williamson in the Williamson-Logan Field. The nearly all-Black town of Giatto, Mercer County, was described as "a very independent town . . . largely owned by colored people. Fifty or more persons own their own property and quite a number of persons are e[x]cavating for the foundation of [new] residences."[21] In the fall of 1916, a number of Black families moved from McDowell County to a settlement near Beckley, Raleigh

County. More than thirteen families moved from Eckman, the *Times* reported, "where they made their first money [in the coal mines of] . . . the Pulaski Iron Company." These people, the reporter concluded, "are proud of their homes and suffice it to say they are at home." [22] The *Times* consistently urged Black miners to save their money and buy homes in Keystone, described as the "Mecca of the Coal Fields." Also, throughout the 1920s the BNWS urged Black workers to buy homes with their savings and earnings as protection against downturns in the economy. [23]

Although some Black miners managed to heed the injunction, Black home-ownership was a highly precarious affair. Located in the least desirable areas, Black privately owned homes were invariably "without modern improvements, such as paving, sewer, water or gas." Less than 40 percent of the Black-owned lots, the BNWS reported, were located in areas with established and stable real estate values. Some real estate sales actually reflected the blatant entrapment of Blacks in fraudulent land deals, in which Blacks purchased "mythical lots in subdivisions which never existed." Still others purchased lots and found it impossible to save or borrow the money necessary to build. During the late 1920s and early 1930s, Blacks increasingly lost both lots and homes as the Great Depression got underway. Buying property, even at bankrupt sales, the *Times* had earlier discovered, was "out of reach" of most Blacks. In an effort to pay mortgages, a growing number of Black homeowners took in boarders, even though their homes could "safely accom[m]odate only a half or a third as many." Making matters worse, coal companies preferred workers who lived in company-owned houses and frequently laid off homeowners first during economic downturns. [24]

Poor housing, as part of poor living conditions, took a disproportionate toll on the health of Black miners and their families according to a 1927–1928 health survey by the BNWS. The survey covered twelve counties, seven of which were located in southern West Virginia. It found that mine accidents were responsible for nearly 9 percent of Black deaths, versus roughly 4 percent for whites, but that tuberculosis was a far worse cause of Black deaths. "The great scourge of the Negro race," tuberculosis was a greater killer than heart disease, pneumonia, nephritis, and premature births, accounting for 13 percent of Black health-related deaths compared to less than 8 percent for whites. In McDowell County, the only southern county tabulated by race, tuberculosis accounted for 12 percent of Black deaths, compared to less than 4 percent for whites. [25] The BNWS concluded that to improve the Black miner's health it would be "necessary to improve his economic position which alone will enable him to improve his living conditions—proper housing, wholesome food and sanitation are prerequisites of good health." The agency reflected the views of Black health professionals like Dr. B. A. Crichlow, superintendent of the all-Black Denmar Sanitarium for tuberculosis patients.[26]

Another factor behind the poor health status of Black miners was the discriminatory health care provided by the coal companies. The *McDowell Times,* the BNWS, and Black miners themselves frequently complained of medical mistreatment of Blacks by the coal companies and their physicians.[27] In 1929, North Dickerson suffered a broken back and two broken ribs in a slate fall. Dickerson was immediately transported from the mine at about 3:00 p.m., but it was not until 7:00 p.m. that he was hospitalized. Upon admittance to the hospital, however, Dickerson bitterly recalled, for three days the medical staff did little to aid his recovery. The doctors believed that he would die, he said, and wished to avoid "the trouble of traction and everything if he was going to die." At one mine, according to interviews conducted by James T. Laing, the company president had a physician son-in-law on the staff of the local hospital who frequently dismissed injured men instead of treating them, ordering them back to work and preventing their full recovery.[28] To be sure, medical abuses like these were perpetrated against white as well as Black miners, but racial discrimination certainly heightened their impact on Blacks.

The segregationist policies of the state reinforced the poor health status of Black workers. In the state-supported medical facilities, Blacks and whites were decidedly separated by race. In McDowell County at Welch Hospital Number 1, formerly "Miners' Hospital No. 1," the superintendent reported, "On the first floor are two entrances—one for white patients and one for colored. The south wing is used exclusively for white patients. . . . The north wing is used exclusively for colored patients." Likewise, in Fayette County at the McKendree Hospital Number 2, formerly Miners' Hospital No. 2, "the first floor consist[ed] of white and colored wards." [29] Although racially segregated health services were discriminatory, their emergence represented an advance over the earlier system of exclusion and neglect.

While the white press ignored discrimination against Blacks, it exaggerated Black criminality. Nevertheless, Black criminal behavior significantly affected the lives of Black coal miners. Blacks comprised less than 7 percent of the state's population throughout the postwar period, but they made up an estimated 25 to 30 percent of the state's prison population. Most of them came from southern West Virginia, but, in fact, a disproportionate number came from the urban areas of northern West Virginia.[30] As elsewhere in industrial America, the most frequently committed crimes by Blacks were larceny, homicide, malicious wounding, and bootlegging.

In early 1915, the *Times* reported that the prohibition law was "helping to fill up the jails" in Raleigh County but had not yet ended the thriving bootlegging business among Blacks. "The bootleggers of 'colored hill' seem to have been making good here of late," the *Times* asserted. Southern West Virginia had the state's highest incidence of prohibition arrests, convictions, and sentences to hard labor on county roads. As mentioned earlier, although some of the arrests and convictions were unfairly made to obtain labor for county road projects, some did involve Blacks who were genuine bootleggers.[31] During the mid-1920s, in addition to importing "moonshine" from as far away as Detroit, Blacks made home brew. The BNWS reported, "Many persons make small quantities in their homes. They do not peddle it in bottles, but 'sell, enough to pay expenses' by the drink. It is more frequently in homes of this kind at such 'liquor parties' that crime[s] of violence are committed or trouble is started which lead to crimes among Negroes."[32]

However common prohibition violations may have been, it was homicide that was the most serious criminal problem for Blacks in southern West Virginia. More than any other crime, homicide reflected the development of intraracial and intra-working-class conflicts within the Black community. Along with the white press, the *Times* consistently reported Black-on-Black homicides, which usually involved firearms and knives. Homicide offenders usually eluded arrest and trial by escaping into the mountains. "On the least provocation," the *Times* reported, "a human life is snuffed out, the 'bad man' backs up the mountain with his smoking revolver until he has had time to make good his escape."[33] However, some homicides involved men of good reputation who were not known for fighting.[34] Still others involved gender conflict within the Black working class. For example, in 1915 one miner shot and killed a woman and severely wounded her friend, when she refused to move into his shanty. The miner escaped into the mountains, eluded police bloodhounds, and caught a freight train out of the area.[35]

Black leaders repeatedly emphasized the connection between Black crime and poverty. Poor Blacks were not only more likely to commit crimes such as larceny and bootlegging, they believed, but were less likely to get professional legal counsel upon arrest.[36] Although Blacks achieved greater access to protection before the law in West Virginia than elsewhere in the South, by the mid-1920s no more than three West Virginia counties impaneled racially mixed juries. Moreover, white offenders were more likely than Blacks to have "interested friends and relatives" among justice officials.[37] Furthermore, the frequency with which Black homicide offenders escaped the law not only demonstrated the difficulties of law enforcement in the mountains but also revealed the laxity of law officers in addressing Black-on-Black crime.[38] Thus the racially discriminatory justice system encouraged Black-on-Black crime and inflated the criminal record of Blacks.

As Black miners faced the problems of crime, health, and housing, southern West Virginia experienced a postwar educational boom.[39] With only ten Black high schools in the entire state on the eve of World War I, southern West Virginia alone boasted thirteen in 1923, and by 1932 the state total had increased to thirty-two.[40] The total state funds spent on the annual salaries of Black public schoolteachers increased from an estimated $160,000 in 1914 to nearly $400,000 in 1920, $700,000 in 1925, $800,000 in 1926, and over $1.2 million in 1929. By the late 1920s, West Virginia had almost fully complied with its educational statute, which required at least an elementary school in any community with ten or more Black students.[41]

Unfortunately, although Black educational facilities increased, they did not keep pace with the rapid expansion of the Black working class. As the Black migration to southern West Virginia accelerated during and after World War I, the number of school-aged Black youth (from five to twenty years old) also rose, increasing from about 19,800 in 1910 to 26,400 in 1920, to 35,600 in 1930. The number of Black youths attending schools likewise increased, from nearly 10,000 in 1910 to 15,000 in 1920 and to nearly 23,500 in 1930. With their parents, the BNWS reported, most Black youths had migrated to West Virginia from other southern states, especially from rural areas and small towns, where schools were few and far between and only met from two to five months each year. Typically these schools were taught by poorly prepared teachers who were seldom paid more than $20 a month. In fact, many of the children had received no schooling whatever.[42]

The state's exclusion of Afro-Americans from the West Virginia state university system and its segregation of them at all other levels of public education hampered the training of Black teachers and administrators. From the outset, then, the educational advancement of Blacks lagged behind that of whites. Scholars often note that, compared to other Southern dual school systems of the period, West Virginia's Blacks received a relatively equal and sometimes disproportionately high percentage of state aid. In 1918, for example, with about 6 percent of the state's Black population, Black colleges received nearly 8 percent of the state's total appropriations for higher education. What figures such as this ignore, though, is that until the late 1920s Black colleges maintained vigorous high school departments because some school districts refused to finance high school training for Black students. As the education historian William P. Jackameit has recently noted, "This situation . . . was, in effect, a shifting of the burden of financing the secondary education of Negroes from the local to the state level."[43]

Local school boards set education for white children as their top priority. Blacks invariably saw white high schools established before Black ones reluctantly were. From the beginning, some counties excluded Blacks from the school construction boom. In early 1915 the state supervisor of free schools reported that several new high schools for whites in McDowell County had been built, ranging in cost from $20,000 to $90,000. At Mt. Hope, Fayette County, school authorities built "a handsome new High School building, a large graded school and a kindergarten." Although white children of "various nationalities" could be found in the town's schools, Blacks were excluded. Where counties failed to establish Black schools, especially high schools, Black parents were forced to send their children elsewhere for postsecondary education, sometimes even out of state. Few Black coal-mining families could afford to, though.[44]

The unequal education of Blacks and whites persisted into the 1920s. In his 1921–1922 biennial report, the state supervisor of Black schools reported that West Virginia was "far behind in its building program for Negro schools" and that only a few districts had provided adequate facilities. Some of the school buildings for Black children were "unsanitary, poorly built and utterly unsuited for school use," and blackboards, seats, maps, books, and suitable playgrounds were generally in short supply. Black teachers were often compelled to hold school in the same public halls as those used by churches, lodges, and the miners' union. The superintendent further lamented, "There seems to be an 'unwritten rule' that whenever a building is to be erected for a Negro school a hill-side site must be selected. Usually these sites are almost inaccessible on account of the steep hill upon which they are located."[45]

Even in the capital city of Charleston, where Black schools were generally better staffed and better equipped, Black education stood on a grossly unequal footing with that of whites. In 1925, upon investigating conditions at the Black Garnet Senior High School, a member of the Charleston Board of Education, Mrs. H. D. Rummel, was "mortified beyond expression at the conditions existing there." Rummel "expressed the hope that no visitors would visit the school before conditions could be corrected" and roundly condemned the state, declaring, "I can't understand why we should be building a million-dollar school for the white children and allow such conditions to exist among the colored children."[46] In 1927, in a vigorous attempt to extend the institutional segregation of Blacks and whites, the Charleston Board of Education sought to establish a segregated Black branch library and barred Blacks from the city's public library. Although a highly aroused and politically active Black community defeated the board's resolution and Blacks retained access to the main building, the board was able to continue segregating Black and white patrons within the building.

Although West Virginia statutes prohibited racial differentials in the payment and training of teachers, some school districts blatantly violated the law. In his 1921–1922 report, the state supervisor of Black schools complained of such illegal discrimination being practiced by a few districts, and the BNWS's 1925–1926 biennial report noted that some districts were notorious for it. As late as 1929, the McDowell County Colored Republican Organization passed a resolution complaining that "in some districts of McDowell county colored school teachers are not receiving the same salaries as white teachers . . . of equal experience and holding the same credentials." [47]

Black teachers also received unequal training. The state excluded Blacks from West Virginia University, yet required high school teachers to have "college degrees." Until 1915, the state's only Black institutions of higher learning, Bluefield State College and West Virginia State College, were ranked in such a way that they could only offer training for elementary teachers. At the same time, state scholarship funds for training elsewhere were insufficient. Not until 1919 did West Virginia State College award its first baccalaureate degrees; Bluefield State College conferred its first bachelor of science degrees in 1929. Although Black access to higher education eventually and gradually improved, its slow development hampered the training of Black teachers. Moreover, when bachelor-level education finally became available, Blacks seeking graduate training had to leave West Virginia to attend school and had to have the funds to do so. [48]

Not only were Black schools deficient in providing opportunities for teacher training, but they also lacked vocational training programs. The BNWS, emphasizing the exclusion of Blacks from several skilled trades, fought for the addition of vocational training to the Black school system. Although over 75 percent of the state's Blacks worked in mining, the bureau noted in 1925, "Negroes [were being] taught no trade or profession which has the remotest connection with mining," but white youth were "being taught at the expense of the State all branches of coal mining." Like Blacks seeking graduate training, Blacks seeking professional training for coal-industry positions had to look elsewhere. In 1926, as noted in chapter 4, in order to pass the state mine foreman and mine safety examinations, Black miner John Patterson took correspondence courses from Pennsylvania State University. [49] Although the state offered some segregated mine safety classes to Black workers by the late 1920s, not until the 1930s would Blacks receive the necessary training to compete for jobs as foremen and for other higher-paying positions requiring formal education and certification.

Although Black miners experienced gradual and, in certain areas, dramatic improvements in their social status, racial inequality persisted in housing and in legal, educational, and health services. Yet, the emergence of segregated public services and institutions represented an advance over the earlier system of exclusion and neglect. Moreover, as the epilogue notes, the expansion of the color line in the institutional life of the region was not entirely led by whites. Black leaders vigorously pushed for more services, even if on a segregated basis. The war and postwar growth of the Black middle class and its small elite would play a crucial role in this process.

—

COMPARATIVE RACE AND ETHNIC RELATIONS

—

During the late twentieth century, a variety of studies transformed our knowledge of class, race, and ethnicity in the development of the U.S. coal industry from its dramatic expansion after the Civil War through its rapid demise in the years after World War II. As early as 1968, social and labor historian Herbert Gutman urged scholars of the U.S. working class to focus attention on the largely hidden history of interracial solidarity in the coal industry, particularly the role of the United Mine Workers of America (UMWA). In a variety of coal-mining strikes in the Northern and Southern coalfields, including West Virginia and Alabama, Gutman underscored the emergence of unity among Black and white miners. He also insisted that such actions represented viable alternatives to the system of ethnic and racial stratification in the workforce and community life of coal-mining towns.[1]

A plethora of studies soon followed Gutman's lead.[2] These studies accented the occasions when class solidarity, spurred by the organizing activities of the UMWA, submerged the color line and challenged the authority of coal-mine operators. Before such understandings of interracial solidarity in coal-miners' lives and struggles could take hold, labor analyst Herbert Hill offered a stinging critique of the shortcomings of research inspired by Gutman's agenda for a new history of coal miners. Hill underscored the persistence of racial hostility within the coal-mining workforce as well as the union despite moments of substantial evidence of unity across the color line.[3]

At about the same time, historian David Roediger and others produced studies emphasizing the salience of "white privilege." The notion of white privilege incorporated workers as well as elites across all sectors of the American economy, society, and politics, including the coercive powers of the state.[4] Partly under the impact of Hill's critique and the emergence of "whiteness" scholar-ship, a fresh wave of studies offered increasingly complicated portraits of labor relations in the coalfields of industrial America. By the turn of the twenty-first century, such studies largely rejected scholarly inquiries into "relations between Black and white workers as either harmonious or antagonistic."[5] Contemporary scholarship underscores the distinctive experiences of each group; it acknowl-edges deep cleavages along the color line; and it notes how the rigors of life and labor in the coal industry (including the ongoing alliance of capital with the military might of the state) nonetheless helped to create a work culture and politics that cut across racial and ethnic divisions.

Drawing upon this expanding body of recent scholarship on the coal indus-try as well as upon my own earlier research on coal miners in southern West Virginia, this chapter addresses a series of debates in the historiography of coal miners in America. First and most important, it confronts the class-race debate ignited by Herbert Hill when he challenged Gutman's interpretation of labor and race relations in the U.S. coal industry. This chapter reinforces Hill's emphasis on the deep racial divide in both the coal-mining workforce and the union, but it also accents the powerful role that the UMWA played in galvanizing interracial unity compared with other industrial unions such as the steelworkers and meatpackers at the time.

While this chapter identifies the color line as the most enduring and pro-nounced division among coal miners in industrial America, it rejects the conclu-sion that the entrenched racial hostility of white workers, employers, and the state largely obliterated the influence of Black miners over their own lives. On the contrary, African American miners forged a variety of strategies for shaping their own experience in the coalfields. Their efforts included the construction of their own coal-mining communities as well as membership in the UMWA when and where possible. In other words, despite powerful recent critiques decrying the limits of an entire generation of scholarship accenting the self-activities of poor and working-class people,[6] this chapter underscores the need for ongoing if more nuanced treatments of this indelible thread in Black workers' culture and politics.

Black miners' history was by no means as uniform or monolithic as some-times suggested in labor and working-class studies. In addition to highlight-ing the "agency" of Black workers, this study addresses questions of variation across regions as well as time in the lives of Black no less than white miners. African Americans first entered the coalfields as enslaved people before the Civil War. In the wake of emancipation, they encountered intense labor exploitation and inequality in the Alabama fields, a measure of equality in southern West

Virginia, and a pattern of stiff resistance and exclusion in Pennsylvania, Ohio, and Illinois.

Finally, this chapter calls attention to the ethnic fragmentation of the immigrant and American-born white coal-mining workforce. Before the gradual emergence of the UMWA, substantial conflict characterized the life and labor even of English-speaking miners. Until the 1960s, however, a voluminous immigration historiography tended to homogenize the experiences of diverse immigrant groups from the British Isles—English, Scottish, and Welsh, although not of the Irish. According to this body of scholarship, British migrants were "absorbed into the general mass of native [American] citizens" and largely lost their identity "almost immediately." It was the arrival of "new immigrants" from southern, central, and eastern Europe that touched off virulent relations among white workers.[7]

During the late twentieth century, immigration historians shifted their attention away from a preoccupation with the "assimilation" of migrants and immigrants into the established culture, politics, and society of the United States. New research focused on conflict and the persistence of Old World forms of politics and institutions in the rapidly industrializing nation.[8] In sum, informed by these larger currents in U.S. labor, ethnic, and social history, this essay explores the numerous ways in which perceived ethnic and racial differences shaped miners' experiences, while emphasizing the distinctive history of African American coal miners and their communities based upon the pervasive ideology and practices of white supremacy.

White Miners' Ethnicity, Conflict, and Solidarity

During the antebellum years, the U.S. coal industry gradually developed on the basis of British immigrant miners in the anthracite district of Pennsylvania. By the 1840s, some 6,800 coal miners produced nearly 2 million tons of coal annually in the United States. In the antebellum South, namely Virginia and Alabama, enslaved African American workers supplemented the early white coal-mining workforce.[9] Following the American Civil War, the U.S. coal industry dramatically expanded. In the eastern Pennsylvania anthracite region alone, coal production rose from 13 million tons in 1870 to 54 million tons in 1910. At the same time, the anthracite coal-mining workforce increased from 36,000 to over 140,000 miners. In addition to American-born migrants from nearby farms and rural settlements, immigrants from England, Scotland, Wales, and Ireland dominated the early postbellum coal-mining workforce.[10]

Nationality, race, and ethnic differences produced significant levels of economic competition, as well as social and political conflict in the U.S. coal industry. While diverse English-speaking immigrants from the British Isles and their American-born counterparts would soon develop forms of solidarity that mitigated their differences, this outcome was by no means a foregone conclusion. In the Mahoning Valley region of Ohio, the Welsh not only spoke their own language, they also "conducted their union meetings entirely in Welsh." In 1874, according to an Illinois miner, each ethnic group forged its own separate institutional and community life: "The English have the St Georges, the Scotch the St Andrews, the Welsh the St David's, and the Irish the St Patrick's." [11]

Despite evidence of nationality and ethnic conflicts in the early postbellum coalfields of the United States, British- and American-born miners soon developed bonds of solidarity in their escalating encounters with the owners of the coal mines. During the final decades of the nineteenth century, they forged a collective identity around their work in the mines, partly honed in the fires of British collieries before migration to America. In 1871 John Hall, an English-born miner, underscored the link between his work as a miner in the United States and his home in England. "I am a miner. . . . I was a miner in the old country, from which I migrated in 1848. I have mined coal in Pennsylvania and also western Virginia. I began mining work when eight years old." [12]

British miners viewed themselves as fiercely "proud," "literate," and "skilled" craftsmen. They also described themselves as "experienced" and independent "contractors, not mere wage earners." In his groundbreaking study of Welsh miners in the U.S., historian Ronald Lewis provides a close and detailed transnational portrait of how the British miners "transferred their scientific knowledge of underground mining to America as well as their practical skills as craftsmen." [13] Skilled "pick miners," as they were sometimes called, not only exercised considerable control over their own daily production of coal and drove up the cost of their labor, they also largely set their own work schedules. They made decisions, too, about the time devoted to their own leisure, home, business, community, and organized labor activities away from the pits. Indeed, some miners earned enough money to purchase and furnish their own homes.

Until the closing decades of the nineteenth century, English-speaking immigrant and American-born colliers made up the majority of the total coal-mining workforce. In addition to pioneering such widely dispersed coalfields as those in the eastern Pennsylvania anthracite district, they initiated coal production in the emerging bituminous coalfields of western Pennsylvania, Ohio, Illinois, and Indiana; the Appalachian South; and the western states of Colorado, Washington, and parts of Wyoming. [14] In the Colorado coalfields, the number of coal miners increased from no more than about fifteen hundred in

The Welsh Strike in the anthracite coalfields of Pennsylvania, 1871. Striking Welsh miners attacked Irish and German strikebreakers at "Tripp's Slope." *Frank Leslie's Illustrated Magazine* 32 (April 29, 1871): 108. Source in public domain.

1870 to a peak of nearly sixteen thousand in 1910. In Colorado and elsewhere, British, Irish, and Welsh miners formed the artisan core of the initial coal-mining workforce.[15]

By the turn of the twentieth century, a variety of forces gradually transformed the character of the U.S. coal industry and undercut the pivotal role of English-speaking and American-born white miners within the workforce. In both the anthracite and bituminous coalfields, the British and American-born "aristocrats" of the coal-mining workforce confronted increasing challenges to their precarious hegemony. As early as 1890, introduction of the coal-undercutting machine dramatically reduced demand for experienced pick miners and opened the door for the recruitment of a large, ethnically and racially diverse, and less skilled hand-loading workforce. The percentage of the coal mechanically undercut for loading increased to nearly 25 percent in 1900 and to over 80 percent by 1930. The new machinery increased the daily output of the individual miner from 2.57 tons in 1891 to 3.71 tons by the beginning of World War I.[16]

Closely intertwined with the expansion of the undercutting machine was massive migration from rural America as well as immigration from eastern, central, and southern Europe to meet the coal industry's growing demand for low-wage hand loaders and general laborers. In rapid succession, operators recruited trainloads of Italian, Slav, Polish, Hungarian, and other new European immigrants for work in the coal mines. Founded in 1897, for example, the coal town of Windber, Pennsylvania, had deep roots in the new immigration. In 1910, according to historian Mildred Beik, four southern, central, and eastern European groups made up nearly 85 percent of the town's total foreign-born population and about 45 percent of its total population.[17]

Established British- and American-born English-speaking white miners resisted the impact of both technological changes and massive southern, central, and eastern European immigration on their work, livelihood, and communities in coal-mining towns. British colliers not only openly disdained the new workers as "ignorant," untrained miners who threatened their safety underground, they also regarded new immigrant culture, work habits, and adherence to Catholicism as a threat to Anglo-Saxon Protestantism. As historian John H. M. Laslett notes, established British colliers responded to the increasing influx of new people with "a mixture of condescension and contempt." In some cases, these workers upped sticks and moved west, describing the new immigrants in nativistic terms such as the "Slav invasion." Violence against Slavs by earlier British and particularly Welsh miners resulted in the Latimar Massacre on September 10, 1897, when armed coal-company guards murdered nineteen Slav strikers in cold blood in the anthracite coalfields of Pennsylvania.[18]

After a period of intense economic, social, and political resistance to the new immigrants, British colliers gradually accepted Italians, Poles, Slavs, and other immigrants into the United Mine Workers of America union, organized in 1890. By World War I, the UMWA had organized old and new immigrants of European descent as well as growing numbers of African Americans. Following the massacre of Slav miners, Welsh miners joined their Slav brothers and walked out under the banner of the UMWA. Although challenged by the rise of the militant Industrial Workers of the World (IWW), founded in 1905, the UMWA became the most ethnically and racially diverse union in the U.S. labor movement. While the UMWA faced an ongoing uphill battle against the coal operators' immense capital and police power, as well as struggling for control over company-owned towns, organized miners achieved significant success in the bituminous coalfields of western Pennsylvania, Ohio, Illinois, and Indiana, though they were far less successful in the anthracite fields of eastern Pennsylvania.[19]

Despite the increasing movement of new immigrants into the coalfields as well as into the UMWA, they nonetheless faced stiff barriers breaking into the higher-skilled, managerial, and supervisory jobs both before and after joining the union. They also confronted obstacles, including ethnic segregation in the housing, institutional, cultural, and political life of coal-mining towns. At the Windber mines, new immigrants constituted 99 percent of all miners in 1910, but they made up only about 10 percent of mine foremen and assistant foremen. Company housing policy also separated English-speaking and earlier immigrant miners from their new immigrant counterparts. At the same time, the Berwind-White Coal Company reinforced the growth of nativist organizations like the Patriotic Order of the Sons of America during the opening decades of the twentieth century and the Ku Klux Klan during the 1920s. Furthermore, English-speaking residents also dominated the town's government, fire, and police departments.[20]

African Americans and the Limits of Working-Class Unity

The incorporation of new immigrant miners into the labor movement of coal-mining towns produced some (though insufficient) benefits, but it was the color line that emerged as the most salient social division that fragmented the coal-mining working class. Nonetheless, similar to the larger U.S. coal industry, the experiences of African American miners varied considerably from region to region and across time. Distinct patterns of "race, class, and community conflict" emerged in the coalfields of "Deep South" Alabama and the Chesapeake region as well as in the Northeast and Midwest.[21] As alluded to earlier, the first generation of Black miners entered the coal industry as enslaved workers in eastern Virginia, the Kanawha Valley, western Virginia, and north-central Alabama. Enslaved antebellum miners gave way in the postbellum years to a predominantly Black prison "convict" coal-mining labor force on the one hand and a sharply racially stratified, free coal-mining working class on the other.

Free Black miners faced a strictly enforced lower wage rate than white workers. They also encountered discriminatory coal-weighing scales based on race and a racially exploitative "contract" labor system. In the contract arrangement, regular white coal loaders hired Black workers as lowly paid helpers and largely passed on the most arduous work of coal-mining labor to their Black counterparts. Partly because of this anti-Black racial imperative, particularly in the coal strikes of 1894 and 1908, coal operators effectively used the "social-equality" issue as a wedge to divide workers and undermine public support for the union cause. Thus, in the Deep South coalfields, the convict lease system disappeared only during the 1890s and the early twentieth century; and it was not until the

1930s that white workers gradually challenged the "social-equality" notion and forged stronger ties with Black miners across the color line.[22]

Whereas Black workers confronted extreme forms of exploitation in the Alabama coal industry, they were largely excluded from the anthracite region of Pennsylvania and only slowly moved into the bituminous fields of western Pennsylvania, Ohio, Illinois, Iowa, and Indiana in small numbers. However, as diverse groups of white miners slowly bridged their differences, created more potent forms of labor solidarity, and walked out on strike for better pay, living, and working conditions in coal towns, Northern coal operators turned increasingly to Black workers as strikebreakers. Beginning during the 1880s, coal companies regularly imported Black workers to break strikes in the Pittsburgh district, the Tuscarawas Valley of Ohio, Virden and Pana in Illinois, and parts of Oklahoma and Kansas. In the small coal-mining town of Buxton, Iowa, the coal company imported Southern Black workers to break the strike among white miners during the 1890s. Blacks soon became the single largest ethnic group in the town's workforce before the town's demise during the 1920s.[23]

In the Pittsburgh district, strikebreaking persisted into the 1920s (including most notably the coal strikes of 1922, 1925, and 1927). Strikebreaking entailed a substantial incidence of violence between striking white workers and African Americans, as well as between white workers, company guards, and police. As economists Abram L. Harris and Sterling Spero noted in their historical study, *The Black Worker* (1931), in western Pennsylvania between September 1927 and February 1928 the results of African American strikebreaking activities "were written largely with violence, bloodshed, loss of life, and the destruction of property." Similar to the earlier reactions of British miners to their southern, central, and eastern European counterparts, old and new white miners of various nationalities and ethnicities treated African American migrants as a "foreign invasion" of their "homes." During labor disputes, white workers often declared in the face of Black workers, "I do not mind the white scab, but I be damned if I will stand for a Negro scab." For their part, Black strikebreakers sometimes boldly retorted, "You would not work with me before the strike. Now I have your job and I am going to keep it."[24]

Despite the recurring use of Black strikebreakers in the coalfields, the United Mine Workers nonetheless reached out to African Americans and opened its doors to Black workers earlier than steel, meatpacking, and other mass-production industries. From its founding in 1890, the UMWA pledged "to unite in one organization, regardless of creed, color or nationality, all workmen . . . employed in and around coal mines." Moreover, the union sought to insure equality of work opportunities among miners in practice. The UMWA constitution included a clause stating that "No member in good standing who holds a dues or transfer card shall be debarred or hindered from obtaining work on account of race, creed or nationality." African American membership in mine unions increased from about one thousand at the union's founding to about five thousand, before declining during the mid-1920s. Black miners not only joined the union, they participated in large-scale strikes in the Northern and Southern coalfields, including the bloody confrontations in Alabama in 1908 and West Virginia (particularly the Paint Creek–Cabin Creek Strikes of 1912–1913 and the Mingo Coal War of 1921).[25]

Coal miners developed some of the most remarkable episodes of interracial as well as interethnic solidarity in the U.S. labor movement. The UMWA soon employed Blacks as union officers, including locals with predominantly immigrant members. African American facility in English made them preferred representatives in some locals with majority immigrant miners. In 1891, the Rendville, Ohio, miner Richard L. Davis was elected to the executive board of the UMWA District 6 (Ohio). He held the Ohio post for six years, and in 1896 and again in 1897 he was elected to the national executive board, the highest position ever held by an African American in the UMWA. Davis's influence was felt at the local, regional, and national levels. He advised miners during bitter industrial disputes in West Virginia, western Pennsylvania, and Alabama as well as Ohio. In 1892, for example, when owners sought to segregate one mine in Rendville by using Black laborers exclusively, paying those workers lower wages and forcing them to work under poorer conditions than had been the case in integrated mines, Davis rallied Black and white workers against the company's effort to divide workers along racial lines.

In another instance Davis opposed the development of segregationist policies in Congo, Ohio. After calling attention to segregated housing, he observed a similar pattern in the mines and urged an end to such racial stratification. Davis resolutely and consistently opposed exclusionary hiring practices, advocated the election of Blacks to leadership positions in the union, and protested white miners' discriminatory attitudes and behavior toward Black workers. On one occasion, he rebuked his white counterparts for referring to Black men in derogatory language: "I assure anyone that I have more respect for a scab than I have for a person who refers to the negro in such way, and God knows the scab I utterly despise."[26]

Although the UMWA forged some of the nation's most significant movements for labor solidarity across the color line, it nonetheless failed to stem the development of racially and ethnically divided coal-mining towns. Segregated and unequal work, living, family, and community environments greeted Black miners across regions and from place to place within the coalfields of the North and South. According to Spero and Harris, "The most frequent complaint one got from the Negro unionist in the coalfields was his inability to use his union card at some mines where the employment of a Negro had caused the white union miners to strike, or where it was believed by the operators that the employment would cause a strike." Black miners regularly complained of the union's "inability or unwillingness to draw any distinction between the absence of racial discrimination in constitutional principle and the appearance of it in every day fact." [27]

In 1988, as noted earlier, the First Baptist Church of Charleston hosted the First Annual Conference on West Virginia's Black History. Spearheaded by the Alliance for the Collection, Preservation, and Dissemination of West Virginia's Black History, subsequent annual conferences have featured a variety of papers, speeches, and comments on the state's Black heritage. They have also reflected an enduring commitment to African American institutions, values, and beliefs in southern West Virginia in particular and West Virginia in general. Mountain State Blacks not only struggled to retain their own institutions, they also joined the Miners for Democracy, an interracial rank-and-file movement against the growing antidemocratic impulses within the leadership of the United Mine Workers of America. But the industrial era had slipped away without a viable economic alternative to fill the void left by the departure of "king coal."

Conclusion

Characterized by enduring patterns of class, ethnic, and racial conflict and inequality, the history of the U.S. coal industry represented not one but many stories. The first generation of British and diverse English-speaking miners emerged at the pinnacle of the early coal-mining workforce as skilled crafts-men, supervisors, and managers, while the later arrival of new immigrants from southern, central, and eastern Europe entailed an uphill battle breaking into the coal industry, first as coal loaders and later as supervisory and managerial employees. But it was the color line that defined the staunchest barriers block-ing the upward mobility of workers in the U.S. coal industry. Even so, Black coal miners' experiences varied from region to region and within the same locale.

Few Blacks found jobs in the Northern anthracite region and only small numbers entered the bituminous fields of the North and Midwest. By contrast, large numbers of Black workers entered the southern Appalachian coalfields of Alabama and West Virginia. In Alabama, many Black miners labored as convict workers alongside a free labor force that was itself racially divided between

Blacks and whites; the latter gained access to a formally instituted wage scale that paid them uniformly higher wages than their Black counterparts. In southern West Virginia, Black and white workers received the same wage for performing the same work, but Mountain State Black miners nonetheless faced ongoing difficulties in using their union card to move around and obtain work during downturns in the coal economy.

Despite important regional and subregional differences in the coal industry, African American coal miners not only joined the UMWA, they also forged their own communities in the face of different levels of economic inequality, institutional segregation, and discrimination. These highly organized Black workers' struggles for freedom and equal rights gained their greatest expression in the southern Appalachian coalfields, but they also characterized life in the Northern and Midwestern fields. In the years after World War II, as increasing mechanization and deindustrialization undercut the coal-loading workforce, Black coal-mining communities declined at a faster rate than their white counterparts. Those who stayed in the coalfields built upon the institutional, political, and cultural foundation established by miners during the industrial era. At the same time, they forged new social struggles within the emerging context of the postindustrial era. How well they ultimately succeed in rebuilding their communities and modes of solidarity is yet to be seen. In that, the color line continues to persist. As in the past, this line is both tenaciously sharp and, at the same time, varyingly dotted.

ACKNOWLEDGMENTS

I am pleased to thank a few of the many people who helped to make this book a reality. As a collection of my previously published essays and book chapters on African American coal miners in the Mountain State and the nation, I owe my first debt to the University of Illinois Press for publishing *Coal, Class, and Color: Blacks in Southern West Virginia, 1915–32* (1990), in both its Blacks in the New World Series and the Working Class in American History series. Special thanks to series editors the late August Meier and David Montgomery, as well as David Brody, Alice Kessler Harris, and Sean Wilentz for envisioning *Coal, Class, and Color* as part of a larger movement to bridge the intellectual divide that too often separated African American and larger U.S. labor history.

Since publication of *Coal, Class, and Color,* a variety of institutions of higher education and public history provided invaluable opportunities to share my research and writing on coal miners with a broad cross-section of students, faculty, staff, and members of the larger community. These events not only entailed extraordinary discussions, debates, and reflections on the past and present of Black people in the coalfields. They also offered forums for imagining alternative paths to the social history of coal mining and race in the twenty-first century. In particular, for hosting lectures and discussions of Black coal miners, I thank the National Mine, Health, and Safety Academy in Beckley, West Virginia; the West Virginia Humanities Council; West Virginia University; Marshall University; the Organization of American Historians; and the international Institute for Advanced Study in the Humanities and Social Sciences in the Netherlands.

Numerous friends, colleagues, educators, administrators, and philanthropic organizations helped to advance my research on African American workers and their communities over the years. At Carnegie Mellon, I offer gratitude to former department head Donna Harsch; current department head Nico Slate; and Richard Scheines, dean of the Dietrich College of Humanities and Social Sciences; members of the Advisory Board for the Center for Africanamerican

Urban Studies and the Economy (CAUSE), especially Kenya Boswell, president of BNY–Mellon Global Philanthropy; and the Giant Eagle Corporation for support of my Giant Eagle University Professorship of History and Social Justice.

Along the road leading to this volume, I have benefited from the scholarship, work, and encouragement of a host of friends and colleagues; to name a few: Earl Lewis (Michigan), Ronald Lewis (West Virginia), Larry Glasco (Pitt), Will Jones (Minnesota), Jacqueline Jones (Texas), Andrew Masich (the Heinz History Center in Pittsburgh), and, at Carnegie Mellon, Wendy Goldman, Joel Tarr, Edda Fields Black, and Eric Anderson. At Carnegie Mellon, Clayton Vaughn-Roberson, PhD (research associate); Hikari Aday (administrative assistant); Jesse Wilson (Webmaster); and Natalie Taylor (business manager) provided indispensable research and administrative work that facilitated the completion of this book.

Most of all, I am especially grateful to Derek Krissoff, director, West Virginia University Press, for supporting publication of this collection. His abiding commitment to research, writing, and education on the history of Black coal miners and their communities made this book possible. Thanks also to Derek's production staff, especially Charlotte Vester, for their work in bringing this volume to fruition. Finally, as always, I thank my wife H. LaRue Trotter, my siblings, the "Trotter-14" (now 12), and nieces and nephews for providing ongoing inspiration for my life and scholarship. In honor of other supportive relatives, I dedicate this book to Willie Frank "Pete" Foster, my cousin and surrogate "Big Brother" while growing up in the southern West Virginia coalfields of McDowell County.

Appendix

———

SCHOLARSHIP, DEBATES, AND SOURCES

———

R esearch on African Americans in West Virginia is gradually expanding. Over the past two decades, historians have produced several studies of Black life in the Mountain State.[1] Mainly the efforts of labor, economic, and social historians, recent studies focus on African American migration to the coalfields, their participation in the organized labor movement, and their energetic community-building activities, especially in southern West Virginia. The new scholarship builds upon a solid, though slim, body of research that emerged during the early to mid-twentieth century. Pioneering studies by Carter G. Woodson, Thomas E. Posey, James T. Laing, John R. Sheeler, and others helped to build the intellectual scaffolding for recent research.[2]

Despite a growing body of scholarship on the subject, however, West Virginia's Black history is replete with blind spots. A variety of topics remain inadequately explored. We need studies of women and children, life in the early rural communities, and life in the major urban centers of Charleston, Huntington, Wheeling, and Parkersburg. Given these gaps in our knowledge, understandably, we also need a comprehensive state study, one that explores the transformation of African American life in West Virginia from its agricultural roots in antebellum Virginia, through its industrial transformation during the late nineteenth and early twentieth centuries, and, more recently, to its emerging postindustrial phase. Without a better understanding of the state's Black history, our knowledge of West Virginia history is also deficient. Therefore, based upon a critique of the historical literature on Blacks in the Mountain State, this appendix identifies blind spots in the established scholarship, draws attention to the need for a state study, and surveys the available primary data for future research.

Carter G. Woodson, "Father of Black History," worked in the coal mines of southern West Virginia before he became the first American-born Black person of former slaves to earn a PhD in history (Harvard, 1912); founder of the Association for the Study of Negro (now African American) Life and History in 1915; and dean at West Virginia Collegiate Institute during the early 1920s. Courtesy of the Ancella Bickley Collection, West Virginia State Archives, Division of Culture and History, Charleston, West Virginia.

Changing Perspectives on West Virginia's Black History

In 1909, George T. Surface, a Yale University geographer, conducted the earliest scholarly study of Black coal miners in southern Appalachia. Covering the aggregate experiences of Blacks in the mines of Kentucky, Tennessee, Virginia, and West Virginia, he compiled useful data on housing, health, and working conditions. Distinguishing between what he called the efficient and inefficient Black miners, he observed that the "great majority" were "irregular in labor or unstable in residence." Moreover, Surface suggested that "the efficiency of this class would be increased by a lower scale of wages." "The negro's moral weakness," he concluded, "is in reality more pronounced than his economic incapacity."[3] Surface ignored the exploitative practices of the coal industry, the role of racial discrimination, and the specific responses of Black workers to these phenomena. Thus, like other scholarly accounts of Blacks at turn-of-the-century America, the geographer's study was marred by the prevailing racial sentiment of the era. Although the pioneer Black historian Carter G. Woodson would soon produce sympathetic antiracist portrayals of Black life in the Mountain State, more than two decades would pass before a more detailed and balanced account of African Americans in West Virginia would appear.[4]

In 1931, the white economist Sterling D. Spero and his Black counterpart Abram L. Harris published their classic study, *The Black Worker: The Negro and the Labor Movement*. By highlighting what they called "the Negro's slave heritage" and the persistence of racial discrimination within the American labor movement, Spero and Harris transcended prevailing racist interpretations of Black workers. "The discrimination which the Negro suffers in industry is a heritage of his previous condition of servitude, kept alive and aggravated within the ranks of organized labor by the structure and politics of American trade unionism."[5] Treating Blacks in the U.S. coal industry from the 1870s to the mid-1920s, chapters titled "The Negro in the Coal Mines" and "The Negro and the United Mine Workers" provide indispensable insights into the experience of Blacks in the Mountain State. In addition to providing detailed data on the numbers, regional distribution, and occupational status of Blacks in the coal industry, Spero and Harris offered useful perspectives on the role of Blacks in the struggle between capital and labor.

Unfortunately, despite its enduring value, *The Black Worker* overlooked the interrelationship between changes in mining employment and transformations in the community life of African Americans in coal-mining towns. The expansion of the Black church, fraternal organizations, social clubs, and civil rights activities received little analysis. Consequently, although providing penetrating insights into the role of Blacks in the UMWA, Spero and Harris overplayed the importance of the union in the socioeconomic and political activities of Black workers.

Subsequent studies illuminated the larger cultural, political, and social life of Blacks in West Virginia. Although some of this scholarship emerged in book form, most of it consisted of PhD dissertations, masters theses, and articles in professional journals. James T. Laing's "The Negro Miner in West Virginia" (1933), Thomas E. Posey's *The Negro Citizen of West Virginia* (1934), and John R. Sheeler's "The Negro in West Virginia" (1954) all considered the interplay of economic, political, and cultural developments in West Virginia's Black history.[6] Focusing mainly on the late 1920s and early 1930s, Laing's PhD dissertation offered a careful assessment of the Black miners' housing, education, health, family life, religion, and leisure activities. Organized around the question of "citizenship," Posey's study traces the shifting political fortunes of Blacks in the Mountain State from statehood through the early years of the Great Depression. Sheeler offers a similar but more detailed treatment of Black life from the colonial era in western Virginia to 1900.

Other studies focused on Black life in individual counties. Studies by Mary V. Brown, Earl C. Clay, Earle H. Diggs, Jack French, and Ralph Minard, respectively, focused on Monongalia, Greenbrier, Fayette, and McDowell Counties.[7] Covering Black life in rural and industrial counties, such studies presented telling sociological data on Black life in the Mountain State. The political, legal, social, and educational history of Blacks also received substantial treatment. Studies by Iola L. Mack, Joel E. High, John R. Drain, Edythe H. Anderson, Edward Grimke Wood, and Laura Pinn Phillips documented the development of Black elementary, secondary, and college education, from the emancipation era through the modern civil rights movement.[8] At the same time, a variety of scholars analyzed the legal, social, and political status of Blacks, emphasizing the shifting nature of race relations.[9]

Under the impact of the modern civil rights movement, scholars deepened our understanding of the state's Black history. They covered a broad range of chronological and topical areas. In addition to MA and PhD dissertations, the journal *West Virginia History* (founded in 1939) also slowly increased its coverage of Black history. In articles appearing in *West Virginia History*, historians like Edward Steel and John C. Stealy documented the history of slavery, antebellum free Blacks, and the Freedmen's Bureau, while others explored the changing legal status of African Americans, the desegregation of public schools, and the life of Booker T. Washington in the Kanawha Valley.[10] Louis R. Harlan's groundbreaking research on Washington culminated in the publication of two monographs and a multivolume collection of private papers and correspondence, all indispensable to the study of Black life in West Virginia.[11]

Studies emphasizing the interrelationship between work, community, and politics would gain their greatest momentum during the rise of the civil rights movement. Before this perspective gained sway, however, scholars returned to Spero and Harris's emphasis on the movement of Blacks into the bituminous coal industry and their role in the organized labor movement. Motivated by contemporary concern with interracial conflict and cooperation, for example, labor historians Stephen Brier and Daniel P. Jordan painted vivid pictures of Black and white miners in militant labor organizations like the Knights of Labor and the United Mine Workers of America. For his part, economic historian Price V. Fishback analyzed the comparative wages and working conditions of Black and white miners between 1900 and 1930.[12] Through their systematic and detailed reconstruction of interracial unionism and the experiences of Black workers in the coal mining labor force, these scholars reinforced the earlier treatment of Spero and Harris. Like *The Black Worker*, however, such studies gave inadequate attention to the interplay of work and community. In order to address these deficiencies, other scholars built upon the tradition charted by Laing and his counterparts. In various studies, David A. Corbin, Ronald L. Lewis, Crandall A. Shifflett, and Joe W. Trotter analyze the connection between coal mining employment and the larger community life of Blacks in coal-mining towns.[13] In a chapter titled "Class Over Caste: Interracial Solidarity in the Company Town," Corbin emphasizes the role of class conflict in shaping the political and institutional life of the Black community. In his book, *Black Coal Miners in America*, Lewis develops chapters on the same subject but stresses the role of race. In my book, *Coal, Class, and Color*, I explore the interplay of class, race, and, to a degree, gender in the larger community life of Blacks in southern West Virginia between 1915 and 1932. Shifflett's book highlights similar themes in West Virginia, although his study focuses mainly on the state of Virginia.

Despite recent strides toward closing the gap between work and community in the lives of West Virginia Blacks, several limitations and blind spots remain. Few treatments of the state's history, Black or white, examine the tremendous socioeconomic changes of World War I and the 1920s, not to mention the depression, World War II, and the postwar era. This was a period in which the coal industry matured and continued to expand, but it also slowly, then rapidly, declined. West Virginia, however, not only was affected by the rise and decline of the coal industry, but also it was influenced by the development of other industries, including lumber, gas, oil, chemical, iron, steel, textile, and electrical power. Moreover, the state's changing African American class structure demands systematic treatment. In a variety of settings (urban, rural, and rural-industrial), the shifting relationship between the Black proletariat, the middle class, and the small Black elite shaped the experiences of Blacks in West Virginia.

Finally, despite recent developments in women's history, the intersection of race and gender is largely absent from historical treatments of Black life in the Mountain State.[14] Without a clear understanding of changing gender and class relations within the Black community, our comprehension of patterns of inter- and intraracial conflict and cooperation will remain impaired. Failure to examine these issues is only partly related to the dearth of documentation. To be sure, compared to materials for research on white economic and political elites, documentation on Black life in West Virginia is slim. See, for example, the standard bibliographies and guides to manuscripts and archives on the state's history: Innis C. Davis, ed., *Bibliography of West Virginia* (Charleston, 1939); Charles Shetler, ed., *Guide to Manuscripts and Archives in the West Virginia Collection* (Morgantown, 1958); and F. Gerald Ham, *A Guide to Manuscripts and Archives in the West Virginia Collection,* No. 2, 1958–1962 (Morgantown, 1965). In his recent synthesis, *West Virginia: A History* (1985), state historian Otis K. Rice reflects the prevailing class and racial biases in the collection and preservation of primary source materials. He devotes little more than a paragraph to the history of Blacks in the state.[15] Still, as shown in the following section, sources for research on African American history in West Virginia are relatively rich. Indeed, a survey of available documentation suggests unusual opportunities for new research on a variety of issues.

A History of Blacks In West Virginia: The Question of Sources

Sources for research on Black life in the Mountain State are much better than available publications on the state's history would have us believe. These data include a variety of state and federal censuses, special reports, newspaper accounts, manuscript collections, oral interviews, and, as suggested above, a growing body of secondary literature. In the absence of comprehensive guides to research sources on Blacks in West Virginia, useful introductions include the bibliographies and essays on primary sources in Posey, *The Negro Citizen*; William H. Turner and Edward J. Cabbell, eds., *Blacks in Appalachia*; Corbin, *Life, Work, and Rebellion*; Lewis, *Black Coal Miners in America*; Trotter, *Coal, Class, and Color*; and Joe W. Trotter and Ancella R. Bickley, eds., *Honoring Our Past: Proceedings of the First Two Conferences on West Virginia's Black History.*[16]

Federal and State Sources

U.S. Census reports offer the primary statistical data for research on Blacks in West Virginia. The reports of the U.S. Census Bureau help to chart the shifting size, sex, age, state of birth, marital status, housing, education, and occupational characteristics of the African American population. Augmenting the regular decennial reports are the detailed household schedules (available for the years 1870 to 1910) and the special compilations on the Black population: *Negro Population in the United States, 1790–1915* (1918; reprint New York, 1968) and *Negroes in the United States, 1920–1932* (1935; reprint New York, 1966). Special reports on religious bodies, business establishments, and employment are also helpful: U.S. Bureau of the Census, *Religious Bodies,* 1906, 1916, and 1926 (Washington, D.C.. respectively, 1910, 1919, and 1930); *Fifteenth Census of U.S.: 1930: Unemployment* (Washington, D.C., 1931); and *Sixteenth Census of U.S.: Census of Business, vol. 1, Retail Trade, 1939* (Washington, D.C., 1941), to name a few. These statistics not only help to quantify important material dimensions of Black life, they also suggest changes in the class structure and social relationships of Blacks in the Mountain State. Nonetheless, the U.S. Census reports have historically undercounted Blacks and must be used with care.

The published records of Congress and other branches of the federal government also illuminate the history of Blacks in the state. From the congressional debates over statehood through the coal wars of the early twentieth century, congressional records offer significant documentation on the state's Black population. On Blacks and the debates over statehood, see the *U.S. Congressional Globe,* 37th Congress, Second and Third Sessions; and, on the coal wars, see the reports of the U.S. Senate Committee on Education and Labor, *Hearings Pursuant to S. 37, Conditions in the Paint Creek District, West Virginia, 1914* (Washington, D.C.); *Hearings Pursuant to S. 80, to Investigate the Recent Act of Violence in the Coal Fields of West Virginia and Adjacent Territory, 1921–22* (2 vols., Washington, D.C.); and *Hearings Pursuant to S. 105, Conditions in the Coal Fields of Pennsylvania, West Virginia, and Ohio, 1928* (2 vols., Washington, D.C.). The congressional hearings help to illuminate the complicated relationship between Blacks and white workers, employers, and the state. Other federal records are discussed below under manuscript and archival materials.

The records of various state departments reinforce the sources provided by the federal government. Located in the West Virginia and Regional History

Collection at West Virginia University and in the State Archives at the Division of Culture and History in Charleston, the official records of the state government help to document a broad range of topics. From the turn of the century through the early 1930s, the annual reports of the State Department of Mines offer statistics on the coal-mining labor force by county, race, and ethnicity.[17] For several years, the state also recorded the number of fatal and nonfatal mine accidents by race and ethnic background. These data enable us to analyze the distribution of Blacks in the coal-mining labor force and to assess the impact of coal mining on the health and welfare of Black miners compared to American-born whites and immigrants.

During the late nineteenth and early twentieth centuries, under increasing pressure from Blacks and their white Republican allies, West Virginia dramatically increased the number of institutions serving African Americans on a segregated basis. In 1909, the state created the State Board of Control to oversee the growing variety of state-supported social welfare institutions for Blacks and whites. In subsequent years, the Board of Control issued biennial reports on the fiscal and programmatic activities of a broad range of Black institutions. These reports offer historical materials on virtually every facet of Black life in the state. See, for instance, the reports of the Department of Negro Schools; West Virginia State College; Bluefield State College; State Home for Aged and Infirm Colored Men and Women; the Industrial School for Colored Boys; the Industrial School for Colored Girls; and the Denmar Tuberculosis Sanitarium.[18]

Other departmental records supplement the reports of the State Board of Control. The State Department of Agriculture and the Department of Health hired Black agents and submitted annual reports by race.[19] On the legislative activities of Black lawmakers, who served in the lower house of the state legislature on a regular basis during the early twentieth century, see the *Journal of the House of Delegates* (Charleston, WV), and, published annually, the *West Virginia Hand Book, Manual, and Official Register,* which provides documentation (including photographs) on the state's Black elected and appointed officials.

Existing court records are also key to research on Blacks in the Mountain State. The records of five landmark cases stand out: *Strauder v. West Virginia,* involving the right of Blacks to serve on juries; the "Birth of a Nation" case, in which the state supreme court upheld a state law prohibiting the showing of racially inflammatory films; the Charleston Public Library Case, in which the court sustained the right of Blacks to use the city's public library along with whites; the *White v. White* case, involving racially restrictive covenants; and the Greenbrier lynching case, which upheld the state's antilynching statute. Transcripts of these cases are in the *Reports of Cases by West Virginia Supreme Court of Appeals*

(Charleston, WV). Since the Strauder case reached the U.S. Supreme Court, data on that case are also in *Reports of the U.S. Supreme Court* (Washington, D.C.).

Created by the legislature in 1921, the West Virginia Bureau of Negro Welfare and Statistics (BNWS) is perhaps the best single source of documentation on the state's Black population. Until its termination in 1956, the BNWS published comprehensive biennial reports on Black socioeconomic, cultural, and political developments throughout the state. Especially useful for students of the early twentieth century, the records of the bureau provide extensive data by county on urban and rural patterns of work and residence, family life and leisure, churches and fraternal orders, politics, newspapers, and virtually every facet of race relations.[20] Since the BNWS utilized sources from a variety of state and federal records, its reports must be used with care and, where possible, corroborated through a broad range of other official records, especially those of the West Virginia State Board of Control.

Manuscript and Archival Collections

Manuscript collections from all branches of the federal government shed light on the history of Blacks in the Mountain State. The voluminous holdings of the National Archives in Washington, D.C., stand out. During the 1920s, for instance, the U.S. Coal Commission surveyed the state's coal-mining towns and provided statistical and descriptive data on the labor force, housing, schools, churches, and recreational facilities by race.

Also at the National Archives are the records of the U.S. Department of Labor. In addition to manuscript materials on labor conditions, the Department of Labor provides illuminating published reports that analyze conditions in the state by race. See especially *Home Environment and Opportunities of Women in Coal Mine Workers' Families* (Washington, D.C., 1925), and *The Welfare of Children in Bituminous Coal Mining Communities in West Virginia* (Washington, D.C., 1923). The files of the U.S. Department of Justice, to take a final example, illuminate patterns of Black migration (including the role of kin and friendship networks) from the rural South into West Virginia. Portions of these records are now available on microfilm (edited by James R. Grossman as *Black Workers in the Era of the Great Migration* (Frederick, MD: University Publications of America, 1985). For further insight into the range of sources available for research on Blacks at the National Archives, see Debra Newman, *Black History: A Guide to Civilian Records in the National Archives* (Baltimore: Smithsonian Institution Press, 1984).

Reinforcing documentation available at the National Archives are the manuscript collections at the Library of Congress. Housed in the Manuscript Division, the papers of the National Association for the Advancement of Colored People (NAACP) offer the most complete manuscript collection on African Americans in the Mountain State. Composed of branches and affiliates throughout the state (more than a dozen in southern West Virginia alone), the NAACP papers help to document the major civil rights and political struggles of Blacks in West Virginia. By offering extensive data on Black men and women members, including the occupational backgrounds of charter members, these papers also illuminate the complex interplay of class, race, and gender in the lives of African Americans. Some of these records are available on microfilm in Randolph Boehm, ed., *A Guide to Papers of the NAACP, Part 1, 1909–1950: Meetings of the Board of Directors, Records of Annual Conferences, Major Speeches, and Special Reports* (Frederick, MD: University Publications of America, 1982).

At the manuscript division of the Library of Congress, the presidential files are important for research on Black political life in West Virginia. For example, the papers of Warren G. Harding and Calvin Coolidge help to document the career of Arthur G. Froe, the Black McDowell County attorney who served as the recorder of deeds for the District of Columbia. The presidential papers shed light on Froe's appointment to office, his connections to the Republican Party on the state and national levels, and his government service.

Other relevant collections at the Library of Congress are the papers of the National Urban League, as well as those of Black spokespersons W. E. B. Du Bois, Booker T. Washington, and Carter G. Woodson. Most important among these are the papers of Booker T. Washington. The Washington papers document the persistent links between Washington and his old hometown, Malden, in Kanawha County. The scholarship of Louis R. Harlan facilitates use of the Washington Papers. See especially Harlan and Raymond W. Smock, eds., *The Booker T. Washington Papers*, 11 vols. (Urbana: University of Illinois Press, 1972–). For research on the relationship between Du Bois and West Virginia, the Du Bois Papers (which deal mainly with his years as editor of the NAACP's *Crisis* magazine) should be supplemented by consulting his private papers, housed at the University of Massachusetts at Amherst. Similarly, researchers using the Woodson papers should also consult the files of West Virginia State College at Institute, where Woodson served as dean of the college during the early 1920s and retained his contacts there.

State, county, and local repositories offer additional manuscript collections for research on Black life in West Virginia. Housed at West Virginia University, the West Virginia and Regional History Collection contains the papers of Justus Collins and Ulysses G. Carter, several Republican and Democratic governors of the state, labor leaders, and Storer College. The papers of Justus Collins, owner of the Winding Gulf Colliery Company and employer of Black miners, contain correspondence with management officials on Blacks in the mines and in the community. The documents include data on women, schools, and the eruption of racial violence during World War I. The files of the Black coal miner and educator, Ulysses G. Carter, illuminate the efforts of African American miners to move up in the occupational hierarchy. Carter offered mine training and safety courses to Black miners during the 1930s.

The Carter papers consist of a variety of programmatic reports, curricula materials, speeches, and news clippings. The political, educational, and labor struggles of African Americans are documented in the records of state officials, white labor leaders, and educational institutions. The papers of Republican governor and U.S. Senator Henry D. Hatfield, Democratic governor John J. Cornwell, and the white UMWA leader Van Amberg Bittner highlight the role of Blacks in the larger political economy. The Storer College Papers provide insight into the early history of Blacks and Black education. Located in Harper's Ferry, Storer College was West Virginia's first institution of higher education for African Americans. The college's records reveal how it was created, developed over the years, and eventually declined, particularly as the center of the state's Black population shifted from the rural counties of the north, east, and central portions of the state to the southern coal-mining areas.

Several local repositories supplement the manuscript collections at West Virginia University. These include the formerly Black colleges, Bluefield State in Bluefield and West Virginia State in Institute, as well as Marshall University in Huntington. The official records of the historically Black colleges are indispensable for research on a broad range of developments in the state's Black history. As Elizabeth Scobell notes in a recent paper at the West Virginia Conference on Black History, Black colleges are the repositories of correspondence, reports, recommendations, programs, brochures, catalogs, photographs, minutes of meetings, and research bulletins.[21] Marshall University is also an important source of manuscript materials on Black life in the state. These include items on the schoolteacher Pauline Fairfax of Huntington, the playwright Ann Kathryn Flagg of Charleston, and Virgie Giles, president of the Colored Civic Welfare League of Parkersburg. For details on these and other items at Marshall University, see Cora P. Teel, "A Guide to the Collections in the Special Collections Department, James E. Morrow Library" (Marshall University, 1990).

The holdings of county and local libraries, courthouses, and municipalities buttress the records available at the college and university levels. The Eastern Regional Coal Archives, housed at the Craft Memorial Library at Bluefield, West

Virginia, contain a collection of visual as well as manuscript materials on Black life. In her research on the development of the Black community in Huntington, Ancella Radford Bickley provides insight into the range of sources for research on Blacks at the local level.[22] She used Cabell County court records, deed books, marriage and death records, city directories, and the reports of the Huntington Public Schools. Similar sources abound for other counties.

Documentation on Black life in the Mountain State is also available in the manuscript collections of other states. Since West Virginia seceded from Virginia during the Civil War, the University of Virginia Library and the Virginia State Library are important repositories of sources on Blacks in West Virginia before and during the struggle for statehood. See especially the records on slavery and secession in *Proceedings and Debates of the Virginia Constitutional Convention, 1829–1830* and *Proceedings on the General Convention of the State of Virginia, 1861.* Even in the twentieth century, however, collections of material on West Virginia's Black history would find their way into repositories outside the state. The papers of the McDowell County Black attorney Thaddeus E. Harris, for example, are housed at Duke University in the Manuscript Division of the William R. Perkins Library. The Harris papers contain correspondence with his wife, materials on his legal activities, and data on his role in the community life of the state.

Newspapers, Magazines, and Oral Recollections

Many white newspapers help to illuminate the history of Blacks in the state. These include the *Wheeling Intelligencer,* the *Greenbrier Independent,* the *Charleston Gazette,* the *Charleston Daily Mail,* and, as the Black population increased in southern West Virginia, the *Welch Daily News, Bluefield Daily Telegraph, Logan Banner,* and the *Raleigh Register,* to name only a few. For insight into the relationship between Blacks and organized labor, see also the *United Mine Workers Journal,* which has published continuously since 1890.

Although the white press constitutes a valuable source for research on the Black experience, the Black press offers a more balanced and sensitive treatment of African American life. Indeed, African Americans have waged ongoing struggles against racist and biased reporting in the white press.[23] Although irregular and often short lived, Black newspapers are most useful in charting the history of Blacks in West Virginia. With the Bureau of Negro Welfare and Statistics, the Black weekly *McDowell Times* is the single best written source of documentation for the early twentieth century. Edited by Matthew Thomas Whittico, a graduate of Lincoln University in Pennsylvania, the paper began publication in 1904 and continued through the early 1940s. It contains local columns on communities throughout the state and parts of Virginia and Kentucky. Unfortunately, extant issues cover only the years 1913–1918 and parts of the late 1930s and early 1940s. These issues are available on microfilm at the West Virginia Division of Culture and History and at the West Virginia and Regional History Collection in Morgantown.

Additional Black newspapers document aspects of Black life before and after the emergence of the *McDowell Times*. Founded in 1882, under the editorship of J. R. Clifford of Martinsburg, the *Pioneer Press* was the state's earliest Black newspaper. It helps document the state's Black history through the early 1900s. Founded in Charleston in 1957, the *Beacon Digest* (originally the *Beacon Journal)* succeeded the *McDowell Times*. Under the editorship of Benjamin R. Starks and, after 1985, his son and daughter-in-law, the *Beacon Digest* enables us to document changes in Black life since World War II and the development of the modern civil rights movement. The paper now claims a circulation of thirty-five thousand.

Other Black publications reinforce the coverage of the *Beacon Digest, McDowell Times,* and *Pioneer Press.* In a paper delivered at the recent conference on West Virginia's Black History, Betty L. Hart discussed a variety of ephemeral Black newspapers: the *West Virginia Spokesman*, the *West Virginia Enterprise, the Advocate,* and the *Huntington Times.* More importantly, however, facets of Black life in West Virginia are documented in nationally circulated Black publications, particularly the *Chicago Defender*, *Pittsburgh Courier,* and *Baltimore Afro-American.* The official organs of national organizations also help to document Black history in West Virginia: the NAACP's *Crisis,* the Urban League's *Opportunity,* the Garvey Movement's *Negro World,* and the Brotherhood of Sleeping Car Porters' *Messenger.* Indicative of the materials in these sources, in 1924 the *Messenger* carried an article by the Black Charleston attorney T. G. Nutter, entitled "These 'Colored' United States [Part] X: West Virginia." Illustrated with twenty-eight photos of prominent Black business and professional people, the essay offered significant insights into the lives of West Virginia's Black men and women.

Despite offering perspective on African American life in the Mountain State, available written accounts are influenced by important class and gender limitations. Compiled mainly by Black and white professional and business men, government reports, manuscript collections, and newspapers reflect conscious efforts to mold rural African Americans into a new but pliant industrial proletariat. They also reveal efforts to define the nature and scope of women's activities and channel them accordingly. Given such prevailing class and gender conventions, oral interviews are important primary sources for scholarship on Black workers, the poor, and women.

Over the past two decades, archivists and individual scholars have collected numerous oral interviews on Blacks in West Virginia. For access to these data, consult the Oral History of Appalachia Project at Marshall University; the West Virginia and Regional History Collection; and *Goldenseal*, a journal of West Virginia's traditional life, published quarterly by the West Virginia Division of Culture and History. Other oral interviews, used in the studies of coal miners by Corbin and Trotter, for example, are held by the individuals who conducted them.

Family history and genealogical projects reinforce the oral interviews and personal recollections of West Virginia Blacks. Indicative of these activities are the papers delivered at the first two conferences on West Virginia's Black History: Nelson L. Barnett Jr., "Seven Generations of Barnetts: A Short History;" Acie McGhee Jr., "The McGhee Family of McDowell County;" and John W. Williams, "The Lawson-Gore Family of Boone County." [24] While the lives of Black women receive close attention in the family histories compiled by Black men, Black women like Anna Evans Gilmer of Institute and Jessie M. Thomas of Gary are family historians in their own right. Their files include painstaking compilations of family trees, written records of births, deaths, sermons, and fraternal orders, and illuminating correspondence between family members.

In addition to the broad range of sources discussed above, documentation on Black teachers and social workers include the following: Minnie Holly Barnes, *Holl's Hurdles* (Radford, VA: 1980), an autobiographical account of a Black teacher; "Fannie Cobb Carter (1872–1973)," a manuscript on the Black teacher, social worker, and administrator of the West Virginia State Home for Colored Girls in Barbara Matz and Janet Craig, eds., *Missing Chapters: West Virginia Women in History* (West Virginia Women's Commission, et al., 1983); and Ahmed P. Williams's recollections on Black women school teachers in McDowell County, in B. B. Maurer, ed., *Mountain Heritage* (Parsons, WV: McClain, 1980). Although meager compared to similar sources on business and professional white women, they are much better than available written accounts of working-class Black women. No accounts of Black domestic and household workers correspond to the accounts of Black teachers and social workers.[25] In short, while oral sources are essential to research on Black workers, the poor, and women, they are most essential to scholarship on working-class African American women.

A critique of the historical literature on Blacks in the Mountain State suggests a variety of primary and secondary sources for future research. Although

uneven and often thin, available sources promise to illuminate the major transformations in African American life, open up new inquiries into a variety of
topics and chronological periods, and create a richer and more varied portrait of
Black life in West Virginia. Only by diligent and systematic effort, however, will
we be able to close gaps and develop a satisfactory synthesis of Black life in the
Mountain State. As suggested, despite substantial research over the past two
decades, few studies focus on the lives of Black women, life in mountain cities,
and changes since the Great Depression and World War II. A firmer grasp of
West Virginia's Black history will not only help us to refine our understanding
of African American history, it will also enable us to redefine the larger history of the state. African American history, like other categories of analysis in
this volume, has broader implications for the state, nation, and world.

NOTES

PREFACE

1. Trotter, "Roots of Health Disparities."
2. Trotter, *Black Milwaukee*, 264.
3. Otis Trotter, "From Vallscreek to Highland Creek."
4. Trotter, *Coal, Class, and Color*, 228–229.
5. Trotter, "Interpreting the African American Working-Class Experience."
6. Greene, "Rethinking the Boundaries of Class."

INTRODUCTION

1. Du Bois, *The Philadelphia Negro*; Wesley, *Negro Labor*; Greene and Woodson, *The Negro Wage Earner*; Spero and Harris, *The Black Worker*; Reid, *Negro Membership*; Cayton and Mitchell, *Black Workers*.
2. Trotter, *The Great Migration*, quoting Woodson.
3. See Trotter, "African American Workers," quoting Brier, 511; Turner and Cabbell, *Blacks in Appalachia*.
4. Trotter, "African American Workers," quoting Jordan, 511.
5. Roediger, *The Wages of Whiteness*, 14. For a critique of the contributions and limitations of emerging whiteness studies at the time, see Kolchin, "Whiteness Studies," and Guglielmo, *White on Arrival*.
6. Also see Burchett, "Promise and Prejudice"; Rice, "The 'Separate but Equal' Schools"; Wilkinson, "Hot and Sweet."
7. See Trotter, "Celebrating the 40-Year History."
8. Fain, *Black Huntington*, 63, 138. This section also draws upon my review of Fain's book in the *American Historical Review*, forthcoming.
9. Armstead, *Black Days, Black Dust*; Bickley and Ewen, *Memphis Tennessee Garrison*; and Otis Trotter, *Keeping Heart*. Cf. Gates, *Colored People*. This memoir covers imminent scholar Henry Louis Gates's hometown near the easternmost part of West Virginia near the Maryland border, where most African Americans and the town's people worked at a paper mill rather than in coal mines.
10. Otis Trotter, *Keeping Heart*, 1.
11. See, for example, Brown, *Gone Home*; Curtin, *Black Prisoners and the World*; Letwin, *Challenge of Interracial Unionism*; Huntley and Montgomery, *Black Workers' Struggle*;

Kelly, *Race, Class, and Power*; Woodrum, *Everybody Was Black*; Shapiro, *A New South Rebellion*.

12. Brown, *Gone Home*, 2–3.
13. Letwin, *Challenge of Interracial Unionism*, 1–7.
14. Curtin, *Black Prisoners and the World*, 5.
15. See, for example, Schwieder, *Black Diamonds*; Schwieder, Hraba, and Schwieder, *Buxton*; Gradwohl and Osborn, *Exploring Buried Buxton*; Chase, *Creating the Black Utopia*; Doppen, *Richard L. Davis*; Jackson, "Impact of the Roslyn Strike"; Rhinehart, *A Way of Work*.
16. Rhinehart, *A Way of Work*.
17. Lewis, *Black Coal Miners*; Lewis, *Welsh Americans*; Long, *Where the Sun Never Shines*; Nyden, *Black Coal Miners*.
18. Goldfield, *The Southern Key*.
19. Long, *Where the Sun Never Shines*, xxiv.
20. Goldfield, *The Southern Key*, 136. This section also draws upon my review of Goldfield's book in *Dissent* magazine, forthcoming.

CHAPTER 2. MIGRATION TO SOUTHERN WEST VIRGINIA

1. Lewis, "Migration of Southern Blacks"; Stuckert, "Black Populations."
2. Eller, *Miners, Millhands, and Mountaineers*; Corbin, *Life, Work, and Rebellion*, 1–7; Barnum, *Negro in the Coal Industry*, 1–24; Spero and Harris, *The Black Worker*, 206–45; Lewis, *Black Coal Miners*, chap. 7; West Virginia Department of Mines, *Annual Reports* (1909, 1910).
3. Williams, *West Virginia*, 109–129; Sullivan, "Coal Men and Coal Towns"; Rice, *West Virginia*, 184–204; Corbin, *Life, Work, and Rebellion*, 3–4; Eller, *Miners, Millhands, and Mountaineers*, 132–140, 165–168; Lawrence, "Appalachian Metamorphosis," 28–42, 64.
4. Corbin, *Life, Work, and Rebellion*, 8, 43–52; Eller, *Miners, Millhands, and Mountaineers*, 129, 165–75; Barnum, *Negro in the Coal Industry*, 1–24; Lawrence, "Appalachian Metamorphosis," 224–228; Fishback, "Employment Conditions," 44–51; Lewis, *Black Coal Miners*, chap. 7; Bailey, "A Judicious Mixture." On the exclusion of blacks from northern industries, see Harris, *The Harder We Run*, 29–50; Foner, *Organized Labor*, 64–135; Spero and Harris, *The Black Worker*, 53–115; U.S. Bureau of the Census, *The Negro Population*, 85; U.S. Bureau of the Census, *Negroes in the United States*, 45; U.S. Bureau of the Census, *Fourteenth Census*, 636–640.
5. Washington, *Up From Slavery*, 26–28; R. G. Hubbard, et al. (Malden Homecoming Committee) to Booker T. Washington, May 29, 1913, in B. T. W. Tuskegee Records, Lecture File, Boxes 811 and 816, Booker T. Washington Papers (Library of Congress); Harlan, *Booker T. Washington: The Making*, 28.
6. Laing, "Negro Miner" (1933), 64–69; Callahan, *Semi-Centennial History*, also quoted in Laing, 64; Taylor, *Negro in the Reconstruction*, also quoted in Laing, 64–65.
7. Laing, "Negro Miner" (1933), 64–69; Callahan, *Semi-Centennial History*, also quoted in Laing, 64; Taylor, *Negro in the Reconstruction*, also quoted in Laing, 64–65.
8. Corbin, *Life, Work, and Rebellion*, 64–65; Lewis, *Black Coal Miners*, chap. 7; and Trotter, *Coal, Class, and Color*, chap. 3.

9. White, "Another Lesson"; Woodson, *A Century of Negro Migration*, 147–166.
10. Lester and Ellen Phillips, interview by author, July 20, 1983; Salem Wooten, interview by author, July 25, 1983; see also Millner, "Conversations with the Ole Man," 58–64; Massey, "I Didn't Think I'd Live," 32–40; Eller, *Miners, Millhands, and Mountaineers*, 165–175; Corbin, *Life, Work, and Rebellion*, chaps. 7, 8, and 9; Fishback, "Employment Conditions," 72–82, 116–120.
11. Wooten, interview by author, July 25, 1983.
12. Robert N. Bell, U.S. attorney, Northern District of Alabama, to U.S. attorney general, October 25, 1916; and Alexander D. Pitts, U.S. attorney, Southern District of Alabama, to Samuel J. Graham, U.S. assistant attorney general, October 27, 1916, both in Department of Justice, Record Group No. 60, Straight Numerical File No. 182363 (Washington, D.C., National Archives); Thelma O. Trotter, conversation with author, August 1, 1983; Solomon Woodson, conversation with author, November 9, 1985.
13. Henri, *Black Migration*, 132–173; Laing, "The Negro Miner" (1933), chap. 4; Eller, *Miners, Millhands, and Mountaineers*, 168–172; Corbin, *Life, Work, and Rebellion*, 61–63; Roy Todd, interview by author, July 18, 1983.
14. Thornton Wright, interview by author, July 27, 1983; W. L. McMillan, Omar, WV, to R. L. Thornton, Three Notch, AL, November 2, 1916, Department of Justice, Record Group No. 60, Straight Numerical File no. 182363; "Migration Study, Negro Migrants, Letters from (Type script), 1916–18," National Urban League Papers, Series 6, Box 86 (Washington, D.C.: Library of Congress).
15. McMillan to Thornton, 2 Nov. 1916; West Virginia Bureau of Negro Welfare and Statistics (WVBNWS), *Biennial Reports* (Charleston, W.Va.), 1921–22, 5, and 1925–26, 8.
16. Phillips and Phillips, interview; Pink Henderson, interview by author, July 15, 1983; Wooten, interview; Lewis, *Black Coal Miners*, chaps. 3 and 4; McMillan to Thornton, November 2, 1916; "From Alabama: Colored Miners Anxious for Organization." *United Mine Workers Journal*, June 1, 1916"; Seals, "Life in Alabama"; Seals, "The Horrors of Convict Mines." The following are in Department of Justice, Record Group No. 60, Straight Numerical File No. 182363: Bell to U.S. attorney, October 25, 1916; Pitts to Graham, October 27, 1916; "Memorandum: Willie Parker" (recorded by Edwin Ball, general manager, Tennessee Coal, Iron, and Railroad Company) and "Statement of Tom Jones."
17. "Wanted at Once," May 12, 1916, and "10 Automobiles Free," May 25, 1917, both in *McDowell Times*; "Safety First," "Go North," "Wanted," and "Employment Office," in U.S. Department of Labor, Box 2, folder 13/25, Record Group No. 174 (Washington, D.C., National Archives).
18. Bell to U.S. attorney general, October 25, 1916; Pitts to Graham, October 27, 1916; "Labor Agents Succeed in Inducing Negroes to Leave Southern Farms," *Atlanta Constitution*; "Memorandum: Willie Parker"; "Statement of Tom Jones"; "Early Surveys . . . Migration Study, Birmingham Summary," National Urban League Papers, Series 6, Box 89 (Washington, D.C., Library of Congress); "Safety First"; "Go North"; "Wanted"; and "Employment Office."
19. "The Exodus," August 18, 1916, and "Southern Exodus in Plain Figures," December 1, 1916, both in *McDowell Times*; White, "Another Lesson"; "Colored Folks Enjoying Universal Industrial and Social Advancement," July 28, 1917, *McDowell Times*.
20. *Conditions in the Coal Fields*; for excerpts of the committee hearings, see *UMWJ*,

March 1, 1928; U.S. Senate Committee on Education and Labor, "Testimony of J. H. Reed," 479–482.

21. "Idlers between Ages of Eighteen and Sixty Will Be Forced to Work," *McDowell Recorder*, May 25, 1917; Hill, "Loafers and Jonahs"; "Dig Coal or Dig Trenches Is the Word to the Miner," *Raleigh Register*, July 12, 1917.

22. Hill, "Loafers and Jonahs."

23. "Educate All the People," April 16, 1915, "To Whom It May Concern," January 29, 1915, and "Good People of McDowell County Outraged," May 17, 1918, all in *McDowell Times*; State Commissioner of Prohibition, *Fourth Biennial Report*, 1921–1922.

24. Wooten interview; Pitts to Graham, October 27, 1916.

25. Todd interview; Watt B. Teal, interview by author, July 27, 1983; Laing, "The Negro Miner" (1933), chap. 4.

26. Phillips and Phillips interview; Campbell, interview by author, July 19, 1983; Bell to U.S. attorney general, October 25, 1916; Pitts to Graham, October 27, 1916; WVBNWS, *Biennial Report*, 1923–1924, 22–23; "Adams-Russel," July 14, 1916, and "Gannaway-Patterson," December 22, 1916, both in *McDowell Times*; *New River Company Employees Magazine* 2, no. 3 (November 9, 1924): 9–10.

27. William M. Beasley, interview by author, July 26, 1983; Henderson interview; Thomas D. Samford, U.S. attorney, Middle District of Alabama, to U.S. attorney general, November 2, 1916, and Samford to U.S. attorney general, October 21, 1916, in Department of Justice Record Group, No. 60, Straight Numerical File No. 182363.

28. Wright interview.

29. Jasper Boykins to U.S. attorney general, October 16, 1916, Department of Justice, Record Group No. 60, Straight Numerical File No. 182363. For a discussion of coercive elements in Southern agriculture, see Mandle, *Roots of Black Poverty*.

30. Pitts to Graham, October 27, 1916.

31. Todd interview.

32. Wooten interview.

33. WVBNWS, *Biennial Reports*, 1921–1922, 57–58, and 1927–1928, 17–19; Phillips and Phillips interview; Laing, "The Negro Miner" (1936); Laing, "The Negro Miner" (1933), chap. 5.

34. "Discrimination against the Negro," *Bluefield Daily Telegraph*, June 20, 1920; "Negro Tricked into Logan County," *UMWJ*, June 15, 1921, includes extensive excerpts of the operator's pamphlet to Black workers.

35. WVBNWS, *Biennial Reports*, especially the reports for 1921–1922, 38–41, and 1923–1924, 29–35.

36. WVBNWS, *Biennial Reports*, 1923–1924, 39–45; Children's Bureau, *Welfare of Children*, 5; U.S. Bureau of the Census, *The Negro Population*, 85; U.S. Bureau of the Census, *Negroes in the United States*, 45; U.S. Bureau of the Census, *Fourteenth Census*, 636–640.

37. Sidney Lee, interview by author, July 19, 1983; Phillips and Phillips interview; Wooten interview; Lawrence, " 'Make a Way out of Nothing.' "

38. North Dickerson, interview by author, July 28, 1983; Charles T. Harris, interview by author, July 18, 1983; Preston Turner, interview by author, July 26, 1983; Lawrence Boling, interview by author, July 18, 1983.

39. WVBNWS, *Biennial Report*, 1921–1922, 57–58, and 1927–1928, 17–19; Laing, "The Negro Miner" (1933), 195. See chapter 3 for more detail.

40. This and the remaining portions of this essay are based on my essay in Salzman, *Encyclopedia*.

CHAPTER 3. INEQUALITY IN THE WORKPLACE

1. For a recent review of this literature, see Trotter, "African American Workers."

2. Laing, "The Negro Miner" (1933), 195.

3. Laing, "The Negro Miner" (1936), 416–422; Laing, "The Negro Miner" (1933), chap. 5; with Dickerson interview. Unless otherwise stated, all interviews were conducted by the author and are in his possession.

4. Teal interview; Laing, "The Negro Miner" (1933), chap. 5. For general insight into the miner's work, see Goodrich, *The Miner's Freedom*, and Dix, *Work Relations*, chaps. 1 and 2.

5. Interviews with Salem Wooten, 25 July 1983, Charles T. Harris, 18 July 1983, and Leonard Davis, 28 July 1983.

6. WVBNWS, *Biennial Report*, 1921–1922, 59; "Safety First," "Go North," "Wanted," and "Employment Office," in Box 2, Folder 13/25, Record Group No. 174, U.S. Department of Labor; "Wanted: Sullivan Machine Men," *Logan Banner* (June 8, 1923); interviews with Roy Todd, July 18, 1983, and William M. Beasley, July 26, 1983. See also Dix, *Work Relations*, chap. 1; Laing, "The Negro Miner" (1933), 264–265; and Fishback, "Employment Conditions," chap. 6.

7. Interview with Pink Henderson, July 15, 1983; Fishback, "Employment Conditions," 182–229; Eller, *Miners, Millhands, and Mountaineers*, 178–182; interview with Walter and Margaret Moorman, July 14, 1983. For reports of Black casualties, see "Six Miners Killed in Explosion at Carswell," *Bluefield Daily Telegraph* (July 19, 1919), "Gary (Among the Colored People)" (December 11, 1923 and January 2, 1924), "Compensation for Six Injured Miners" (December 10, 1923), "Russel Dodson Killed Monday by Slate Fall" (July 14, 1925), and "Walter McNeil Hurt in Mine (July 22, 1925), all in the *Welch Daily News*; "Negro Miner Is Killed at Thorpe" (June 12, 1929), "Colored Miner Killed Friday in Slate Fall" (March 5, 1930), "McDowell County Continues Out in Front in Mine Fatalities" (July 24, 1929), "Negro Miner Electrocuted in Tidewater Mines" (October 9, 1929), and "Hemphill Colored Miner Killed in Mining Accident" (January 8, 1930), all in the *McDowell Recorder*.

8. For a discussion of these processes in the urban-industrial context, see Gottlieb, *Making Their Own Way*; Grossman, *Land of Hope*; Lewis, *In Their Own Interests*; and Trotter, *Black Milwaukee*.

9. Interviews with Lawrence Boling, July 18, 1983, Andrew Campbell, July 19, 1983, William M. Beasley, July 26, 1983, and Charles T. Harris, July 18, 1983; "Annual Garden Inspection at Gary Plants," (July 17 and 23, 1925), "Annual Inspection of Yards and Gardens: Consolidation Cola Company" (July 27, 1925), all in *Welch Daily News*; Agricultural Extension Service, *Annual Reports*, 1921–1932, especially "Negro Work" and "Extension Work with Negroes"; "The Annual Garden and Yard Contest Complete Success," *New River Company Employees' Magazine* 3, no. 1 (September 1925): 3–4, and 2, no. 2 (October 1924): 8–9; "55 Individual Awards Made Today in Yard and Garden Contests," *McDowell Recorder* (July 31, 1929).

10. Peters Sisters, *War Poems*, 7.
11. WVBNWS, *Biennial Report*, 1923–1924, 25–28; interview with Walter and Margaret Moorman, July 14, 1983; Women's Bureau, *Home Environment*, 47; interviews with Thornton Wright, July 27, 1983, and Andrew Campbell, July 19, 1983; "Goes South on Vacation," March 5, 1915, and "Giatto Rapidly Progressing," May 29, 1915, both in *McDowell Times*.
12. Interview with Leonard Davis, July 28, 1983.
13. Obituaries, *McDowell Times*, 1915–1918, especially January 28, 1916, and August 13, 1915.
14. Susie Norwell to W. E. B. Du Bois, January 10, 1928; Du Bois to Norwell, May 16, 1928, reel no. 27, W. E. B. Du Bois Papers, Library of Congress; Barnes, *Holl's Hurdles*, 24–27; interviews with Thornton Wright, July 27, 1983, Walter and Margaret Moorman, July 14, 1983, Lester and Ellen Phillips, July 20, 1983, Watt Teal, July 27, 1983, and Leonard Davis, July 28, 1983.
15. Millner, "Conversations with the 'Ole Man," 58–64; "Looking for a Helpmate," *McDowell Times* (November 19, 1915); "Among Our Colored People," *New River Company Employees' Magazine* 2, no. 3 (November 1924): 11–12; interviews with Charles T. Harris, July 18, 1983, and Walter and Margaret Moorman, July 14, 1983.
16. "Idlers between Ages," *McDowell Recorder* (May 25, 1917); Hill, "Loafers and Jonahs"; "Dig Coal or Dig Trenches," *Raleigh Register* (July 12, 1917).
17. "How a Coal Miner Can Save Money," *McDowell Times* (February 19, 1915); Laing, "The Negro Miner" (1933), chaps. 2, 3, and 4. Also see "Local Items," *McDowell Times* (March 26, 1915); WVBNWS, *Biennial Reports*, 1921–1922, 5–11, 38–41, and 1923–1924, 8–10, 39–45; "Kimball (Colored News)," *Welch Daily News* (January 28, 1924); "Among Our Colored," in various issues of the *New River Company Employees' Magazine* (1924–1930); "Agricultural Extension Work in Mining Towns," in Agricultural Extension Service, *Annual Reports*, 1921–1926.
18. Anderson, "News of the Colored People" (December 28, 1930); WVBNWS, *Biennial Reports*, 1929–1932, 12–14.
19. Cherniack, *The Hawk's Nest Incident*, 18–19, 89–91; Rowh, "The Hawk's Nest Tragedy."
20. Chemiack, *The Hawk's Nest Incident,* 18–19, 90–91; Rowh, "The Hawk's Nest Tragedy."
21. Interviews with Pink Henderson, July 15, 1983, and Leonard Davis, July 3, 1983; U.S. Bureau of the Census, *Fifteenth Census*, 6:1428.
22. W. H. Harris, "Exceptional Opportunities"; Fishback, "Employment Conditions," 284–285.
23. WVBNWS, *Biennial Reports*, 1921–1922, 58–59, and 1927–1928, 15–17; newspaper clipping, *Welch Daily News* (September 21, 1926), in U. G. Carter Papers (West Virginia Collection, West Virginia University).
24. Laing, "The Negro Miner" (1933), 182–183, 213; W. H. Harris, "Exceptional Opportunities."
25. Morris, *Plight*, 297–298; Fishback, "Employment Conditions," 308–309; West Virginia State College Mining Extension Service, *Annual Report*, 1942–1943, in U. G. Carter Papers.
26. WVBNWS, *Biennial Reports*, 1921–1922, 86–87, and 1923–1924, 36–37.

27. Fuetter, "Mixed Labor in Coal Mining," 137, quoted in Lewis, *Black Coal Miners*, 144–145; Henderson interview.
28. "Memorandum, Willie Parker," Straight Numerical Files, No. 182363, U.S. Department of Justice Records, RG 60, National Archives, Washington, D.C.; interviews with Henderson and Harris; Laing, "The Negro Miner" (1933), 242.
29. "Memorandum, Willie Parker"; interviews with Leonard Davis, July 28, 1983, and Roy Todd, July 18, 1983.
30. Fishback, "Employment Conditions," 284–285; Laing, "The Negro Miner" (1933), 191, 242, 249–250.
31. Laing, "The Negro Miner" (1933), 234–236.
32. Massey, "I Didn't Think I'd Live," 32–40.
33. Davis interview; Laing, "The Negro Miner" (1933), 225–228.
34. Interviews with Moorman and Moorman and Todd.
35. Interviews with Campbell, Henderson, and Phillips and Phillips.
36. Interviews with Dickerson and Boling.
37. Davis interview; Laing, "The Negro Miner" (1933), 189; Witt and Dolter, "Before I'd Be a Slave."
38. Laing, "The Negro Miner" (1933), 225–228.
39. Laing, "The Negro Miner" (1933), 225–228, 474.
40. Trotter, *Coal, Class, and Color*, chaps. 3, 4.
41. Laing, "The Negro Miner" (1933), 222–224; Fishback, "Employment Conditions," 169.
42. For the debate on the role of race and class in the coalfields, see Hill, "Myth-Making as Labor History"; and Brier, "In Defense of Gutman."
43. Interviews with Todd and Harris; Lewis, *Black Coal Miners*, 179–180, citing *Color: A Tip Top World Magazine* 4 (February 1948): 13; "Among Our Colored People," 8.
44. Boling interview.
45. Harris interview.
46. Interviews with Beasley and Todd; Laing, "The Negro Miner" (1933), 264–265.
47. Todd interview; "First Aid Contest at Gary" (June 4, 1915), and "Working Hard to Stop Accidents" (August 4, 1916), both in *McDowell Times*; "Pocahontas Wins Safety Meet," *McDowell Recorder* (August 22, 1929).
48. Harris interview; Massey, "I Didn't Think I'd Live," 32–40; Millner, "Conversations with the 'Ole Man."
49. Harris interview; interviews with Dickerson and Beasley.
50. Interviews with Moorman and Moorman and Harris.
51. Todd interview.
52. Interviews with Harris, Todd, Henderson, Dickerson, and Boling.
53. For membership statistics on UMWA Districts 17 and 29, see Corbin, *Life, Work, and Rebellion*, 76–77, 184; "Delegate [Frank] Ingham," in *Proceedings*, 1:173; Records of Districts 17 and 29, UMWA Papers, UMWA Archives, Washington, D.C.
54. Hill, "Coal Strike and Negro Miners"; WVBNWS, *Biennial Reports*, 1923–1924, 22–24, and 1925–1926, 131. For insight into Black and white occupancy of the UMWA tent colonies of striking miners, see Box 2, Folders 9, 10, Van Amberg Bittner Papers, West Virginia Collection, West Virginia University.
55. "From Iowa; A Word to the West Virginia Miners," *UMWJ* (June 1, 1916); Edmunds, "West Virginia on Tap"; "District 29 Holds a Splendid Special

Convention," *UMWJ* (February 1, 1919); and "Assignment of Speakers for 1921 Labor Day" *UMWJ* (September 1, 1921).

56. Jordan, "The Mingo War"; Corbin, *Life, Work, and Rebellion*, 195–224; Hill, "Coal Strike and Negro Miners"; *Charleston Gazette* (September 1, 1921) and "Confessed Murderer of John Gore Is Given Life Sentence," *Logan Banner* (October 19, 1923); Witt and Dolter, "Before I'd Be a Slave," 23–47. Blankenhorn, "Marching through West Virginia," 289. Blankenhorn estimates there were two thousand Blacks among the eight thousand marchers.

57. See *Charleston Gazette* (September 1, 1921) and "Confessed Murderer of John Gore"; "From Silush, W.Va.," *UMWJ* (September 1921).

58. Testimony of Frank Ingham, *West Virginia Coal Fields*, vol. 1, 26–38.

59. Testimony of Frank Ingham.

60. Testimony of Frank Ingham.

61. Testimonies of George Echols and J. H. Reed, both in *West Virginia Coal Fields*, 469–482.

62. Testimonies of George Echols and J. H. Reed.

63. "Agreement between Carbon Fuel Company and Its Employees," 1923–1925, in "Kanawha/Coal River," Mining Community Schedule-A, Box 28, U.S. Coal Commission Records, Record Group 68, National Archives.

64. "Agreement between Carbon Fuel Company."

65. "Easy," *United Mine Workers Journal*, January 15, 1925.

66. "Agreement between Carbon Fuel Company."

67. WVBNWS, *Biennial Reports*, 1921–1922, 54–60; "The Coal Strike and Negro Miners in West Virginia" (c. 1922), in "Early Surveys," Series 6, Box 89, National Urban League Papers.

68. WVBNWS, *Biennial Report*; "Coal Strike and Negro Miners."

69. WVBNWS, *Biennial Report*; "Coal Strike and Negro Miners."

70. "Discrimination against the Negro," *Bluefield Daily Telegraph*, June 20, 1920.

71. "Negro Tricked into Logan County," *United Mine Workers Journal*, June 15, 1921 (includes extensive excerpts from the operators' pamphlet directed toward Black workers; testimony of Langdon Bell, director of the Red Jacket Consolidated Coal Company, in U.S. Senate Committee on Interstate Commerce, *Conditions in the Coal Fields*.

72. W. H. Harris, "Exceptional Opportunities." See also Agricultural Extension Service, *Annual Report,* 1923, 98–110.

73. Anderson, "News of the Colored People" (September 2, 9, 22, and 23, 1920; November 15, 1924; and January 1, 1925).

74. White, "Weyanoke"; "Lynwin Coal Company: Offering Great Extra Inducements" (May 11, 1917); "Lynwin Coal Company: Offering Great Opportunities for Money" (May 4, 1917); "Sycamore C. Company: Located in Mingo County, W.Va.: Doing Good Work" (July 23, 1915); "The Coal Miners Provided For" (February 26, 1915); Blenkinsopp, "Colored Miner 'Don'ts' "; "Improved Conditions in the Winding Gulf Fields" (September 17, 1917), all in *McDowell Times*. See also Anderson, "News of the Colored People" (September 23, 1920); and Farley, "Homecoming."

75. U. G. Carter, "Public Address" and "Speech to New River Colored Mining Institute, Fayette County," in Box 1, Folder 8, Carter Papers; "McDowell County Colored Republican Organization," *McDowell Recorder* (October 23, 1920); Fishback,

"Employment Conditions," 231 n9; Lewis, *Black Coal Miners*, 223 n18; and Laing, "The Negro Miner" (1933), 180–182.

76. Carter, "Public Address" and "Speech," Box 1, Folder 8, Carter Papers; "McDowell County," *McDowell Recorder* (October 23, 1929); Fishback, "Employment Conditions," 231 n9; Lewis, *Black Coal Miners*, 223 n18; Laing, "The Negro Miners" (1933), 180–182.

77. For documentation of the following comparative discussion, see Trotter, *Coal, Class, and Color*, chap. 11, especially notes 9–11.

78. Laing, "The Negro Miner" (1933), 462, 487.

79. Lewis, *Black Coal Miners*, 81.

CHAPTER 4. COMMUNITY FORMATION

1. Harris, *The Harder We Run*, 29–50; Foner, *Organized Labor*, 64–135; Spero and Harris, *The Black Worker*, 53–115.

2. Eller, *Miners, Millhands, and Mountaineers*, 128–140; Corbin, *Life, Work, and Rebellion*, 1–7; Barnum, *Negro in the Coal Industry*, 1–24; Spero and Harris, *The Black Worker*, 206–245; Lewis, *Black Coal Miners*, chap. 7; West Virginia Department of Mines, *Annual Reports* (1909, 1910).

3. For fuller figures on the population change in southern West Virginia, see table 1.1 in Trotter, *Coal, Class, and Color*, 11.

4. Corbin, *Life, Work, and Rebellion*, 8, 43–52; Eller, *Miners, Millhands, and Mountaineers*, 129, 165–175; Barnum, *Negro in the Coal Industry*, 1–24; Lawrence, "Appalachian Metamorphosis," 224–228; Fishback, "Employment Conditions," 44–51; Lewis, *Black Coal Miners*, chap. 7; Bailey, "A Judicious Mixture"; U.S. Bureau of the Census, *Report on the Population*, 435; U.S. Bureau of the Census, *Thirteenth Census*, 3:1032–1041.

5. For further discussion of these adjustments in the labor force and the genesis of a black working class, see Trotter, *Coal, Class, and Color*, chap. 1.

6. Sheeler, "Negro in West Virginia," 256–257; Washington, *Up from Slavery*, 57–58; Harlan, *Booker T. Washington: The Making*, 33–51, 84–85, and 137–138.

7. U.S. Bureau of the Census, *Religious Bodies, 1906*, 140; U.S. Bureau of the Census, *Religious Bodies, 1926*, 133, 998; "Sacred Concert," December 5, 1913, "Services at Keystone" and "Locals," May 15, 1914, "The Presbyterian Sunday School Relief Department," October 16, 1914, "The Mt. Olivet Baptist Ass'n," July 18, 1913, "The Flat Top Baptist Association," May 9, 1913, all in *McDowell Times*; Sheeler, "Negro in West Virginia," 251–274; Washington, *Up from Slavery*, 57–58; Harlan, *Booker T. Washington: The Making*, 33–51, 84–85, and 137–138.

8. U.S. Bureau of the Census, *Twelfth Census*, 410–414; U.S. Bureau of the Census, *Thirteenth Census*, 4:529–530; "Bluestone Baptist Church Rally," May 9, 1913, "Rally at Anawalt," July 4, 1913, and "Welch News," June 13, 1913, all in *McDowell Times*.

9. "Welch News," *McDowell Times*, June 13, 1913.

10. "McAlpin Notes," May 1, 1914, "Locals," May 23, 1913, "Coalwood News," May 22, 1914, and "Slabfork," December 11, 1914, all in *McDowell Times*. For insight into Black religion during the industrial era, see Levine, *Black Culture*, chap. 3; Frazier, *The Negro Church*, chaps. 3, 4, 5; and Bethel, *Promiseland*, 69–91, 136–144.

11. "Baptizing at Wingfield Baptist Church: Fifteen Hundred People . . . Witness Ceremony," May 9, 1913, "Bramwell News," November 28, 1913, "Giatto News," December 12, 1913, "Kimball Notes," October 23, 1914, all in *McDowell Times*.

12. "Death at Gilliam," *McDowell Times*, July 4, 1913.

13. See various issues of the *McDowell Times*, 1913–1914; Lawrence, "Appalachian Metamorphosis," 13–35.

14. For works on Black religion in the South, see note 10 above.

15. "The Flat Top Baptist Association Holds Successful Session in City," July 25, 1913, and "Pastor Installed at First Baptist Church," November 14, 1913, both in *McDowell Times*; Boris, *Who's Who in Colored America*, vol. 1, 1927, 108–109; Spradling, *In Black and White*, 517; Robinson, *Historical Afro-American Biographies*, 215–216.

16. "In Memory: Rev. Nelson Barnett," and Rev. I. V Bryant, "Funeral-Sermon of Rev. Nelson Barnett," both in private files of Capt. Nelson L. Barnett, U.S. Air Force (retired), Huntington, WV (copies in author's possession).

17. "In Memory: Rev. Nelson Barnett," and Rev. I. V Bryant, "Funeral-Sermon of Rev. Nelson Barnett," both in private files of Capt. Nelson L. Barnett, U.S. Air Force (retired), Huntington, WV (copies in author's possession).

18. "In Memory: Rev. Nelson Barnett," and Rev. I. V Bryant, "Funeral-Sermon of Rev. Nelson Barnett," both in private files of Capt. Nelson L. Barnett, U.S. Air Force (retired), Huntington, WV (copies in author's possession).

19. "The Flat Top Baptist Association," "Rev. Coger Preaches Able Sermon," July 25, 1913, "Jenkinjones Notes," August 8, 1913, and "Colored Member Elected," October 30, 1914, all in *McDowell Times*.

20. "Giatto News," December 12, 1913, "Rally at First Baptist Church, Kimball," April 10, 1914, "Services at Keystone," May 1, 1914, "Great Baptist Meeting at Tams," July 24, 1914, "Glen White," October 2, 1914, "Religious Services at Keystone," March 20, 1914, all in *McDowell Times*.

21. For spirited revivals at African Methodist Episcopal churches, see "A Voice from the A.M.E. Church," May 8, 1914, "Locals," May 15, 1914, and "Great Revival at Landgraff," May 16, 1913, all in *McDowell Times*. Black Presbyterians in West Virginia also retained important links to the spiritual traditions of Southern Blacks. See especially "Back from Vacation," *McDowell Times*, September 5, 1913.

22. "Successful Evangelistic Services Conducted at Northfork," April 24, 1914, and "Rev. Gipson and His Church Work," September 24, 1914, both in *McDowell Times*.

23. "Sacred Concert," *McDowell Times*, December 5, 1913.

24. Hill, "My Dream of the Future Church." Also see "The Prisoners' Friend," June 5, 1914, "The Presbyterian Sunday School Relief Department," October 16, 1914, and "McDowell County Applies for 150 State Convicts," June 20, 1913, all in *McDowell Times*.

25. See various issues of the *McDowell Times*, 1913–1914.

26. "Golden Rule News," May 9, 1913, "Address of Rev. R. H. McKoy, D.D.," June 13, 1913, "2000 Wanted," January 16, 1914, and "Golden Rule Association: Hold 10th Annual Meeting in Tazewell," June 12, 1914, all in *McDowell Times*.

27. "Golden Rule News," "Address," and "2000 Wanted."

28. "John Panell Killed by Falling Slate," September 5, 1913, "Death at Gilliam," July 4, 1913, and "Landgraff Loses a Good Citizen," July 25, 1913, all in *McDowell Times*.

29. "Colored Odd Fellows Parade: Hold Great Thanksgiving Service," 16 May 1913, *McDowell Times*.

30. "Keystone Lodge A.F. and A.M. Hold Services," 27 June 1913, and "Pythian Anniversary Ceremonies Held," 3 April 1914, both in *McDowell Times*.

31. "Colored Odd Fellows Parade: Hold Great Thanksgiving Service," May 6, 1913, and "Mayor: Delivers Address of Welcome to Colored Pythians of State," August 8, 1913, both in *McDowell Times*.

32. Sheeler, "Negro in West Virginia," 191–194. For patterns of Black disfranchisement in other parts of the South, see Williamson, *The Crucible of Race*.

33. Lawrence, "Appalachian Metamorphosis," 183–186.

34. Sheeler, "Negro in West Virginia," 202–203; Washington, *Up from Slavery*, 64–65; Harlan, *Booker T. Washington: The Making*, 93–96.

35. Otis K. Rice, *West Virginia*, 165–173, 204–216; Williams, *West Virginia: A History*, 115–129; Corbin, *Life, Work, and Rebellion*, 10–18.

36. Sheeler, "Negro in West Virginia," 207–212; U.S. Bureau of the Census, *Thirteenth Census*, 3:1032–1041; Otis K. Rice, *West Virginia*, 172, 206, 208.

37. Otis K. Rice, *West Virginia*, 207; Williams, *West Virginia: A History*, 115–119; Corbin, *Life, Work, and Rebellion*, 10–18; quote in *New York World*, July 23, 1899, reprinted in *Public Addresses, etc., of Governor G. W. Atkinson*, courtesy of Gary L. Weiner, Clarksburg, WV.

38. Williams, *West Virginia: A History*, 115–129; Corbin, *Life, Work, and Rebellion*, 10–18; Sheeler, "Negro in West Virginia," 207–212; U.S. Bureau of the Census, *Thirteenth Census*, 3:1032–1041; Swisher, *Manual of the State*, 114; "Great Meeting of the McDowell County Colored Republican Organization," November 21, 1913, "Republicans Together," July 31, 1914, and "Prof. Sanders Promoted," July 31, 1914, all in *McDowell Times*; WVBNWS, *Biennial Report*, 1921–1922, 67.

39. "Great Meeting," "Republicans Together," "Prof. Sanders Promoted," all in *McDowell Times*; "State Librarian," in John T. Harris, *West Virginia Legislative Hand Book* (1916), 809.

40. Sheeler, "Negro in West Virginia," 223–226, 230–246; "The School Attendance," May 9, 1913, and "West Virginia Colored Institute," June 27, 1913, both in *McDowell Times*; Harlan, *History of West Virginia State College*.

41. Sheeler, "Negro in West Virginia," 234–239; "Storer College" and "State of W.Va. Correspondence on Appropriations to Storer, 1914–1941," box 1, Storer College Papers, West Virginia Collection, West Virginia University.

42. See Storer College to Governor H. D. Hatfield, February 1915, box 1, Storer College Papers.

43. "Interracial Racial Relations," WVBNWS, *Biennial Report*, 1925–1926, 118–120.

44. Sheeler, "Negro in West Virginia," 251–260, 207–213; "In Memory" and "Funeral Sermon," in private files of Capt. Nelson L. Barnett, Huntington, WV; "Pythians Capture the City of Baltimore," September 5, 1913, "National Baptist Convention," September 26, 1913 and September 25, 1914, and "Locals," September 5, 1913, all in *McDowell Times*; John T. Harris, *West Virginia Legislative Hand Book* (1916), 809; John T. Harris, *West Virginia Legislative Hand Book* (1928), 220; John T. Harris, *West Virginia Legislative Hand Book* (1929), 201.

45. "Elks Hold Great Meeting" and "Nutter Elected Grand Exalted Ruler," September 5, 1913, "Convention of Elks," July 17, 1914, "Elks Hold Big Meeting," September 4,

1914, "Fifteenth Annual Session of the I.B.P.O.E. of the World," September 11, 1914, all *in McDowell Times*; Harlan, *Booker T. Washington: The Wizard of Tuskegee*, 125–127; and Trotter, *Coal, Class, and Color*, chap. 2.

46. For the *Times'* antiunion position, see "We Still Adhere to Our Policy," July 4, 1913, "Illimitable as the Wind: We Blow on Whom We Please," July 11, 1913, "Unfair Attitude of Union Men toward the Negro," July 18, 1913, Reverend M. L. Shrum to M. T. Whittico, June 20, 1913, reprinted, July 4, 1913, and "Clean Up and Swat the Flies," May 9, 1913, all in *McDowell Times*. See also Corbin, *Life, Work, and Rebellion*, 75–79.

47. Corbin, *Life, Work, and Rebellion*, 41, 77–105; Lawrence, "Appalachian Metamorphosis," 63, 133–138, 184–185, 262–263, 288; Lewis, *Black Coal Miners*, chaps. 7 and 8, especially 141–142; Sayles, *Thinking in Pictures*; Spero and Harris, *The Black Worker*, chap. 7; Laing, "The Negro Miner" (1933), 493–496.

48. "Split Skirts," *McDowell Times*, July 4, 1913.

49. "Attend to Your Duties," *McDowell Times*, July 25, 1913.

50. "Literary Program," March 13, 1914, and "Woman's Auxiliar[y] National Baptist Convention," September 5, 1913, both in *McDowell Times*.

51. "St. Luke News," May 9, 1913, "Mrs. Malinda Cobbs: A Successful Deputy," August 10 and August 31, 1917 (includes a photo and summary of Cobbs's lodge activities), "Woman's Auxiliar[y]," all in *McDowell Times*.

52. "Bluefield Police" and "Brave Colored Woman Defends Her Honor and Home Shoots at Cops," July 18, 1913, "Colored Odd Fellows," "The Annual Thanksgiving Services," May 30, 1913, and "The Ninth Annual Meeting," June 13, 1913, all in *McDowell Times*.

53. Brier, "Interracial Organizing"; Lewis, *Black Coal Miners*, 136–140.

54. Brier, "Interracial Organizing," 29.

55. For the upsurge of interracial unionism in 1913–1914, see Corbin, *Life, Work, and Rebellion*, 87–101; Lewis, *Black Coal Miners*, 14–42; Lunt, *Law and Order*; Wheeler, "Mountaineer Mine Wars."

56. Brier, "Interracial Organizing," 32–33.

57. See note 36 above, especially Sheeler, "Negro in West Virginia," 207–212, and *McDowell Times*, November 21, 1913, July 31, 1914, and May 16, 1913. See also "Editor Air. Whittico," February 23, 1917, and "Whittico Dead," June 23, 1939, both in *McDowell Times*.

58. "Colored Odd Fellows Parade."

CHAPTER 5. ENVIRONMENTAL CONDITIONS

1. Lillian B. Waller to E. C. Lewis, February 18, 1920, Lewis to John R. Shillady, February 16, 1920, "Bloodthirsty Murder in Thug-Rule Logan," news clipping, *Charleston Federationist*, December 18, 1919, "Report of the Charleston Branch," February 18, 1920, all in Charleston Branch Files, Box G-215, Records of the National Association for the Advancement of Colored People (NAACP Papers), Library of Congress; James Weldon Johnson to Howard Sutherland, West Virginia senator, December 16, 1919, "West Virginia Senators Notified of Lynching in Their State," news release, December 17, 1919, Lewis to Governor John J. Cornwell, March 13, 1920, Shillady to Cornwell, February 12, 1920, Cornwell to Shillady, February 17, 1920, Cornwell to Lewis, March 15, 1920, "Two Negroes Taken Off

Train Tied to Freight Car and Shot to Death by Coal Field Mob," news clipping, *New York Herald*, December 16, 1919, all in Administrative File, Box C-370, NAACP Papers.

2. Lewis to Walter White, December 13 and 19, 1922, White to Lewis, December 19 and 16, 1922, White to T. G. Nutter, February 28, 1922, "A Negro Woman," letter to editor, *New York Age,* n.d., news clipping from *Cincinnati Post,* February 23, 1922, all in Charleston Branch Files, Box G-215, NAACP Papers; letter of petition for clemency, Charleston NAACP to Governor E. F. Morgan, February 21, 1922, Nutter to White, March 3, 1922, both in Legal Files, Box D-2, NAACP Papers; "First Baptist Church," the *Bulletin,* May 28,1922, in Charleston Branch Files, Box G-216, NAACP Papers; WVBNWS, *Biennial Report* 1923–1924, 96–98.

3. "Henry Grogan," testimony of plaintiff and the accused, Nutter to Robert Bagnall, August 16, 1928, Albert Kyselka to Roger Baldwin, American Civil Liberties Union, August 24, 1928, Baldwin to Bagnall, August 24, 1928, "State of West Virginia vs. Henry Grogan," defense attorney's petition for a writ of error, all in Charleston Branch Files, Box G-215, NAACP Papers.

4. WVBNWS, *Biennial Reports,* 1925–1926, 114–118, and 1921–1922, 52. See also the following news clippings in Charleston Branch Files, Box G-216, NAACP Papers: "Has Never Heard of God: Girl Tells Court," October 19, 1923, and "Three Negro[e]s Are Dead," November 2, 1926, both in *Logan Banner;* "Negro is Placed on Trial Today in Assault Case," July 25, 1925, "Jury in Watt Wall Case," July 29, 1925, both in *Welch Daily News;* "Negro Murders White Man," c. January 1922, "Negro Attacks Girl in Holdup Case: Makes Escape," January 22, 1922, in *Charleston Gazette.*

5. "Billy Sunday Bids Logan Fond Farewell," June 22, 1923, "Ku Klux Klan Gives Billy Pleasant Surprise," June 22, 1923, "Klansmen Celebrate Independence Day," July 6, 1923, "Klan's Greatest Ceremonial Tonight," November 2, 1923, "Klan Ceremonial Was Witnessed by Multitude," November 9, 1923, "Logan Klan Have Special Train," August 22, 1924, "Logan Klan is Prominent at State Meeting," August 29, 1924, "Logan Klan Gives Money to Christian Church," August 22, 1924, all in *Logan Banner.* For the revival of the Ku Klux Klan after World War I, see Jackson, *Ku Klux Klan in the City;* and Chalmers, *Hooded Americanism.*

6. "Packed Theatre to Hear Speech on Ku Klux Klan," news clipping, *Bluefield Daily Telegraph,* March 6, 1924, "The Negro Situation," KKK circular letter, in Charleston Branch Files, Box G-215, NAACP Papers; WVBNWS, *Biennial Report,* 1921–1922, 52–54.

7. Interviews with Campbell, Charles T. Harris, Henderson, John L. Page, July 13, 1983, and Boling. See also Witt and Dolter, "Before I'd Be a Slave"; Laing, "The Negro Miner" (1933), 409–411.

8. "Welch Has No Accom[m]odation for Colored People—Hotel Greatly Needed," August 31, 1917, and articles on April 6, August 10, and October 12, 1917, all in *McDowell Times;* interview with Henderson.

9. Lawrence, "Appalachian Metamorphosis," 180; interviews with Dickerson, Campbell, Teal, and Charles T. Harris; "Memorandum: Willie Parker," U.S. Department of Justice, Record Group No. 60, Straight Numerical File No. 182363; Laing, "The Negro Miner" (1933), 480–481, 483.

10. Interviews with Dickerson, Campbell, Teal, and Charles T. Harris; "Memorandum: Willie Parker," U.S. Department of Justice; Laing, "The Negro Miner" (1933), 480–481, 483.

11. Interview with Preston Turner; S. R. Anderson, a Black journalist, to Justin Collins, August 13, 1923, Series 1, Box 14, Folder 101, Justus Collins Papers, West Virginia Collection, West Virginia University.

12. Obie McCollum to Walter White, October 17, 1930, Charleston Branch Files, Box G-215, NAACP Papers; "Rich Coal Operator," *United Mine Workers Journal*, October 15, 1930.

13. Laing, "The Negro Miner" (1933), 348–349; "Why," *McDowell Times*, November 17, 1916; Wolfe, "Putting Them in Their Places." Also see "International Convention Goes on Record in Favor of Traditional Policy of Observance of Contracts," *UMWJ*, October 1, 1921, and "Living Conditions in Many Mine Fields against Which the Union Continues to Fight," *UMWJ*, March 15, 1924.

14. Women's Bureau, *Home Environment*, 55–59; Children's Bureau, *The Welfare of Children*, 6–17, 47.

15. Women's Bureau, *Home Environment*, 17, 55–59.

16. Women's Bureau, *Home Environment*, 17, 55–59; Children's Bureau, *The Welfare of Children*, 6–17, 47.

17. "Sycamore Coal Company," *McDowell Times*, July 23, 1915.

18. W. H. Harris, "Exceptional Opportunities"; White, "Weyanoke."

19. Wolfe to Collins, August 25, 1917, Series 1, Box 15, Folder titled, "August," Wolfe to Collins, September 19, 1918, Series 1, Box 14, Folder 101, both in Justus Collins Papers; "Annual Garden Inspection at Gary Plants," July 17 and 23, 1925, "Gary Colored News," July 25, 1925, "Annual Inspection of Lands and Gardens: Consolidation Coal Company," July 27, 1925, all in *Welch Daily News*.

20. Laing, "The Negro Miner" (1933), 340–341; "Mining Community Schedule—A," Record Group No. 68, U.S. Coal Commission, National Archives; "Annual Garden Inspection," and "Gary Colored News"; "Agricultural Extension Work in Mining Camps" and "Negro Work," in Agricultural Extension Service, *Annual Reports*, 1921–1932.

21. U.S. Bureau of the Census, *Fifteenth Census*, 6:1427–1429; WVBNWS, *Biennial Reports*, 1921–1932; "Miners Own Homes and Automobiles," reprint from a Charleston newspaper in *McDowell Times*, March 5, 1915; "Giatto for Judge Ira E. Robinson," *McDowell Times*, March 31, 1916; Laing, "The Negro Miner" (1933), 295, 317.

22. "Mt Carbon and Kimberly," July 28, 1916, "McDowell Citizens," October 13, 1916, "Lilly Land Company," November 26, 1915, and "Great Land Sale," May 28, 1915, all in *McDowell Times*.

23. See the Keystone-based *McDowell Times*, 1915–1918; "Lot Sale Going On," *McDowell Recorder*, May 18, 1917; "Housing Conditions" and "Home Ownership" in WVBNWS, *Biennial Reports*, 1921–1922, 45–49, and 1925–1926, 59–61.

24. WVBNWS, *Biennial Report*, 1923–1924, 47–48; "Evils of Bad Housing," in WVBNWS, *Biennial Report*, 1929–1932, 6–10; "Great Land Sale"; Laing, "The Negro Miner" (1933), 295, 317.

25. WVBNWS, *Biennial Report*, 1927–1928, 5–14. The BNWS based its study on Federal Registration Area data. Also see WVBNWS, *Biennial Reports*, 1921–1922, 16, 1923–1924, 14–15, 1925–1926, 10–11, and 1929–1932, 49. See also West Virginia State Board of Control (WVSBC), *Biennial Report*, 1924–1925, 145–163; West Virginia State Health Department (WVSHD), *Annual Reports*, 1918–1932.

26. WVBNWS, "Health and Mortality," *Biennial Report*, 1927–1928, 5–14.

27. W. H. Harris, "The Negro Doctors"; WVSBC, "State Tuberculosis Sanitarium," *Biennial Report*, 1914–1916, 172–192.

28. Interviews with Walter and Margaret Moorman, Dickerson, Wright, and Teal; Laing, "The Negro Miner" (1933), 314. For the role of Black midwives, refer to interviews with Davis and Campbell.

29. WVSBC, "Welch Hospital," *Biennial Report*, 1918–1919, 172–184, and 1924–1925, 165–166; WVSBC, "McKendree Hospital Number 2," *Biennial Report*, 1924–1925, 185–187. Also see WVSBC, "Weston State Hospital," *Biennial Report*, 1916–1917, 48–90.

30. "What is the Cause?" *McDowell Times*, July 23, 1915; WVSBC, "Penitentiary," *Biennial Reports*, 1918–1919, 218–235; WVBNWS, *Biennial Reports*, 1921–1922, 34–36, and 1923–1924, 92; WVSBC, "Penitentiary," *Biennial Reports*, 1920–1930.

31. W. F. Denny (sometimes misprinted as D. F. Denny), "People Have Rights," April 30, 1915, "Criminal Court at Princeton," July 9, 1915, "To Whom It May Concern," January 29, 1915, and "Educate All the People," April 16, 1915, all in *McDowell Times*; State Commissioner of Prohibition, *Fourth Biennial Report*, 1921–1922; "Thirty Gallon Still Is Found Near Church," December 21, 1923, "Two Plead Guilty to Liquor Charges," December 31, 1923, and "Three Give Bond," January 5, 1924, all in *Welch Daily News*.

32. "Negro Has Special Jacket to Carry His Moonshine In," July 21, 1925, "Three Colored Men Pose as Officers and Carry Liquor," January 15, 1925, both in *McDowell Recorder*; "Whoopee," May 28, 1915, "Again," July 30, 1915, "Thousands of Dollars Worth of Liquor . . . Destroyed," March 30, 1917, "Still Captured: Fire Water Destroyed," March 29, 1918, all in *McDowell Times*; WVBNWS, *Biennial Report*, 1923–1924, 92.

33. "What Is the Cause?"

34. "Man Murdered at Eureka," March 19, 1915, W. H. Harris, "Murder on King's Operation," March 26, 1915, "Murder for Revenge," May 7, 1915, and "Murder at Landgraf," July 23, 1915, all in *McDowell Times*; "Miner Shot to Death and Murderer Escapes," *Charleston Daily Mail,* July 14, 1918; *Welch Daily News*, February 4, 1924, July 28, 1925, and November 4, 1926.

35. "Murder at Crumpler: Woman Killed, Another Shot," July 30, 1915, and "Kills Husband," September 17, 1915, both in *McDowell Times*; "Bullets Aimed at Fast Moving Auto," December 13, 1923, and "Woman Kills Husband, Another Shoots Hers," both in *Welch Daily News*; "Crazed Negro Slays Wife, Shoots Brother," August 21, 1929, and "Negro Inflicts Fatal Wound on Girl," March 5, 1930," both in *McDowell Recorder.*

36. WVBNWS, *Biennial Reports*, 1925–1926, 110–114, and "Crime," 1927–1928, 56–61, and 1929–1932, 55–57.

37. "Why" and "The Climax," September 10, 1915, both in *McDowell Times*; WVBNWS, *Biennial Report*, 1923–1924, 96–98; E. C. Lewis to Walter White, December 13 and 19, 1922, White to Lewis, December 19 and 16, 1922, in Charleston Branch Files, Box G-215, NAACP Papers.

38. WVBNWS, Biennial Report, 1923–1924, 96–98.

39. Ambler, *A History of Education*, 503–504; Otis K. Rice, *West Virginia*, 239–254.

40. Jackameit, "A Short History"; Ambler, *A History of Education*, 454–456, 489–495; Harlan, *History of West Virginia State College*, chaps. 4, 5, and 6; WVBNWS, *Biennial Reports*, 1923–1924, 64–67, and 1921–1932; State Supervisor of Negro Schools,

Biennial Report, 1921–1922, 1–35; "West Virginia Collegiate Institute" and "Bluefield Colored Institute," in WVSBC, *Biennial Reports,* 1916–1930.

41. WVBNWS, *Biennial Reports,* 1921–1922, 25, 1923–1924, 64–69, and 1929–1932, 15; "Ten High Schools Receive State Aid," *Welch Daily News,* February 9, 1923; State Supervisor of Negro Schools, *Biennial Report,* 1921–1922, 1–35; State Superintendent of Free Schools, *Biennial Report,* 1929–1930, 88; Jackameit, "A Short History," 309–324; Ambler, *A History of Education,* 409.

42. U.S. Bureau of the Census, *Fourteenth Census,*1172; U.S. Bureau of the Census, *Fifteenth* Census, 1263–1277; "Education of the Negro," WVBNWS, *Biennial Reports,* 1921–1922, 25, 1923–1924, 64–69, and 1929–1932, 15; State Supervisor of Negro Schools, *Biennial Report,* 1921–1922, 1–35; State Superintendent of Free Schools, *Biennial Report,* 1929–1930, 88; Jackameit, "A Short History," 309–324; Ambler, *A History of Education,* 409.

43. Jackameit, "A Short History," 312; WVSBC, *Biennial Report,* 1916–1918, 17–18; Ambler, *A History of Education,* 489–495; Harlan, *History of West Virginia State College,* chaps. 4, 5, and 6. Cf. Lewis, *Black Coal Miners,* 155, and Corbin, *Life, Work, and Rebellion,* 70.

44. "Successful School Year," June 11, 1915, "Account of High Schools in McDowell Co.," January 15, 1915, "The Mining Town School System," March 5, 1915, "Prof. W. W. Sanders Makes Statement," June 21, 1916, "Are Fees of High School Pupils Paid by District Boards of Education?" February 16, 1917, all in *McDowell Times.*

45. "Education Made by Teacher," *McDowell Times,* March 19, 1915. Also see *McDowell Times,* February 19 and October 6, 1915 and October 13 and September 8, 1916; State Supervisor of Negro Schools, *Biennial Report,* 1921–1922, 1–35; "Education of the Negro," WVBNWS, *Biennial Reports,* 1921–1922, 22–25, 64–69; WVSBC, "State Aid to Students Outside the State," *Biennial Report,* 1930–1931, 530–531.

46. "Colored High School Will be Improved Upon," *Charleston Gazette,* December 9, 1925; WVBNWS, *Biennial Report,* 1925–1926, 84–91; "Resolutions, Charleston Board of Education," October 13, 1927, "The Board of Education of the Charleston Independent School District: Minutes of a Special Meeting," February 21, 1928, T. G. Nutter, president of the Charleston NAACP, to William T. Andrews, special legal assistant, NAACP headquarters, February 28, 1928, March 15, 20, and 28, 1928, April 21, 1928, and May 28, 1928, "R. S. Spillman, Member and Attorney of Charleston Board of Education," February 27, 1928, and Charleston NAACP, Lewis to National Office, October 23, 1918, all in Charleston Branch Files, Box G-215, NAACP Papers.

47. State Supervisor of Negro Schools, *Biennial Report,* 1921–1922, 1–35; WVBNWS, *Biennial Report,* 1925–1926, 87–91; "McDowell County Colored Republican Organization," *McDowell Recorder,* October 23, 1929; Laing, "The Negro Miner" (1933), 376.

48. "College Department for Negroes," *McDowell Times,* January 8, 1915; State Supervisor of Negro Schools, *Biennial Report,* 1–35; WVSBC, *Biennial Report,* 1930–1931, 530–531; WVBNWS, *Biennial Report,* 1923–1924, 64–69; Jackameit, "A Short History," 309–324; Harlan, *History of West Virginia State College,* chaps. 4, 5, and 6.

49. WVBNWS, *Biennial Report,* 1925–1926, 84–91; speeches and correspondence of U. G. Carter, Mining Extension Service, West Virginia State College, in the U. G. Carter Papers, West Virginia Collection.

EPILOGUE

1. Gutman, "Negro and the United Mine Workers of America," 49–127.
2. Early studies following Gutman's lead include Corbin, *Life, Work, and Rebellion*; Worthman, "Black Workers and Labor Unions"; Brier, "Interracial Organizing"; and Jordan, "The Mingo War."
3. Hill, "Myth-Making as Labor History"; Painter, "The New Labor History."
4. Roediger, "History Making and Politics"; Roediger, *The Wages of Whiteness*; Kolchin, "Whiteness Studies"; Arnesen, "Whiteness and the Historians' Imagination"; and responses to Arnesen's essay by James Barrett and others in *International Labor and Working Class History* 60 (2001), 33–80.
5. Letwin, *Challenge of Interracial Unionism*, 6. For more examples of studies in this vein, see Shapiro, *A New South Rebellion*; Kelly, *Race, Class, and Power*; Lewis, *Black Coal Miners*; Shifflett, *Coal Towns*; Trotter, *Coal, Class, and Color*.
6. For a provocative critique of this notion, see Johnson, "On Agency."
7. Bukowczyk, "Introduction, Forum"; Lewis, *Welsh Americans*, 4. For helpful theoretical and empirical assessments of assimilationist theory, see also, respectively, O'Connor, *Poverty Knowledge*; and Beik, *The Miners of Windber*.
8. Gjerde, "New Growth on Old Vines." For an initial synthesis of this scholarship, see Bodnar, *The Transplanted*.
9. Long, *Where the Sun Never Shines*, 3–5, 19–23. See also Lewis, *Coal, Iron, and Slaves*; Starobin, *Industrial Slavery in the Old South*.
10. Long, *Where the Sun Never Shines*, 3–5, 56–57.
11. Lewis, *Welsh Americans*, ix–x, 1–9.
12. Lewis, *Welsh Americans*, 51–90; John Hall is quoted from Long, *Where the Sun Never Shines*, 7.
13. Laslett, *United Mine Workers of America*, 14; Lewis, *Welsh Americans*, 59–60, 120–21.
14. Laslett, *United Mine Workers of America*, 1–25; Laslett, *Nature's Noblemen*, 1–9; Fox, *United We Stand*, 21–23, 56–74, 82–101; Blatz, *Democratic Miners*, 1–35.
15. Andrews, *Killing for Coal*, 95–96, 102–103.
16. Dix, *What's a Coal Miner to Do?*, 6–7, 28–32, 217.
17. Beik, *The Miners of Windber*, xx–xxx, 1–51; Beik, "UMWA and New Immigrant Miners"; Laslett, " 'A Parting of the Ways,' " 320–325, 417–437.
18. Lewis, *Welsh Americans*, 236–237; Blatz, *Democratic Miners*, 55–60.
19. Lewis, *Welsh Americans*, 238–239; Cohen, "Monopoly, Competition," 415–416; Long, *Where the Sun Never Shines*, 248–249, 321–323.
20. Beik, "UMWA and New Immigrant Miners," 329.
21. Lewis, *Black Coal Miners*, iv–xv.
22. Lewis, *Black Coal Miners*, viii–xv; Lewis, *Coal, Iron, and Slaves*, 3–10; Letwin, *Challenge of Interracial Unionism*, 1–30; Kelly, *Race, Class, and Power*, 3–15. In her groundbreaking study of resistance against convict labor in Tennessee, historian Karin Shapiro shows how Black and white miners forged greater interracial solidarity in the eastern Tennessee coal towns of Coal Creek, Briceville, and Oliver Springs than they did in the southeastern town of Tracy City. See Shapiro, *A New South Rebellion*, 12–13. Coal companies provided wider screens for weighing coal mined by Blacks than they did for whites, thus creating a racial differential in pay. Such practices reinforced the idea that white men were both materially and socially

"superior" to Black workers. Thus, any evidence of Black-white solidarity through labor unions flirted with the idea of social equality of all workers and threatened white-worker privileges such as discriminatory weighing practices. See Lewis, *Black Coal Miners*, 47.

23. Spero and Harris, *The Black Worker*, 210–213; Nelson, *Divided We Stand*, 167; Schwieder, Hraba, and Schwieder, *Buxton*, 3–12, 209. See also Schwieder, *Black Diamonds*.

24. Spero and Harris, *The Black Worker*, 233; Nelson, *Divided We Stand*, 167.

25. Spero and Harris, *The Black Worker*, 356–357. See also Letwin, *Challenge of Interracial Unionism*, 89–123; Corbin, *Life, Work, and Rebellion*, 45–46, 65–77, 87–101; Shapiro, *A New South Rebellion*, 31–32, 229–230.

26. Richard L. Davis's coal-mining career is well documented in the columns of the *United Mine Workers' Journal* and the *National Labor Tribune*. See also Gutman, "Negro and the United Mine Workers of America."

27. Spero and Harris, *The Black Worker*, 336–337.

APPENDIX: SCHOLARSHIP, DEBATES, AND SOURCES

1. Lewis, *Black Coal Miners*; Trotter, *Coal, Class, and Color*; Lewis, "The Black Presence"; Shifflett, *Coal Towns*; Trotter and Bickley, *Honoring Our Past*; Turner and Cabbell, *Blacks in Appalachia*; Barnum, *Negro in the Coal Industry*; Corbin, *Life, Work, and Rebellion*; Bailey, "A Judicious Mixture"; and two PhD dissertations: Lawrence, "Appalachian Metamorphosis" and Fishback, "Employment Conditions."

2. Woodson, "Disruption of Virginia"; Woodson, *Early Negro Education in West Virginia*; Posey, *The Negro Citizen of West Virginia*; Laing, "The Negro Miner" (1933); Sheeler, "The Negro in West Virginia before 1900."

3. Surface, "The Negro Mine Laborer."

4. Woodson, "Disruption of Virginia"; Woodson, *Early Negro Education*.

5. Spero and Harris, *The Black Worker*, xv and chs. 10 and 17. Also see essays by Abram L. Harris, "Negro in the Coal Mining Industry," and "Plight of the Negro Miner."

6. See note 2.

7. This and the following discussion in notes 8 and 9 are primarily based upon Duncan, "Master's Theses and Doctoral Dissertations." See especially, Brown, "A History of the Negroes"; Clay, "The Negro in Greenbrier County"; Diggs, "Socio-Economic Status"; and French, "Segregation Patterns." See also Minard, "Race Relationships." Minard conducted his field work in 1946.

8. See Mock, "Rise of Negro Elementary Education"; Hight, "History of Negro Secondary Education"; Drain, "History of West Virginia State College"; Anderson, "Legislative Acts"; Wood, "Development of Secondary Education"; and Phillips, "Development of Education for Negroes."

9. Monico, "Negro and the Martinsburg Gazette"; Wynne, "Reconstruction and the Negro"; Moore, "Slavery as a Factor" (1947); Moore, "Slavery as a Factor" (1956); and Jones, "Civil Status of Negroes."

10. Thompson, "An Appeal for Racial Justice"; Zerber, "An Analysis"; Smith, "West Virginia Human Rights Commission"; Steel, "Bypath to Freedom"; Steel, "Black Monongalians"; Cresswell, "Case of Taylor Strauder"; Stealey, "Freedmen's Bureau"; Stealey, "Reports of Freedmen's Bureau District Officers"; Stealey, "Reports of

Freedmen's Bureau Operations"; Smith, "Race Relations"; Jackameit, "A Short History"; Duran and Duran, "Integration in Reverse"; Louis R. Harlan, "Booker T. Washington's West Virginia Boyhood"; Louis R. Harlan, "Booker T. Washington and the Kanawha Valley"; John C. Harlan, "Booker T. Washington"; Mongin, "A College in Secession"; John C. Harlan, *History of West Virginia State College*. With the exception of articles on John Brown and the Harpers Ferry story, few articles on Blacks appeared in *West Virginia History* before the 1960s. See, for example, Draper, "Legal Phases"; Stutter, "John Brown's Letter"; Stutter, "John Brown"; Jellison, "Martyrdom of John Brown"; Lord, "John Brown"; Moreland, "Early Iron Industry."

11. Louis R. Harlan, *Booker T. Washington: The Making*; Louis R. Harlan, *Booker T. Washington: The Wizard of Tuskegee*; Harlan and Smock, *The Booker T. Washington Papers*.

12. Brier, "Interracial Organizing"; Jordan, "The Mingo War"; Fishback, "Employment Conditions."

13. Corbin, *Life, Work, and Rebellion*; Lewis, *Black Coal Miners*; Trotter, *Coal, Class, and Color*; Shifflett, *Coal Towns*.

14. See Pudup, "Women's Work." In the same issue, see other essays on women in West Virginia's history, especially Melosh, "Recovery and Revision."

15. Rice, *West Virginia*.

16. See notes 1 and 2.

17. West Virginia Department of Mines, *Annual Reports*.

18. West Virginia State Board of Control, *Biennial Reports*.

19. See Agricultural Extension Service, *Annual Reports*; West Virginia State Health Department, *Annual Reports*.

20. West Virginia Bureau of Negro Welfare and Statistics, *Biennial Reports*.

21. Scobell, "Preserving the History."

22. Bickley, "Black People."

23. This analysis of black publications is based upon Hart, "The Black Press," and Trotter, *Coal, Class, and Color*.

24. See Trotter and Bickley, *Honoring Our Past*.

25. Cf. Linn, "The Lieutenant Governor." This article offers insight on the life of Walter Thomas Ferguson, the messenger and chauffeur for the West Virginia Liquor Commissioner and later for seven governors of the state.

BIBLIOGRAPHY

Agricultural Extension Service. *Annual Reports*. Morgantown, WV. Various years.

Ambler, Charles H. *A History of Education in West Virginia: From Early Colonial Times to 1949*. Huntington, WV: Standard, 1951.

Anderson, Edyth H. "Legislative Acts Pertaining to the Education of Negroes in West Virginia." EdM, University of Cincinnati, 1953.

Anderson, S. R. "News of the Colored People." *Bluefield Daily Telegraph*, various dates.

Andrews, Thomas G. *Killing for Coal: America's Deadliest Labor War*. Cambridge, MA: Harvard University Press, 2008.

Armstead, Robert. *Black Days, Black Dust: The Memories of an African American Coal Miner*. Knoxville: University of Tennessee Press, 2002.

Arnesen, Eric. "Whiteness and the Historians' Imagination." *International Labor and Working-Class History* 60 (2001): 3–32.

Bailey, Kenneth R. "A Judicious Mixture: Negroes and Immigrants in the West Virginia Mines, 1880–1917." *West Virginia History* 34 (1973): 141–161.

Barnes, Minnie Holly. *Holl's Hurdles*. Radford, VA: Commonwealth, 1980.

Barnum, Darold T. *The Negro in the Bituminous Coal Mining Industry*. Philadelphia: University of Pennsylvania Press, 1970.

Beik, Mildred A. *The Miners of Windber: The Struggles of New Immigrants for Unionization, 1890s–1930s*. University Park: Pennsylvania State University Press, 1996.

———. "The UMWA and New Immigrant Miners in Pennsylvania Bituminous: The Case of Windber." In John H. M. Laslett, *The United Mine Workers of America*, 320–325. University Park: Pennsylvania State University Press, 1996.

Bethel, Elizabeth R. *Promiseland: A Century of Life in a Negro Community*. Philadelphia: Temple University Press, 1981.

Bickley, Ancella R. "Black People and the Huntington Experience." In Trotter and Bickley, eds., *Honoring Our Past*, 132. Charleston: Alliance for the Collection, Preservation and Dissemination of West Virginia's Black History), 1991.

Bickley, Ancella R., and Lynda Ann Ewen. *Memphis Tennessee Garrison: The Remarkable Story of a Black Appalachian Woman*. Athens: Ohio University Press, 2001.

Blankenhorn, Heber. "Marching through West Virginia." *Nation* 113 (September 1921): 288–289.

Blatz, Perry K. *Democratic Miners: Work and Labor Relations in the Anthracite Coal Industry, 1875–1925*. Albany: State University of New York Press, 1994.

Blenkinsopp, Lawson. "The Colored Miner 'Don'ts' for Safety First." *McDowell Times*, January 15, 1915.

Bodnar, John. *The Transplanted: A History of Immigrants in Urban America*. Bloomington: Indiana University Press, 1985.

Boris, Joseph J. *Who's Who in Colored America*, vol. 1, 1927. New York: Who's Who in Colored America, 1927.

Brier, Stephen. "In Defense of Gutman: The Union's Case." *International Journal of Politics, Culture and Society* 2, no. 3 (Spring 1989): 383–395.

———. "Interracial Organizing in the West Virginia Coal Industry: Participation of Black Aline Workers, 1880–1894." In Gary M. Fink and Merle E. Reed, eds., *Essays in Southern Labor History,* 18–43. Westport, CT: Greenwood, 1977.

Brown, Karida L. *Gone Home: Race and Roots through Appalachia*. Chapel Hill: University of North Carolina Press, 2018.

Brown, Mary V. "A History of the Negroes of Monongalia County, from the Pioneer Days to the Close of the Nineteenth Century." MA thesis, West Virginia University, 1930.

Bukowczyk, John J. "Introduction, Forum: Thomas and Znaniecki's *The Polish Peasant* in Europe and America." *Journal of American Ethnic History* 16 (1996): 3–15.

Burchett, Michael H. "Promise and Prejudice: Wise County, Virginia and the Great Migration, 1910–1920." *Journal of Negro History* 82, no. 3 (Summer 1997): 312–327.

Caldwell, A. B. *The History of the American Negro: West Virginia Edition*. Morgantown: West Virginia University Press, 2012. Originally published as volume 7. Atlanta: A. B. Caldwell, 1923.

Callahan, J. M. *Semi-Centennial History of West Virginia*. Charleston: Semi-Centennial Commission, 1913.

Cayton, Horace R., and George S. Mitchell. *Black Workers and the New Unions*. Chapel Hill: University of North Carolina Press, 1939.

Chalmers, David M. *Hooded Americanism: The History of the Ku Klux Klan*. Durham, NC: Duke University Press, 1981.

Chase, Rachelle. *Creating the Black Utopia of Buxton, Iowa*. Charleston: History Press, 2019.

Cherniack, Martin. *The Hawk's Nest Incident: America's Worst Industrial Disaster*. New Haven, CT: Yale University Press, 1986.

Children's Bureau, U.S. Department of Labor. *The Welfare of Children in Bituminous Coal Mining Communities in West Virginia*. Washington, D.C.: Government Printing Office, 1923.

Clay, Earl C. "The Negro in Greenbrier County, West Virginia: A Social, Economic, and Educational Study." EdM, Virginia State University, 1946.

Cohen, Isaac. "Monopoly, Competition, and Collective Bargaining: Pennsylvania and South Wales Compared." In John H. M. Laslett, *United Mine Workers of America*, 415–416. University Park: Pennsylvania State University Press, 1996.

Conditions in the Coal Fields of Pennsylvania, West Virginia, and Ohio: Hearings before the Committee on Interstate Commerce. Washington, D.C.: Government Printing Office, 1928.

Corbin, David A. *Life, Work, and Rebellion in the Coal Fields: Southern West Virginia Miners, 1880–1922*. Urbana: University of Illinois Press, 1981.

Cresswell, Stephen. "The Case of Taylor Strauder." *West Virginia History* 44 (Spring 1983): 193–211.

Curtin, Mary Ellen. *Black Prisoners and the World, Alabama, 1865–1900*. Charlottesville: University Press of Virginia, 2000.

"Delegate [Frank] Ingham." In *Proceedings of the 28th Consecutive and 5th Biennial*

Convention of the United Mine Workers of America, Indianapolis, Indiana, 20 Sept. to 5 Oct. 1921, vol. 1. Indianapolis: Bookwalter-Ball-Greathouse, 1922.

Dickerson, Dennis. *Out of the Crucible: Black Steelworkers in Western Pennsylvania, 1875–1980.* Albany: State University of New York Press, 1986.

Diggs, Earle H. "Socio-Economic Status of the Negro Miner of Fayette County, West Virginia." MA thesis, Ohio University, 1944.

Dix, Keith. *What's a Coal Miner to Do? The Mechanization of Coal Mining.* Pittsburgh: University of Pittsburgh Press, 1988.

———. *Work Relations in the Coal Industry: The Handloading Era, 1880–1930.* Morgantown: West Virginia University Press, 1977.

Doppen, Frans H. *Richard L. Davis and the Color Line in Ohio Coal: A Hocking Valley Mine Labor Organizer, 1862–1900.* Jefferson, NC: McFarland & Company, 2016.

Drain, John R. "The History of West Virginia State College from 1892 to 1950." MA thesis, West Virginia University, 1951.

Draper, Daniel C. "Legal Phases of the Trial of John Brown." *West Virginia History* 1 (January 1940): 87–103.

Du Bois, W. E. B. *The Philadelphia Negro: A Social Study.* 1899; reprint Philadelphia: University of Pennsylvania, 1996.

Duncan, Richard R., ed. "Master's Theses and Doctoral Dissertations on West Virginia History." *West Virginia History* 46 (1985–1986): 159–180.

Duran, Elizabeth C., and James A. Duran Jr. "Integration in Reverse at West Virginia State College." *West Virginia History* 45 (1984): 61–78.

Edmunds, G. H. "West Virginia on Tap." *United Mine Worker's Journal,* April 11, 1917.

Eller, Ronald D. *Miners, Millhands, and Mountaineers: Industrialization of the Appalachian South, 1880—1930.* Knoxville: University of Tennessee Press, 1982.

Fain, Cicero M. *Black Huntington: An Appalachian Story.* Urbana: University of Illinois Press, 2019.

Farley, Yvonne S. "Homecoming." *Goldenseal* 5, no. 4 (October–December 1979): 7–16.

Fishback, Price V. "Employment Conditions of Blacks in the Coal Industry, 1900–1930." PhD diss., University of Washington, 1983.

Foner, Philip S. *Organized Labor and the Black Worker, 1619–1973.* New York: International, 1974.

Fox, Maier B. *United We Stand: The United Mine Workers of America 1890–1990.* Washington D.C.: United Mine Workers of America, 1990.

Frazier, E. Franklin. *The Negro Church in America.* New York: Schocken Books, 1963.

French, Jack "Segregation Patterns in a Coal Camp." MA thesis, West Virginia University, 1953.

Fuetter, C. F. "Mixed Labor in Coal Mining." *Coal Age* 10 (July 22, 1916): 137.

Gates, Henry Louis, Jr., *Colored People: A Memoir.* New York: Alfred A. Knopf, 1994.

Gjerde, Jon. "New Growth on Old Vines—The State of the Field: The Social History of Immigration to and Ethnicity in the United States." *Journal of American Ethnic History* 18 (1999): 40–65.

Goldfield, Michael. *The Southern Key: Class, Race, and Radicalism in the 1930s and 1940s.* New York: Oxford University Press, 2020.

Goodrich, Carter G. *The Miner's Freedom.* 1925; reprint New York: Arno, 1971.

Gottlieb, Peter. *Making Their Own Way: Southern Blacks' Migration to Pittsburgh, 1916–30.* Urbana: University of Illinois Press, 1987.

Gradwohl, David M., and Nancy M. Osborn. *Exploring Buried Buxton: Archaeology of an*

Abandoned Iowa Coal Mining Town with a Large Black Population. Iowa City: University of Iowa Press, 2006.

Green, James. *The Devil is Here in These Hills: West Virginia's Coal Miners and Their Battle for Freedom*. New York: Atlantic Monthly Press, 2015.

Greene, Julie. "Rethinking the Boundaries of Class: Labor History and Theories of Class and Capitalism." *Labor: Studies in Working-Class History of the Americas* 18, no. 2 (May 2021): 92–112.

Greene, Lorenzo J., and Carter G. Woodson. *The Negro Wage Earner*. 1930; reprint New York: Russell and Russell, 1969.

Grossman, James. *Land of Hope: Chicago, Black Southerners, and the Great Migration*. Chicago: University of Chicago Press, 1989.

Guglielmo, Thomas A. *White on Arrival: Italians, Race, Color, and Power in Chicago, 1890–1945*. New York: Oxford University Press, 2003.

Gutman, Herbert. "The Negro and the United Mine Workers of America: The Career and Letters of Richard L. Davis and Something of Their Meaning, 1890–1900." In Julius Jacobson, ed., *The Negro and the American Labor Movement*, 49–127. Garden City, NY: Doubleday, 1968. Reprinted in Herbert Gutman, *Work, Culture, and Society in Industrializing America: Essays in American Working-Class and Social History*, 121–208. New York: Vintage, 1977.

Harlan, John C. "Booker T. Washington." *West Virginia History* 32 (January 1971): 121–123.

———. *History of West Virginia State College, 1890–1965*. Dubuque, IA: Wm. C. Brown, 1968.

Harlan, Louis R. "Booker T. Washington and the Kanawha Valley, 1875–1879." *West Virginia History* 33 (January 1972): 124–141.

———. *Booker T. Washington: The Making of a Black Leader, 1856–1901*. New York: Oxford University Press, 1972.

———. *Booker T. Washington: The Wizard of Tuskegee, 1901–1915*. New York: Oxford University Press, 1983.

———. "Booker T. Washington's West Virginia Boyhood." *West Virginia History* 32 (January 1971): 63–85.

Harlan, Louis R., and Raymond W. Smock, eds. *The Booker T. Washington Papers*. Two vols. Urbana: University of Illinois Press 1972.

Harris, Abram L. "Plight of the Negro Miner." *Opportunity* 3 (October 1925): 312.

———. "The Negro in the Coal Mining Industry." *Opportunity* 4 (February 1926): 45–47.

Harris, John T., ed. *West Virginia Legislative Hand Book*. Charleston: Tribune, 1916.

———, ed. *West Virginia Legislative Hand Book*. Charleston: Tribune, 1928.

———, ed. *West Virginia Legislative Hand Book*. Charleston: Tribune, 1929.

Harris, W. H. "Exceptional Opportunities . . . at Olga Shaft, Coalwood, W.Va." *McDowell Times*, September 8, 1916.

——— "The Negro Doctors Should Be Employed . . . by the Coal Companies." *McDowell Times*, July 28, 1916.

Harris, William H. *The Harder We Run: Black Workers Since the Civil War*. New York: Oxford University Press, 1982.

Hart, Betty L. Powell "The Black Press in West Virginia: A Brief History." In Trotter and Bickley, eds., *Honoring Our Past*, 156–179. Charleston: Alliance for the Collection, Preservation and Dissemination of West Virginia's Black History, 1991.

Henri, Florette. *Black Migration: Movement North, 1900–1920*. Garden City: Anchor Press Doubleday, 1975.

Hight, Joel E. "History of Negro Secondary Education in McDowell County, West Virginia." EdM thesis, University of Cincinnati, 1946.

Hill, Herbert. "Myth-Making as Labor History: Herbert Gutman and the United Mine Workers of America." *International Journal of Politics, Culture and Society* 2, no. 2 (Winter 1988): 132–200.

Hill, T. Edward. "The Coal Strike and Negro Miners in West Virginia" (c. 1922). In "Early Surveys," Series 6, Box 89, National Urban League Papers, Library of Congress.

———. "Loafers and Jonahs." *McDowell Times*, May 25, 1917.

———. "My Dream of the Future Church." *McDowell Times*, December 12, 1913.

Huntley, Horace, and David Montgomery, eds. *Black Workers' Struggle for Equality in Birmingham*. Champaign: University of Illinois Press, 2007.

Jackameit, William P. "A Short History of Negro Public Higher Education in West Virginia, 1890–1965," *West Virginia History* 37, no. 4 (July 1976): 309–324.

Jackson, Frederick O. "The Impact of the Roslyn Coal Miners' Strike on African American Migration into the State of Washington: 1888 through 1910." PhD diss., Western Washington University, 1995.

Jackson, Kenneth T. *The Ku Klux Klan in the City, 1915–1930*. New York: Oxford University Press, 1967.

Jellison, Charles A. "The Martyrdom of John Brown." *West Virginia History* 18 (July 1957): 243–255.

Johnson, Walter. "On Agency." *Journal of Social History* 37 (2003): 113–124.

Jones, Lawrence Neale. "The Civil Status of Negroes in West Virginia as Reflected in Legislative Acts and Judicial Decisions, 1860–1940." MA thesis, University of Chicago, 1948.

Jordan, Daniel P. "The Mingo War: Labor Violence in the Southern West Virginia Coal Fields, 1919–1922." In Gary M. Fink and Merle E. Reed, eds., *Essays in Southern Labor History*, 102–143. Westport, CT: Greenwood, 1977.

Kelly, Brian. *Race, Class, and Power in the Alabama Coalfields, 1908–1921*. Champaign: University of Illinois Press, 2001.

Kolchin, Peter. "Whiteness Studies: The New History of Race in America." *Journal of American History* 89, no. 1 (June 2002): 154–173.

Laing, James T. "The Negro Miner in West Virginia." PhD diss., Ohio State University, 1933.

———. "The Negro Miner in West Virginia." *Social Forces* 14 (1936): 416–422.

Laslett, John H. M. *Nature's Noblemen: The Fortunes of the Independent Collier in Scotland and the American Midwest, 1855–1889*. Los Angeles: University of California Institute of Industrial Relations, 1983.

———. " 'A Parting of the Ways': Immigrant Miners and the Rise of Politically Conscious Trade Unionism in Scotland and the American Midwest, 1865–1924." In John H. M. Laslett, ed., *The United Mine Workers of America*, 417–437. University Park: Pennsylvania State University Press, 1996.

———, ed. *The United Mine Workers of America: A Model of Industrial Solidarity?* University Park: Pennsylvania State University Press, 1996.

Lawrence, Randall G. "Appalachian Metamorphosis: Industrializing Society on the Central Appalachian Plateau, 1860–1913." PhD diss., Duke University, 1983.

———. " 'Make a Way Out of Nothing': One Black Woman's Trip from North Carolina to the McDowell County Coalfields." *Goldenseal* 5, no. 4 (October–December 1979): 27–31.

Letwin, Daniel. *The Challenge of Interracial Unionism: Alabama Coal Miners, 1878–1921.* Chapel Hill: University of North Carolina Press, 1998.

Levine, Lawrence. *Black Culture and Black Consciousness: Afro-American Folk Thought from Slavery to Freedom.* Oxford: Oxford University Press, 1977.

Lewis, Earl. *In Their Own Interests: Race, Class, and Power in Twentieth-Century Norfolk, Virginia.* Berkeley: University of California Press, 1991.

Lewis, Ronald L. *Black Coal Miners in America: Race, Class, and Community Conflict, 1780–1980.* Lexington: University Press of Kentucky, 1987.

———. "The Black Presence in the Paint-Creek Strike, 1912–13." *West Virginia History* 46 (1985–1986): 59–71.

———. *Coal, Iron, and Slaves: Industrial Slavery in Maryland and Virginia, 1715–1865.* Westport, CT: Praeger, 1979.

———. "Migration of Southern Blacks to the Central Appalachian Coalfields: The Transition from Peasant to Proletarian." *Journal of Southern History* 55, no. 1 (February 1989): 77–102.

———. *Welsh Americans: A History of Assimilation in the Coalfields.* Chapel Hill: University of North Carolina Press, 2008.

Linn, Carolyn J. "The Lieutenant Governor of West Virginia." *West Virginia History* 32 (April 1971): 194–199.

Long, Priscilla. *Where the Sun Never Shines: A History of America's Bloody Coal Industry.* New York: Paragon House, 1989.

Lord, Jeanette Mather. "John Brown: They Had a Concern." *West Virginia History* 20 (April 1959): 163–183.

Lunt, Richard D. *Law and Order versus the Miners: West Virginia, 1907–1933.* Hamden, CT: Archon Books, 1979.

Mandle, Jay R. *The Roots of Black Poverty: The Southern Plantation Economy after the Civil War.* Durham, N.C.: Duke University Press, 1978.

Margo, Robert A. *Race and Schooling in the South, 1880–1950.* Chicago: University of Chicago Press, 1990.

Melosh, Barbara. "Recovery and Revision: Women's History and West Virginia." *West Virginia History* 49 (1990): 3–6.

Massey, Tim R. "I Didn't Think I'd Live to See 1950: Looking Back with Columbus Avery." *Goldenseal* 8 (Spring 1982): 32–40.

Millner, Reginald. "Conversations with the 'Ole Man: The Life and Times of a Black Appalachian Coal Miner." *Goldenseal* 5 (January–March 1979): 58–64.

Minard, Ralph. "Race Relationships in the Pocahontas Coal Field." *Journal of Social Sciences* 8 (1952): 29–44.

Mock, Iola L. "The Rise of Negro Elementary Education in West Virginia." EdM thesis, University of Cincinnati, 1935.

Mongin, Alfred. "A College in Secession: The Early Years of Storer College." *West Virginia History* 23 (July 1962): 263–264.

Monico, Francis W. "The Negro and the Martinsburg Gazette, 1799–1833." MA thesis, West Virginia University, 1959.

Moore, George Ellis. "Slavery as a Factor in the Formation of West Virginia." MA thesis, West Virginia University, 1947.

————. "Slavery as a Factor in the Formation of West Virginia." *West Virginia History* 18 (October 1956): 5–89.

Moreland, James R. "Early Iron Industry in the Cheat Mountains." *West Virginia History* 8 (October 1946): 105–118.

Morris, Homer L. *The Plight of the Bituminous Coal Miner*. Philadelphia: University of Pennsylvania Press, 1934.

Nelson, Bruce. *Divided We Stand: American Workers and the Struggle for Black Equality*. Princeton, NJ: Princeton University Press, 2002.

Nyden, Paul. *Black Coal Miners in the United States*. New York: American Institute for Marxist Studies, 1974.

O'Connor, Alice. *Poverty Knowledge: Social Science, Social Policy, and the Poor in Twentieth-Century U.S. History*. Princeton, NJ: Princeton University Press, 2001.

Painter, Nell Irvin. "The New Labor History and the Historical Moment." *International Journal of Politics, Culture, and Society* 2 (1989): 367–370.

Peters Sisters. *War Poems*. Charleston: Union, 1919.

Phillips, Laura Pinn. "Development of Education for Negroes in West Virginia." MA thesis, Howard University, 1937.

Posey, Thomas E. *The Negro Citizen of West Virginia*. Institute, WV: West Virginia State College Press, 1934.

Pudup, Mary Beth. "Women's Work in the West Virginia Economy." *West Virginia History* 49 (1990): 7–20.

Rachleff, Peter. *Black Labor in Richmond, 1865–1890*. 1984; reprint Urbana: University of Illinois Press, 1989.

Reid, Ira De Augustine. *Negro Membership in American Labor Unions*. New York: National Urban League, Department of Research and Investigation, 1930.

Rhinehart, Marilyn D. *A Way of Work and a Way of Life: Coal Mining in Thurber, Texas, 1888–1992*. College Station: Texas A&M University Press, 1992.

Rice, Connie L. "The 'Separate but Equal' Schools of Monongalia County's Coal Mining Communities." *Journal of Appalachian Studies* 2, no. 2 (Fall 1996): 323–335.

Rice, Otis K. *West Virginia: A History*. Lexington: University Press of Kentucky, 1985.

Robinson, Wilhelmina S. *Historical Afro-American Biographies*. Cornwells Heights, PA.: Publishers Agency, 1978.

Roediger, David. "History Making and Politics." *International Journal of Politics, Culture, and Society* 2 (1989): 371–372.

————. *The Wages of Whiteness: Race and the Making of the American Working Class*. London: Verso, 1991.

Rowh, Mark. "The Hawk's Nest Tragedy: Fifty Years Later," *Goldenseal* 7, no. 1 (1981): 31–32.

Salzman, Jack, ed., *Encyclopedia of African American Culture and History*. New York: Macmillan, 1996.

Sayles, John. *Thinking in Pictures: The Making of the Movie "Matewan."* Boston: Houghton Mifflin, 1987.

Schwieder, Dorothy. *Black Diamonds: Life and Work in Iowa's Coal Mining Communities, 1895–1925*. Ames: Iowa State University Press, 1983.

Schwieder, Dorothy, Joseph Hraba, and Elmer Schwieder. *Buxton: Work and Racial Equality in a Coal Mining Community*. Ames: Iowa State University Press, 1987.

Scobell, Elizabeth. "Preserving the History of West Virginia State College." In Trotter and Bickley, eds., *Honoring Our Past*. Charleston: Alliance for the Collection, Preservation and Dissemination of West Virginia's Black History, 1991.

Seals, Rev. T. H. "The Horrors of Convict Mines of Alabama." *United Mine Workers Journal*, August 19, 1915.

———. "Life in Alabama." *United Mine Workers Journal*, September 15, 1924.

Shapiro, Karin A. *A New South Rebellion: The Battle against Convict Labor in the Tennessee Coalfields, 1871–1896*. Chapel Hill: University of North Caroline Press, 1998.

Sheeler, John R. "The Negro in West Virginia before 1900." PhD diss., West Virginia University, 1954.

Shifflett, Crandall. *Coal Towns: Life, Work, and Culture in Company Towns of Southern Appalachia, 1880–1960*. Knoxville: University of Tennessee Press, 1990.

Smith, Douglas C. "In Quest of Equality: The West Virginia Experience." *West Virginia History* 37, no. 3 (April 1976): 213–216.

———. "Race Relations and Institutional Responses in West Virginia: A History." *West Virginia History* 39 (October 1977): 30–48.

———. "The West Virginia Human Rights Commission during the Govett-McKinney Era." PhD diss., West Virginia University, 1975.

Spero, Sterling D., and Abram L. Harris. *The Black Worker: The Negro and the Labor Movement*. 1931; reprint New York: Atheneum, 1968.

Spradling, Mary M., ed. *In Black and White: A Guide to Magazine Articles, Newspaper Articles, and Books Concerning More than 6,700 Black Individuals and Groups*. Detroit: Gale Research, 1980.

Starobin, Robert S. *Industrial Slavery in the Old South*. New York: Oxford University Press, 1970.

State Commissioner of Prohibition. *Biennial Reports*. Charleston: Office of the State Commissioner on Prohibition. Various years.

State Superintendent of Free Schools. *Biennial Reports*. Charleston: Office of the State Superintendent of Free Schools. Various years.

State Supervisor of Negro Schools. *Biennial Report of the State Supervisor of Negro Schools, 1921–1922*. Charleston: Office of the State Supervisor of Negro Schools.

Stealey, John E., III, "The Freedmen's Bureau in West Virginia." *West Virginia History* 39, nos. 2–3 (January–April 1978): 99–142.

———, ed. "Reports of Freedmen's Bureau District Officers on Tours and Surveys in West Virginia." *West Virginia History* 43 (Winter 1982): 145–155.

———, ed. "Reports of Freedmen's Bureau Operations in West Virginia: Agents in the Eastern Panhandle." *West Virginia History* 42 (1980–1981): 94–129.

Steel, Edward M., Jr., "Black Monongalians: A Judicial View of the Negro in Monongalia County, 1776–1865." *West Virginia History* 34 (July 1973): 331–359.

———. "Bypath to Freedom." *West Virginia History* 31 (October 1969): 33–39.

Stuckert, Robert P. "Black Populations of the Southern Appalachian Mountains." *Phylon* 48, no. 2 (Summer 1987): 141–151.

Stutter, Boyd B. "John Brown and the Oberlin Lands." *West Virginia History* 12 (April 1951): 183–199.

———. "John Brown's Letter." *West Virginia History* 9 (October 1947): 1–25.

Sullivan, Charles Kenneth. "Coal Men and Coal Towns: Development of the Smokeless Coalfields of Southern West Virginia, 1873–1923." PhD diss., University of Pittsburgh, 1979.

Surface, George T. "The Negro Mine Laborer: Central Appalachian Coal Field." *Annals of the American Academy of Political and Social Science* 33 (1909): 115–128.

Swisher, C. W., ed. *Manual of the State of West Virginia, 1907–1908*. Charleston: Tribune, 1907.

Taylor, A. A. *The Negro in the Reconstruction of Virginia*. Washington, D.C.: Associated, 1926.

Thomas, Richard Walter. *Life for Us Is What We Make It: Building Black Community in Detroit, 1915–1945*. Bloomington: Indiana University Press, 1992.

Thompson, Bruce A. "An Appeal for Racial Justice: The Civic Interest Progressives' Confrontation with Huntington, West Virginia, and Marshall University, 1963–1965." MA thesis, Marshall University, 1986.

Trotter, Joe William, Jr. "African American Workers: New Directions in U.S. Labor Historiography." *Labor History* 35, no. 4 (Fall 1994): 495–523.

———. *Black Milwaukee: The Making of an Industrial Proletariat, 1915–45*. Urbana: University of Chicago Press, 1985; reprint 1988.

———. "Celebrating the 40-Year History of the Working Class in American History Series from the University of Illinois Press, 1978–2018: A Perspective from the African American Field." Symposium, Newberry Library and the University of Illinois Press, Chicago, Illinois, October 27, 2018, online.

———. *Coal, Class, and Color: Blacks in Southern West Virginia, 1915–32*. Urbana: University of Illinois Press, 1990.

———, ed. *The Great Migration in Historical Perspective: New Dimensions of Race, Class, and Gender*. Bloomington: Indiana University Press, 1991.

———. "Historical Afterword." In Ancella R. Bickley and Lynda Ann Ewen, eds., *Memphis Tennessee Garrison: The Remarkable Story of a Black Appalachian Woman*, 223–224. Athens: Ohio University Press, 2001.

———. "Interpreting the African American Working-Class Experience: An Essay on Sources." In Trotter, *Workers on Arrival: Black Labor in the Making of America*, 185–210. Oakland: University of California Press, 2019.

———. "Introduction: African Americans in West Virginia." In A. B. Caldwell, *History of the Negro: West Virginia Edition*, xvi–xvii. Morgantown, WV: West Virginia Classics, 2012.

———. "The Roots of Health Disparities in African American History." Forthcoming essay.

Trotter, Joe W., and Ancella R. Bickley. *Honoring Our Past: Proceedings of the First Two Conferences on West Virginia's Black History*. Charleston: Alliance for the Collection, Preservation and Dissemination of West Virginia's Black History, 1991.

Trotter, Otis. "From Vallscreek to Highland Creek: A Memoir of Family Struggle, Race and Medicine." Unpublished manuscript, 2012.

———. *Keeping Heart: A Memoir of Family Struggle, Race, and Medicine*. Athens: Ohio University Press, 2015.

Turner, William H., and Edward Cabbell, eds. *Blacks in Appalachia*. Lexington: University Press of Kentucky, 1985.

U.S. Bureau of the Census. *Fifteenth Census of the United States, 1930*. Vol. 3. Washington, D.C.: Government Printing Office, 1932.

———. *Fifteenth Census of the United States, 1930*. Vol. 6. Washington, D.C.: Government Printing Office, 11933.

———. *Fourteenth Census of the United States, 1920*. Vol. 2. Washington, D.C.: Government Printing Office, 1922.

———. *Negroes in the United States, 1920–1932*. Washington, D.C.: Government Printing Office, 1935; reprint, New York: Amo Press 1966.

———. *The Negro Population in the United States, 1790–1915*. Washington, D.C.: Government Printing Office, 1918; reprint New York: Arno Press 1968.

———. *Religious Bodies, 1906*. Washington, D.C.: Government Printing Office, 1910.

———. *Religious Bodies, 1926*. Washington, D.C.: Government Printing Office, 1929.

———. *Report on the Population of the United States, Eleventh Census of the United States, 1890*. Washington, D.C.: Government Printing Office, 1895.

———. *Thirteenth Census of the United States, 1910*. Vols. 3–4. Washington, D.C.: Government Printing Office, 1913.

———. *Twelfth Census of the United States, 1900: Special Reports, Occupations*. Washington, D.C.: Government Printing Office, 1904.

U.S. Senate Committee on Education and Labor. Various testimonies. In *West Virginia Coal Fields: Hearings before the Committee on Education*. Washington, D.C.: Government Printing Office, 1921.

U.S. Senate Committee on Interstate Commerce. *Conditions in the Coal Fields of Pennsylvania, West Virginia, and Ohio: Hearings before the Committee on Interstate Commerce, 1838–41*. Washington, D.C.: Government Printing Office, 1928.

Wagner, John A. "West Virginia." In *Black America: A State-by-State Historical Encyclopedia*, Alton Hornsby Jr., ed., 913–930. Santa Barbara, CA: Greenwood, 2011.

Washington, Booker T. *Up from Slavery*. 1901; reprint, New York: Bantam Books, 1967.

Wesley, Charles H. *Negro Labor in the United States, 1850–1925: A Study in American Economic History*. 1927; reprint New York: Russell and Russell, 1967.

West Virginia Bureau of Negro Welfare and Statistics. *Biennial Reports*. Charleston: WVBNWS. Various dates.

West Virginia Department of Mines. *Annual Reports*. Charleston: WVDM. Various dates.

West Virginia Human Rights Commission. *Annual Reports*. Charleston: WVHRC. Various dates.

West Virginia Human Rights Commission. Public Hearing in Wheeling. Charleston: WVHRC, February 1971.

West Virginia State Board of Control. *Biennial Reports*. Charleston: WVSBC. Various dates.

West Virginia State Health Department. *Annual Reports*. Charleston: WVSHD. Various dates.

Wheeler, Hoyt N. "Mountaineer Mine Wars: An Analysis of the West Virginia Mine Wars of 1912–13 and 1920–21." *Business History Review* 50 (Spring 1976): 69–91.

White, Ralph W. "Another Lesson from the East St. Louis Lynching." *McDowell Times*, July 20, 1917.

———. "Weyanoke: The Eldorado of the Coal Fields in Its Section of State." *McDowell Times*, July 13, 1917.

Wilkinson, Christopher. *Big Band Jazz in Black West Virginia, 1930–1942*. Jackson: University Press of Mississippi, 2012.

———. "Hot and Sweet: Big Band Music in Black West Virginia before the Swing Era." *American Music* 21, no. 2 (Summer 2003): 159–179.

Williams, John A. *West Virginia: A History*. New York: W.W. Norton, 1984.

———. *West Virginia and the Captains of Industry*. Morgantown: West Virginia University, 1976.

Williamson, Joel. *The Crucible of Race: Black-White Relations in the American South since Emancipation*. New York: Oxford University Press, 1984.

Witt, Matt, and Earl Dolter. "Before I'd Be a Slave." In Matt Witt, ed., *In Our Blood: Four Coal Mining Families*, 23–47. New Market, TN: Highlander Research Center, 1979.

Wolfe, Margaret R. "Putting Them in Their Places: Industrial Housing in Southern Appalachia, 1900–1930." *Appalachian Journal* 7, no. 3 (Summer 1979): 27–36.

Women's Bureau. *Home Environment and Employment Opportunities for Women in Coal Mine Workers' Families*. Washington, D.C.: U.S. Department of Labor, 1925.

Wood, Edward Grimke. "Development of Secondary Education for Negroes in West Virginia." EdM, University of Cincinnati, 1937.

Woodrum, Robert H. *Everybody Was Black Down There: Race and Industrial Change in the Alabama Coalfields*. Athens: University of Georgia Press, 2007.

Woodson, Carter G. *A Century of Negro Migration*. 1918; reprint New York: AMS Press, 1970.

———. "Disruption of Virginia." PhD diss., Harvard University, 1912.

———. *Early Negro Education in West Virginia*. Institute: West Virginia State College Bulletin, 1921.

Worthman, Paul. "Black Workers and Labor Unions in Birmingham, Alabama, 1897–1904." *Labor History* 10 (1969): 375–407.

Wynne, Anne Marie. "Reconstruction and the Negro in West Virginia." MA thesis, University of Maryland, 1972.

Zerber, Carter. "An Analysis of Negro Political Behavior in Junction City." MA thesis, Marshall University, 1967.

Zieger, Robert H., ed. *Organized Labor in the Twentieth-Century South*. Knoxville: University of Tennessee Press, 1991.

SOURCES AND PERMISSIONS

Chapter 1: Originally published as "Introduction: African Americans in West Virginia." In A. B. Caldwell, *History of the American Negro: West Virginia Edition* (Morgantown: West Virginia University Press), 2012.

Chapter 2: Originally published as "Black Migration to Southern West Virginia." In Ken Fones-Wolf and Ronald L. Lewis, eds., *Transnational West Virginia: Ethnic Communities and Economic Change, 1840–1940* (Morgantown: West Virginia University Press), 2002. Portions of the chapter also appeared in Joe William Trotter Jr., *Coal, Class, and Color: Blacks in Southern West Virginia, 1915–32* (Urbana: University of Illinois Press), 1990.

Chapter 3: Originally published as "Black Miners in West Virginia: Class and Community Responses to Workplace Discrimination, 1920–1930." In John H. M. Laslett, ed., *The United Mine Workers of America: A Model of Industrial Solidarity?* (University Park: Pennsylvania State University Press, in association with the Pennsylvania University Libraries), 1996. Portions of the chapter also appeared in Joe William Trotter Jr., *Coal, Class, and Color: Blacks in Southern West Virginia,1915–45* (Urbana: University of Illinois Press), 1990; and in Rober H. Zieger, ed., *Organized Labor in the Twentieth-Century South* (Knoxville: University of Tennessee Press), 1991.

Chapter 4: Originally published as "The Formation of Black Community in Southern West Virginia Coalfields." In John Inscoe, ed., *Appalachians and Race: The Mountain South from Slavery to Segregation* (Lexington: University Press of Kentucky), 2001. An earlier version of this chapter appeared in Joe William Trotter Jr., *Coal, Class, and Color: Blacks in Southern West Virginia, 1915–32* (Urbana: University of Illinois Press), 1990.

Chapter 5: From Joe William Trotter Jr., *Coal, Class, and Color: Blacks in Southern West Virginia, 1915–32.* Copyright 1990 by the Board of Trustees of the University of Illinois. Used with permission from the University of Illinois Press.

Epilogue: Originally published as "The Dynamics of Race and Ethnicity in the U.S. Coal Industry from the Civil War through Recent Times." *International Journal of Social History* 60, no. 51 (December 2015): 145–164. Used with permission from Cambridge University Press.

Appendix: Originally published as "Blacks in West Virginia: A Critique of the Secondary Literature and a Survey of the Primary Sources." In Ronald L. Lewis and John C. Hennen Jr., eds., *Essays on West Virginia History: Critical Essays on the Literature*, 187–201 (Dubuque, IA: Kendall/Hunt), 1993.

INDEX